Freedom Is Your Destiny!

May you find this book encouraging as you fight the good fight of faith.

Dan

Daniel T. Eismann

Freedom Is Your Destiny!

Daniel T. Eismann

Desert Sage Press
Eagle, Idaho

Daniel T. Eismann

ISBN: 978-0-9897133-9-9
Library of Congress Control Number: 2013945042

To order additional copies of this book please contact:
Desert Sage Press
P. O. Box 357, Eagle, Idaho 83616 or **www.desertsagepress.com**
E-book is available from **www.amazon.com**

DEDICATION

This book is dedicated to my fellow Vietnam veterans, to all who have served in our military, and to my fellow soldiers in Christ.

Freedom Is Your Destiny!

Table of Contents

Freedom Is Your Destiny!

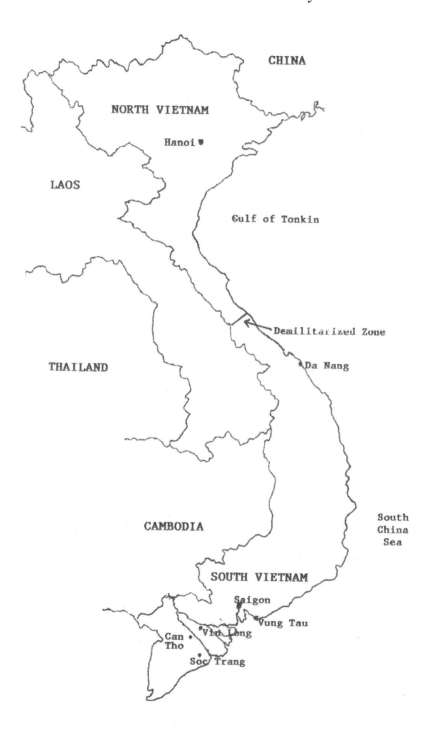

Daniel T. Eismann

Prologue

I had joined the Army in September 1967 after two years of college. I wanted to be a helicopter pilot, but at the recruiter's suggestion I enlisted to be a helicopter mechanic. He said I could request flight school after I was in helicopter maintenance school. When I arrived at Ft. Lewis, Washington, for basic training, I first went through a battery of written tests with hundreds of others who had just arrived. When we were done, two of us were called out and asked if we would be willing to be in the Special Forces. I said, "Sure," but at the end of basic training I was still destined for helicopter maintenance school. I did not know at the time that a UH-1 ("Huey") helicopter mechanic was the most critical MOS (Military Occupational Specialty) in the Army at that time.

Once I was in helicopter maintenance school at Ft. Eustis, Virginia, I decided not to apply for flight school. To become a pilot, I would have to go through warrant officer school, ground school, and flight school. I was told there would be delays before starting each school. Nobody could tell me how long it would take to become a pilot, and I would have a five-year commitment upon graduating. When I had finished basic training, I had to wait two weeks doing KP (kitchen patrol) for them to correct a one-letter typographical error in my orders. When I arrived at Ft. Eustis, I had to wait over a month doing KP and other similar jobs because they did not want to start our training until after Christmas. Considering how my training had progressed so far, I decided I was not willing to risk more lengthy delays. At the end of helicopter maintenance school, I did volunteer for airborne training. However, a few days after passing the physical requirements (including running a timed mile on an ankle I had sprained playing basketball), we were told there had been a paperwork foul-up that would take at least two weeks to straighten out. For me, that was the last straw. I immediately submitted a written request to be sent to Vietnam. The Army processed that paperwork expeditiously, and within a few days I was headed home for a two-week leave before departing for Vietnam.

In 1959, North Vietnam had sought to defeat the government in South Vietnam through the Viet Cong, which were Vietnamese who lived or had lived in the South. They were organized into main force units (2,000-man regiments), which were well-trained and equipped full-time soldiers; regional force units (500-man battalions) which were also full-time soldiers, but not as well-trained and equipped; and local force units (10-12 man squads), which were poorly trained and equipped. In response, President Kennedy substantially increased both American aid to the government in the South and the number of American advisors. In August 1964, North Vietnam began sending divisions of its regular army into the South, and in response President Johnson committed America to the war with the landing of the 9th Marine Expeditionary Brigade in Da Nang on March 8, 1965. More American troops followed, so that during 1965 American troop strength increased from 23,300 to 184,300. It continued increasing to a high of over 543,000 in April, 1969.

I arrived in Vietnam on May 12, 1968, two days after the beginning of peace talks to end the war began. I left two years later with the peace talks still ongoing. During the years I was in Vietnam (1968, 1969, 1970), America suffered respectively the second highest, the highest, and the fourth highest numbers of casualties in the war.

For all but a few months of that time, I was stationed at Soc Trang in the Mekong Delta, about 95 miles southwest of Saigon. The airfield had been created by the Japanese during World War II, where they stationed fighters and observation planes. One of the pilots in my company told me that his father had bombed the airfield during that war. After the war, the French took over the airfield and improved it. Most of the buildings were single-story structures reflecting French architecture. The sign in front of the operations building said that the elevation was two feet above sea level.

When I arrived, there was a 3,000-foot paved runway that ran north and south. Unfortunately, it had been built perpendicular to the prevailing winds, and during the windier times of the year fixed-wing aircraft, including C-130's, could not take off and land, except for an Air America airplane designed to operate on short runways. During windy days, it could land and take off crossways on the runway. In fact, on especially windy days it needed a shorter distance in which to take off than did our helicopter gunships. All of the buildings were located on the west side of the runway. There was a chain-link fence surrounding the perimeter, with concrete bunkers just inside the fence.

Two helicopter companies operated out of the airfield: the 121st Aviation Company (Assault Helicopter) and the 336th Aviation Company (Assault Helicopter). I was assigned to the 121st, which was the first Army aviation unit in the Mekong Delta. It occupied the buildings along the northern half of the runway. It had about 290 men divided into five platoons: a headquarters platoon, a service platoon, and three helicopter platoons. Two of the helicopter platoons were "airlift platoons," which transported soldiers into and out of landing zones (LZ's). The third was the gunship platoon. In addition to the helicopter companies, there was a group of combat engineers living in tents at the southern end of the runway, an artillery battery located at the northern end of the runway, battalion headquarters located in the middle, and a reconnaissance airplane company.

Soc Trang had three creature comforts that were very appreciated—lukewarm showers, flush toilets, and a paved runway. In Soc Trang, we had bathroom buildings probably built by the French in which there were flush toilets and lukewarm showers. For a few months I was stationed at Vinh Long, which had cold showers located outdoors on the side of a building and toilets that were like multi-seat outhouses, except that the refuse did not go into a hole in the ground, but into 55-gallon steel drums that had been cut in half. The steel drums were removed each day through doors in the back of the outhouse, and the refuse was burned, using diesel fuel. Not very sweet smelling. In Vinh Long, the runway and adjoining flight lines were "paved" with interlocking steel panels that had baseball-sized holes throughout them. The soil below panels was very sandy, and so when helicopters took off and landed, they stirred up a small sandstorm. Anyone standing nearby got sand in his hair, his ears, and down his neck. That did not happen on the asphalt-paved runway and flight lines at Soc Trang.

When I was stationed at Vinh Long, I was a crew chief for a Cobra helicopter gunship. One day, the Cobras were operating out of Soc Trang, and I was flown to Soc Trang so that there would be a crew chief there in case one of the Cobras needed repairs. During the noon hour, one of the Cobra pilots was resting in a hammock attached to his helicopter that was parked on the flight line. He was a friend of mine and knew I had been stationed at Soc Trang. When I walked up, he said, "This is heaven."

Unfortunately, he was later killed along with the other pilot in his Cobra. Taps was played during their memorial service, and for years after that I teared up whenever I heard Taps.

Daniel T. Eismann

1

WELCOME TO VIETNAM

Beloved, do not think it strange concerning the fiery trial which is to try you, as though some strange thing happened to you.

1 Peter 4:12

The explosion jolted me out of a deep sleep. Then there was another explosion, and another, and another. It was my second night at the small Army airfield near Soc Trang, Vietnam, where I had just been stationed. I had been asleep on a cot in the supply room with about a dozen other soldiers who had also arrived two days earlier. Because there was no room in the hootches (single story barracks), we were all sleeping in the supply room. It was an old, single-story, two-room building that had barely enough empty floor space for us to set up our cots each night.

As I listened to the explosions, some of which sounded close while others sounded farther away, I realized I was experiencing my first mortar attack. I looked up at the tin roof above my head (there was no ceiling), and recalled the two-story, wooden barracks building I had seen at the processing center at Binh Long a few days earlier when I had arrived "in country." It had been hit dead center by an enemy rocket, and the middle of it looked like a wooden crater. There was a large hole where most of the roof had been, and the interior was a shambles. I decided that the tin roof of the supply building would not provide much protection if a mortar round hit it, so I crawled under a small desk near the door (the only cover available) and sat there waiting for the explosions to stop.

For some reason, I looked at my watch to see what time it was. I think it was about 11:00 p.m. As I lay under the desk, I wanted to go outside just to see what was going on, but I did not do so because I assumed someone would yell at me as being a stupid "new guy." Finally, the explosions ceased. I again looked at my watch, and it was about 12:30 a.m.

Not long after the explosions stopped, the door to the supply building swung open, and the officer who stepped inside ordered, "Get out to the perimeter bunkers." I stood up and responded, "We have not been issued any weapons." I was hoping he would get us some weapons, but he merely said, "Go to the bunkers anyway." I left the supply room and ran across the runway to a bunker located at the far end of the runway. The bunker was a concrete box with a doorway in the back wall and a horizontal window opening in the front wall, facing the perimeter fence. I did not want to be sitting inside a cement box, so I climbed up a wooden ladder leaning against the back wall to the top of the bunker. The flat, concrete roof had a row of sandbags on both sides and the front. I sat down leaning against the sandbags on the left side, peering intently out into the blackness, wondering what I could do without a weapon if there was a ground attack. I looked around, and there was nothing I could use as a weapon. There were not even any rocks I could throw at the enemy. I remember thinking that even the Russian peasants had pitchforks to use against the attacking German army.

As I was sitting there in the silence focusing on the blackness beyond the perimeter fence, straining to see if any of the shadows were moving, I heard a metallic click-click sound behind me. Suddenly, a loud kaboom ripped through the night. If I could have clawed my way down through the top of the bunker, I would have. I then realized that my bunker was near an artillery battery, and it was just a howitzer (cannon) answering the enemy.

Welcome to Vietnam! If I had any doubt before, I now knew that the war was upon me, and I did not even have a weapon with which to fight back.

* * * * * * * *

All physical war is, at its core, a spiritual conflict. As Jesus said, evil thoughts and actions come out of the hearts of men.[1]

Even though you may not be in a physical war, you are in a war—a spiritual war. All of us were born into a world at war—Satan's war against God. Although the outcome of Satan's rebellion is not in doubt, there will be many casualties until the final battle.

There are those who will hate you without cause and will seek to harm you in any way they can. You have an evil enemy who wants to steal your joy and peace, who wants you to worship something other than God, and who does not want you to fulfill your God-ordained destiny. You cannot make the enemy go away by ignoring him. You cannot make peace with the enemy. You cannot compromise with him.

God has a life plan, a destiny, for each of us. "For we are His workmanship, created in Christ Jesus for good works, which God prepared beforehand that we should walk in them."[2] Living out God's destiny for your life will bring you your greatest joy and satisfaction. That is why the enemy's primary goal is to keep each of us from fulfilling our destinies. The enemy uses many weapons to keep us from doing so, such as alcohol, drugs, sex, entertainment, the cares of life, and the love of money and/or power. Fortunately, God is longsuffering and full of mercy. Even if you have strayed from the path He has planned for you, He will welcome you back.

Many of the events in our lives were not simply random occurrences. Fulfilling your God-given destiny will depend upon the attitude of your heart. You must have the same heart attitude to prevail in the struggle for your destiny as that of a soldier in physical combat. You must have, what is often called, the heart of a warrior. The purpose of this book is to explain aspects of the heart attitude that will enable you to live your life in victory and to fulfill all that God has planned for you.

I asked two combat veterans to read what I have written to see whether I had, in their opinions, covered the aspects of a warrior's heart. One was a tank driver under General Patton in World War II and fought in the Battle of the Bulge. The other fought 18 months in Korea as an infantryman, where he was given a battlefield commission after the first Battle of Pork Chop Hill. He later served as an Army helicopter pilot in Vietnam, where he earned the Congressional Medal of Honor (our nation's highest award for heroism) and the Distinguished Service Cross (the Army's second highest award for heroism). After they had read it, I asked them whether I had covered the aspects of a warrior's heart. They told me that I had.

Historically in our nation, only men were involved regularly in physical combat, and from what I have read only about 10% of those in the military during a war were actually involved in combat. Whether we want to be or not, all of us are involved in spiritual warfare. To prevail, we all, both men and women, must have the heart of a warrior. It was because both Deborah and Jael were warriors that Israel had peace for forty years.[3] Rahab saved two of the Israelites who were spying out the Promised Land, and she was included in the genealogy of Christ.[4] In Christ, there is neither male nor female.[5] We are all one in the Lord. Upon believing in Jesus Christ, we all enlist as His soldiers to fight in this spiritual battle.[6] The war is upon you. The question is, "Will you fight? Will you be a warrior?"

---

[1] Mark 7:21-23.
[2] Ephesians 2:10.
[3] Judges 4-5.
[4] Joshua 2; Matthew 1:5.
[5] Galatians 3:28.
[6] 2 Timothy 2:3-4.

Freedom Is Your Destiny!

2

GOD WANTS YOU TO KNOW WAR

Now these are the nations which the LORD left, that He might test Israel by them, that is, all who had not known any of the wars in Canaan (this was only so that the generations of the children of Israel might be taught to know war, at least those who had not formerly known it).

Judges 3:1-2

In Judges 3:1-4 we are told that God left five nations in the Promised Land "so that the generations of the children of Israel might be taught to know war." Why would God want the Israelites to be taught to know war? He did not need the Israelite's help to eliminate the enemy in the Promised Land. The Angel of the LORD killed 185,000 Assyrian soldiers in one night.[1] I believe that it was because in war, they would have to learn to trust God and demonstrate that trust by relying upon and obeying Him. The nations possessing the Promised Land were greater and mightier than were the Israelites.[2] They could not prevail in their own strength. Requiring the Israelites to enter the battle tested their trust in God. Trust can only be proved genuine when there is risk—when you have something to lose. Taking possession of the Promised Land meant that they had to risk not only their own lives, but those of their families. What greater risk is there than that? What greater test of faith is there than that? They had to trust Him not only in the physical battles, but they had to do so by obeying Him in all aspects of their lives.

The battle for the Promised Land was not just a physical war. It was also a spiritual war. God was keeping the promise He made to Abram to give the land to him and his descendants,[3] and He was using the Israelites to bring judgment against the inhabitants of the land because of their wickedness.[4] Just before Joshua led the Israelites into the battle of Jericho, the pre-incarnate Christ appeared to him and said, "[A]s the Commander of the army of the LORD I have now come."[5] The battle for Jericho was God's. He was not joining the Israelites in their battle; He was permitting them to join in His. We must do likewise.

In order to live out our destinies, we must prevail in this spiritual war into which we have been thrust. Our enemies in spiritual warfare are principalities, powers, and rulers of the darkness—the "spiritual *hosts* of wickedness."[6] They are more powerful than we are.[7] Because they are spiritual beings, we cannot see them nor can we harm them physically. Trying to fight them in our own power would be futile. Praise God, however, that the Holy Spirit in us is greater than they are.[8] Thus, just as the Israelites were required to trust, rely upon, and obey God in order to take possession of the Promised Land, in spiritual warfare we also must trust, rely upon, and obey God in order to prevail. We cannot prevail in our own strength.

God wants you to learn to rely upon Him. If we trust in Him, we will rely upon Him and not upon the things of the world.[9]

When Jeroboam was king of Israel, he brought his army against Judah. The army of Israel had twice the number of soldiers as did Judah's army and surrounded it. The king of Judah cried out to God, and He struck the army of Israel and brought the victory. "Thus the children of Israel were subdued at that time; and the children of Judah prevailed, because they relied on the LORD God of their fathers."[10]

Asa then became king of Judah, and it was attacked by the army of Ethiopia, which also had about twice the number of soldiers as did Judah. Asa cried out to God, saying, "LORD, *it is* nothing for You to help, whether with many or with those who have no power; help us, O LORD our God, for we rest on You, and in Your name we go against this multitude. O LORD, You *are* our God; do not let man prevail against You!" God struck the Ethiopian army, and it fled.[11] However, later in Asa's reign, a new king of Israel came against Judah. Rather than relying upon God, Asa took silver and gold from the temple and purchased a treaty with the king of Syria, who attacked Israel and caused its army to withdraw from Judah. God then sent a prophet to deliver a rebuke to king Asa. The prophet reminded Asa that the Ethiopian army had been huge, and then said, "Yet, because you relied on the LORD, He delivered them into your hand. For the eyes of the LORD run to and fro throughout the whole earth, to show Himself strong on behalf of *those* whose heart *is* loyal to Him." Relying upon God shows that our hearts are loyal to Him. The prophet concluded by saying, "In this you have done foolishly; therefore from now on you shall have wars."[12] If we want the victory, we must rely upon God.

"The LORD *is* a man of war."[13] "He is the Lord of hosts,"[14] which literally means the Lord of armies. God could have ended Satan's rebellion before he tempted Eve in the garden, but God did not choose to do so. God could have ended Satan's rebellion before we were born, but again He did not choose to do so. God has His timetable for doing so. He has left the enemy in the land. As a result, we are in a spiritual war, and we must fight.

We can learn about spiritual warfare from physical battle. Throughout Scripture there are references to physical battle to illustrate spiritual truths. Paul referred to Epaphroditus as "my brother, fellow worker, and fellow soldier"[15] and to Archippus as "our fellow soldier."[16] Paul told Timothy to "endure hardship as a good soldier of Jesus Christ."[17] He also wrote, "No one engaged in warfare entangles himself with the affairs of *this* life, that he may please him who enlisted him as a soldier."[18] We are told to "put on the armor of light,"[19] "the armor of righteousness,"[20] and "the whole armor of God."[21] The "word of God" is called a sword,[22] and we have "weapons of our warfare"[23] and are to "wage the good warfare,"[24] and we have "fleshly lusts which war against the soul."[25] God included in Scripture the physical battles for the Promised Land for a reason.

The life we are to live is not one of safety; it is one of risk. It is "fight[ing] the good fight of faith."[26] There is an added benefit. When we participate with God in the battle, He enables us to share in the victories. The Israelites lost faith because of the giants in the land.[27] If we have faith in God, nothing He asks us to do will be impossible for us.[28] The bigger the giants, the sweeter is the victory.

1 John 5:4 says, "And this is the victory that has overcome the world—our faith." What better way to develop faith than by joining with God in this battle? Revelation 12:11 says that the Christians overcame Satan "by the blood of the lamb and the word of their testimony." Our testimony has to be based upon personal experiences. We cannot testify about something without having first-hand knowledge. Where better to get personal experiences

regarding God than in joining Him in battle? More importantly, how can we better know our heavenly Father than by working and fighting with Him?

I was not a believer in Jesus Christ when I was in Vietnam. I did not accept Christ as my Lord and Savior until over thirteen years after my return. Nevertheless, my faith in God has been greatly strengthened by my experiences there. I hope that by sharing those experiences, your faith will also be strengthened.

---

[1] Isaiah 37:36.
[2] Deuteronomy 7:1.
[3] Genesis 12:7, 13:14-15, 15:18-21; Exodus 6:2-4, 8; Deuteronomy 34:1-4; Joshua 1:1-2, 6.
[4] Deuteronomy 9:4.
[5] Joshua 5:14.
[6] Ephesians 6:12.
[7] Hebrews 2:9; 2 Peter 2:11.
[8] Matthew 12:28; 1 John 4:4.
[9] Isaiah 30:12; 31:1; Ezekiel 33:26.
[10] 2 Chronicles 13:3, 13-18.
[11] 2 Chronicles 14:8-12.
[12] 2 Chronicles 16:1-9.
[13] Exodus 15:3a.
[14] 1 Chronicles 11:9.
[15] Philippians 2:25.
[16] Philemon :2.
[17] 2 Timothy 2:3.
[18] 2 Timothy 2:4.
[19] Romans 13:12.
[20] 2 Corinthians 6:7.
[21] Ephesians 6:11, 13.
[22] Ephesians 6:17.
[23] 2 Corinthians 10:4.
[24] 1 Timothy 1:18
[25] 1 Peter 2:11
[26] 1 Timothy 6:12.
[27] Numbers 13:31-14:4.
[28] Matthew 17:20.

Freedom Is Your Destiny!

3

WHO'S IN CHARGE?

"Not everyone who says to Me, 'Lord, Lord,'
shall enter the kingdom of heaven, but he
who does the will of My Father in heaven."

Matthew 7:21

After enlisting in the Army, I had to go through boot camp (basic training). One of the primary purposes behind boot camp was to teach us to submit to authority, to obey orders without questioning them, to become disciplined. This learning process actually began before boot camp while we were at the reception center where we spent about a week before starting basic training.

We underwent some testing at the reception center, but most of the time there was nothing "officially" for us to do. However, the assistant drill sergeant had other ideas. Whenever he came into the barracks, we were to jump to attention. Whenever he yelled, "Fall in," we were to immediately stop whatever we were doing, run outside to the front of the barracks, line up in formation, and stand at attention, looking straight ahead. Throughout the day, he would enter the barracks and yell, "Fall in!" Often, he would not come outside immediately, but would stand at a second floor window watching to see whether anyone moved, talked, or looked anywhere but straight ahead while standing in formation. If anyone did, he would impose immediate consequences. After we had stood at attention for a while, he would march us around in formation for an hour or so. He was beginning to teach us that we were to submit to authority, we were to obey immediately without asking questions. That training continued throughout boot camp.

For example, one of the things we had to do during basic training was stand guard duty, usually over some inanimate object such as a tree or garbage can. The purpose was not to teach us how to guard a tree or garbage can. It was to teach us to obey—to submit to authority. If feels pretty silly guarding a tree, or a garbage can, or other similar object.

We want to be given some more important task. But, if we do not obey when it seems unimportant, how can we be trusted to obey when it is important? We must prove ourselves first to be faithful in the little things. As Jesus said in the Parable of the Minas, when the nobleman returned after having given each of his servants one mina to invest, one servant had used the one mina to earn ten minas. The nobleman responded, "Well *done*, good servant; because you were faithful in a very little, have authority over ten cities."[1]

King David was one of the greatest warriors in the Bible. God described him as "a man after My own heart, who will do all My will."[2] Although King David did not obey perfectly (none of us can), the desire of his heart was to obey God. When He walked the earth, Jesus demonstrated the type of relationship we were to have with God and with Him. During His incarnation, Jesus lived a life of complete obedience to the Father, thereby demonstrating how we are to live.

First, He came down from heaven not to do His own will, but to do the will of the Father, who sent Him.[3] We too must desire to do God's will, not our own.

Second, Jesus did not seek His own glory; He sought to bring glory to the Father.[4] We likewise must not seek our own glory, but we should live to bring glory to God.

Third, Jesus did and said only what the Father told Him to.[5] We also must strive to do and say what the Father would have us.

Fourth, Jesus did not seek to assert His own authority, but His doctrine and judgment were from the Father.[6] His authority came from the fact that He was in such complete obedience to the Father that they were one.[7] He could say, "He who has seen Me has seen the Father."[8] Likewise, our spiritual authority comes from being in obedience to Jesus as to what we do and say and as to our doctrine.

Finally, Jesus did not take credit for the works that He did. Instead, He said, "[T]he Father who dwells in Me does the works."[9] We likewise must not take credit for the things that Jesus enables us to do.

At the same time He was living in obedience to the Father, Jesus was also teaching His disciples how they were to live. Jesus imitated the Father, and His disciples were to imitate Him. A disciple is an adherent who accepts the teacher's instruction as his or her rule of conduct and seeks to imitate the teacher. Thus, Jesus said, "It is enough for a disciple that he be like his teacher"[10] and "[E]veryone who is perfectly trained will be like his teacher."[11]

That is the relationship we are to have with Jesus. He is *the* Teacher,[12] and we are His disciples. That is why Jesus commanded, "Go therefore and make disciples of all the nations . . . teaching them to observe [obey] all things that I have commanded you."[13] To be Jesus's disciple, we must seek to learn from Him, conforming our conduct to His teaching.[14] We must make that the highest priority in our lives.[15] Thus, to walk in fellowship with Christ, we must be His disciples. "If we say that we have fellowship with Him, and walk in darkness [live a life of disobedience to God], we lie and do not practice the truth."[16]

What we call the Lord's Prayer includes, "Your kingdom come, Your will be done on earth as *it is* in heaven."[17] Jesus instructed that we are to pray that God's kingdom will come and that His will be done. That is to be the focus of our hearts—His reign and His will. As Peter and the other apostles told the high priest, "We ought to obey God rather than men."[18]

Although "God is love,"[19] it is the kingdom of God, not the social club of God, or the democracy of God. For there to be a kingdom, there must be a King, and those in the kingdom must be the King's subjects, who are to submit to the King's authority. As Jesus said, "But why do you call Me 'Lord, Lord," and not do the things which I say?"[20] He warned:

> "Not everyone who says to Me, 'Lord, Lord,' shall enter the kingdom of heaven, but he who does the will of My Father in heaven. Many will say to Me in that day [the day of judgment], 'Lord, Lord, have we not prophesied in Your name, cast out demons in Your name, and done many wonders in Your name?' And then I will declare to them, 'I never knew you; depart from Me you who practice lawlessness!' "[21]

The people Jesus was talking about in this passage prophesied in His name, cast out demons in His name, and did many wonders in His name. They were probably viewed by others as being very righteous believers. Yet, Jesus said He never knew them.

"The Lord knows those who are His."[22] The people in the passage quoted above were not His because they practiced lawlessness. The Greek word translated "practice" means to labor or work as in a field or trade in order to produce something. The Greek word translated "lawlessness" means to violate the law. Jesus was not referring to the fact that they did not live lives of perfect obedience. Rather, their lifestyles, the focus of their lives, what they worked at, was sin. They had not submitted to Jesus's lordship.

Each of us became a soldier in a spiritual army when we became a believer, when we accepted Jesus as our Lord and Savior and became His disciple. Jesus is the Commander of the army of God.[23] As He said after His resurrection from the dead, "All authority has been given to Me in heaven and on earth."[24] The Greek words translated "all authority" mean all possible authority in heaven and on earth, absolute authority. Nowhere does Scripture state that Jesus has given up His authority. In fact, "He must reign till He has put all enemies under His feet."[25] If we are going to be warriors in Jesus's army, we must submit to His authority in how we conduct our lives.

As we fight this spiritual battle for our destinies, we must seek God's strategy. Every morning before we took off, the pilots would be briefed as to our mission for that day. They did not devise the overall strategy, nor were they told what all other groups of the military would be doing. They were simply told what part we were to play. Every combat unit was not simply told to go out and do what it thought best. What each unit did had to be part of an overall strategy, even if we did not know that strategy.

Throughout the battles in the Promised Land, God

gave the Israelites the strategy for their battles. Although God also fought for them, they were usually required to participate in the battle in some way, and the strategy differed from battle to battle. For example, at Jericho God removed the enemy's insurmountable defenses so that the Israelites could ravage the enemy stronghold.[26] At Ai God had the Israelites lure the enemy into an ambush, and He told Joshua when to spring the ambush.[27] When they came to the aid of the people of Gibeon, God rained large hailstones upon their enemies, so that more died from the hailstones than were killed by the Israelites, and He caused the sun to stand still to give them more time to take revenge upon their enemies.[28] There were times when the Israelites apparently had to attack the enemy directly, because there is no reference to strategy, although God did deliver the enemies into the hand of Israel.[29] When the Moabites, Ammonites, and others came against Jehoshaphat the king of Judah, God told the Israelites they would not need to fight, and He caused their enemies to fight among themselves until they were all destroyed.[30] When the Philistines came against Israel at Mizpah, God "thundered with a loud thunder upon the Philistines" and so confused them that Israel overcame them.[31] When Sennacherib, king of Assyria, came against Jerusalem, God had the angel of the LORD kill 185,000 Assyrian soldiers during the night.[32] God's instructions to Joshua for the attack against Jericho differed from His instructions to Joshua for the attack against Ai, and both differed from His instructions at Gibeon.

As shown by King David, a man after God's own heart, we must continually seek God's direction even when fighting the same enemy. When the Philistines heard that David had been anointed king over Israel, they came against him. "David inquired of the LORD, saying, 'Shall I go up against the Philistines? Will You deliver them into my hand?' And the LORD said to David, 'Go up, for I will doubtless deliver the Philistines into your hand.'"[33] David defeated them, but the Philistines came against him again. David did not assume that because the LORD had previously told him before to go up against them that he should do it again. Instead, when David inquired of the LORD, He said: " 'You shall not go up; circle around behind them, and come upon them in front of the mulberry trees. So it shall be, when you hear the sound of marching in the tops of the mulberry trees, then you shall advance quickly. For then the LORD will go out before you to strike the camp of the Philistines.' "[34]   David did as the LORD directed, and prevailed.   When David saw that the Philistines were attacking Keilah, a city in Judah near the Philistine border, he did not assume that his men should go to Keilah's aid simply because the Philistines were the enemy. Rather, he inquired of the LORD, asking whether he should attack the Philistines, and then did so after God said He would deliver the Philistines into David's hand.[35]

God will not always give the victory immediately. When the Israelites went against Benjamin, they inquired of God and He said for Judah to go first in battle.[36] The children of Benjamin killed 22,000 Israelites.[37] That night, the children of Israel again inquired of God, and He said to go up against Benjamin.[38] They did, and Benjamin killed 18,000 more Israelites.[39]   The children of Israel again inquired of God, and He said, "Go up, for tomorrow I will deliver them into your hand."[40] The Israelites did so, and prevailed.[41]

We must follow God's directions, even if they seem illogical (e.g., marching around Jericho) or do not produce immediate victory (e.g., the Israelites against Benjamin). We may also need to combine prayer with fasting. For example, when the Moabites, Ammonites, and others came against Jehoshaphat the king of Judah, Jehoshaphat "feared, and set himself to seek the LORD, and proclaimed a fast throughout all Judah," and the LORD answered their prayers.[42] We see throughout the Bible that fasting often precedes or accompanies prayer.[43] We must realize that our strength comes from our relationship with God.

We have a tendency to create formulas for success. If we did something and had a good outcome, then we should be able to repeat that outcome by doing the same thing again. In physical battle, there is a saying that the battle plan lasts only for the first five minutes of the battle. Then it must be adjusted to the changing circumstances and how the enemy is responding. In spiritual battles, we cannot expect success by using formulas that "worked" in the past. The battle requires a relationship with God, which means we must hear from Him what we are to do in each specific circumstance.

God told the Israelites to take the ark of the covenant into battle against Jericho.[44] They did so, and prevailed. Years later, after being defeated by the Philistines, the Israelites took the ark into battle thinking that it would save them.[45] After all, that strategy had worked before. However, the ark was not a talisman. The Philistines defeated the Israelites and captured the ark.[46] The Israelites were defeated because of their sin, which separated them from God. In the battle, they could not simply do what they had done before or think that taking the ark with them would obligate God to intervene on their side. Likewise, we cannot seek to devise or learn formulas that will make us victorious in the battles for our destinies.

Various false doctrines have been created to make us believe that we can be the masters of our own destinies. Some claim that if our faith is strong enough, we can bring about what we will. Others teach that if we recite specific words in our prayers (similar to an incantation), God must answer the prayers as we desire. Others claim that if we do certain things or perform certain acts, then God will be obligated to reward us by doing what we want. These and other similar false doctrines are devised simply to appeal to our fleshly desire to be in control.

Obedience to God will be one of the greatest challenges and struggles of our lives. Our very natures are constantly demanding that we be in charge. We want to exercise our own authority. We want to do what pleases us. We want to be in control.

Submission to God's will in all things is absolutely necessary in this war. That is the only way we can live in victory. That is the only way we can fulfill our individual destinies. God exalted Christ Jesus because "He humbled Himself and became obedient to *the point of* death, even death on the cross."[47] If Jesus was exalted because of His humble obedience, how can we expect God to exalt us if we are disobedient?

I do not mean that we must obey perfectly in everything that we do in order to live out our destinies. None of us can do that. After his conversion, Paul sought to do all that God had called him to do, regardless of the opposition or adverse circumstances. He set his heart to obey God and endured many hardships in the process. Yet, he still lamented: "For what I am doing, I do not understand. For what I will to do, that I do not practice; but what I hate, that I do."[48] Even so, at the end of his life, Paul was able to write, through the inspiration of the Holy Spirit, "I have fought the good fight, I have finished the race, I have kept the faith."[49] Oh, that each of us could say that at the end of our lives!

Although our sins have been forgiven, God

disciplines us because we are His children.[50] That does not mean that He punishes every act of disobedience. The purpose of discipline is to correct the attitude of the heart, not merely to punish wrongdoing. If we are truly repentant when we stumble, there is no need for us to be disciplined for disobedience.

However, obedience should not be based upon the fear of punishment. Pagans seek to appease their gods to keep them from getting angry. The desire of our hearts should be to please God, not to appease Him. The difference between appeasing and pleasing is God's unconditional love.

When we came to God through Christ, we became God's adopted children,[51] and He "sent forth the Spirit of His Son into []our hearts, crying out, 'Abba, Father!' "[52] "God has not given us a spirit of fear, but of power and of love and of a sound mind."[53] "God demonstrate[d] His own love toward us, in that while we were still sinners, Christ died for us."[54] "In Him we have redemption through His blood, the forgiveness of sins, according to the riches of His grace."[55] Therefore, we should love Him because of the love He has shown us. We must not give up our struggle against sin because of our love for Him. He will help us through the work of the Holy Spirit in our hearts.[56]

Jesus said, "If you love Me, keep My commandments."[57] He also said, "He who has My commandments and keeps them, it is he who loves Me."[58] Love for Him comes first, and it then produces the desire to obey Him. Keeping His commandments is a sign of our love for Him, not a way to earn His love.

With respect to obedience, actions speak louder than words.[59] It is not enough to simply say that we love and obey God. For it to be genuine, it must be reflected in our conduct. Jesus taught that in the Parable of the Two Sons.[60]

A father asked his two sons to work in his vineyard, and the first refused, but later did so, while the second said he would, but did not. It was the one who actually went to the vineyard who obeyed, not the one who said he would, but did not.

True obedience is doing what we are asked even when we do not know why. Our obligation is to obey. The results of our obedience are up to God. We will not always know why God asks us to do something, or whether anything good comes from it. We often cannot see or understand the part we are playing in God's larger plan.

Obedience is more than simply living our lives according to Biblical principles. It is more than attending church on Sundays and putting money in the offering plate. For example, Jesus said, "Go into all the world and preach the gospel to every creature."[61] Yet, when Paul, Silas, and Timothy were on Paul's second missionary journey, "they were forbidden by the Holy Spirit to preach the word in Asia," and "they tried to go into Bithynia, but the Spirit did not permit them."[62] God wanted them to go to Macedonia, to preach the gospel there.[63] God had a specific plan for them that was part of His larger plan for the church. Simply knowing God's larger plan (going into all the world to preach the gospel) was not sufficient to guide them in the part they were to play at that time. They had to hear from Him regarding the specific work He wanted them to do.

We must actively seek direction from God to know what He desires us to do at any point in time. We cannot simply wait until He gets our attention. "[S]hould not a people seek [inquire of] their God?"[64] We see with Uzziah, "He sought God in the days of Zechariah, who had understanding in the visions of God; and as long as he sought the LORD, God made him prosper."[65] Jesus often went out alone to pray in order to seek direction from the

Father. Certain prophets and teachers were seeking the Lord by prayer and fasting when the Holy Spirit directed them, "Now separate to Me Barnabas and Saul [Paul] for the work to which I have called them."[66] To live out our destinies, we need to actively seek God's will, direction, and help. As stated at Proverbs 19:21, "There are many plans in a man's heart, nevertheless the LORD's counsel—that will stand."

Ephesians 2:10 states, "For we are His workmanship, created in Christ Jesus for good works, which God prepared beforehand that we should walk in them." I do not believe that God simply prepared a list of good works so that we could pick the ones we wanted to do. Rather, He has made a specific plan for each of our lives. As we live out our destinies, He will have different good works for each of us to do. They will be good works from God's perspective, not necessarily from man's. Their purpose will be to bring glory to God, not to ourselves. Any good works we perform will be because "it is God who works in [us] both to will and to do for *His* good pleasure."[67]

We must be careful not to rely upon worldly principles in our spiritual battles. Isaiah 31:1 says, "Woe to those who go down to Egypt for help, *and* rely on horses, who trust in chariots because *they are* many, and in horsemen because they are very strong, but who do not look to the Holy One of Israel, nor seek the LORD!" Egypt symbolizes the world.

As we grow in Christ, obedience will become easier. We simply must have an attitude of obedience and seeking His direction. As God told the Israelites, "If you are willing and obedient, you shall eat the good of the land."[68]

David longed for water from the well of Bethlehem, which was held by the Philistines. Upon hearing David express that desire, three of his mighty men broke through the camp of the Philistines, drew water from the well, and brought it back to David.[69]   What devotion to their commander!   What are you willing to do for your Commander, Jesus Christ?

---

[1] Luke 19:17.
[2] Acts 13:22.
[3] John 6:38.
[4] John 7:16-18.
[5] John 5:19; 8:28-29; 10:32, 36-38; 14:10-11, 31.
[6] John 5:26-27, 30; 7:16-18.
[7] John 10:30.
[8] John 14:9.
[9] John 14:10.
[10] Matthew 10:25.
[11] Luke 6:40.
[12] Matthew 23:10.
[13] Matthew 28:19-20.
[14] Matthew 10:25; Luke 6:40; John 13:34-35; John 15:7-8.
[15] Luke 14:25-33; Mark 8:34-35.
[16] 1 John 1:6.
[17] Matthew 6:10.
[18] Acts 5:29.
[19] 1 John 4:16.
[20] Luke 6:46.
[21] Matthew 7:21-23.
[22] 2 Timothy 2:19.
[23] Joshua 5:14; Revelation 19:1-16.
[24] Matthew 28:18.
[25] 1 Corinthians 15:25.
[26] Joshua 6.
[27] Joshua 8.
[28] Joshua 10:1-14.
[29] Joshua 10:28-43; 11.
[30] 2 Chronicles 20:1-24.
[31] 1 Samuel 7:7-10.
[32] 2 Kings 19.
[33] 2 Samuel 5:19.
[34] 2 Samuel 5:23-24.
[35] 1 Samuel 23:1-5.
[36] Judges 20:18.
[37] Judges 20:19-21.

[38] Judges 20:22-23.
[39] Judges 20:24-25.
[40] Judges 20:26-28.
[41] Judges 20:29-35.
[42] 2 Chronicles 20:3, 5-24.
[43] Ezra 8:23; Daniel 9:3; Judges 20:26-27; Acts 13:1-3.
[44] Joshua 6:2-5.
[45] 1 Samuel 4:1-4.
[46] 1 Samuel 4:10-11.
[47] Philippians 2:8-9.
[48] Romans 7:15.
[49] 2 Timothy 4:7.
[50] Hebrews 12:3-11.
[51] Ephesians 1:5.
[52] Galatians 4:6.
[53] 2 Timothy 1:7.
[54] Romans 5:8.
[55] Ephesians 1:7.
[56] Romans 2:28-29; 5:5; 8:1-17; Colossians 2:11-12; Ephesians 3:14-19.
[57] John 14:15.
[58] John 14:21.
[59] Isaiah 29:13; Matthew 21:28-32; Titus 1:16.
[60] Matthew 21:28-32.
[61] Mark 16:15.
[62] Acts 16:6-7.
[63] Acts 16:9-10.
[64] Isaiah 8:19.
[65] 2 Chronicles 26:5.
[66] Acts 13:1-2.
[67] Philippians 3:13.
[68] Isaiah 1:19.
[69] 1 Chronicles 11:16-18.

4

WHAT ARE WE FIGHTING FOR?

For we are His workmanship, created in Christ Jesus for good works, which God prepared beforehand that we should walk in them.

Ephesians 2:10

"I will be their God, and they shall be My people. . . . [F]or all shall know Me, from the least of them to the greatest of them."

Hebrews 8:10-11

A question often raised is, "What are we fighting for?" When one is actively engaged in combat, when the bullets are zipping past, the answer is easy. "I am fighting to stay alive, to keep those fighting alongside me alive, and to defeat the enemy." However, that answer does not explain how we happened to be in combat in the first place. That is not why people join the military. They join for other reasons, such as love of country and sense of duty.

So, the question is, "What are we fighting for in spiritual warfare?" To answer that question, let's first look at the Israelites. What were they fighting for?

The Israelites had been slaves in Egypt for 430 years.

By celebrating the first Passover, they were saved from God's judgment (the death of the firstborn) through their faith in the blood of the lamb.[1] The Passover foreshadowed salvation through faith in the shed blood of Christ, "our Passover."[2] They were then freed from bondage,[3] and after they left Egypt, they were baptized, they ate spiritual food, and they drank of Christ.[4] Then, they were to enter the Promised Land. Because the Passover foreshadowed salvation and was followed by baptism and drinking of Christ, entering the Promised Land represents the next part of their spiritual journey.

By taking the Promised Land, the Israelites were fulfilling their destiny. They were fighting to take possession of their inheritance—the Promised Land.[5] It was a good and large land flowing with milk and honey.[6] In addition, they would receive beautiful cities they did not build, houses full of all good things they did not fill, hewn-out wells they did not dig, and vineyards and olive trees they did not plant.[7]

God told Joshua: "[A]rise, go over this Jordan [River], you and all this people, to the land which I am giving to them—the children of Israel. Every place that the sole of your foot will tread upon I have given you."[8] God did not say that He would give them the land. He said that He had already given it to them. It was their destiny to receive it, but they would have to fight for it. They would get every place that the sole of their feet tread.

God's plan for the Israelites was larger than merely providing them with temporal possessions in a land that was their own. They were part of God's plan to bring His salvation to the ends of the earth. Thus, their battle was partly secular or temporal and partly spiritual or eternal.

The most important aspect of their battle was that which is eternal—intimacy with God. They were created for

God's glory and to declare His praise.[9] He brought them out of Egypt into the Promised Land so that He would be their God and they would be His people.[10] It would be a place where He would have fellowship with them and provide for them, and they would learn from Him and about Him. In other words, they would come to know Him.

We fight for the same things. God wants us to know Him. Although our sins separated us from Him,[11] He has provided a way for us to receive forgiveness of our sins and a new heart so that He can be our God, and we can be His people and come to know Him.[12]

The first step in knowing God is realizing who you are to God. You are always on His mind. He never stops thinking and caring about you. To Him, you are significant. God loves you and cherishes you. Why else would He send His Son to die for your sins?[13] He accepts you and wants a relationship with you. Why else would He desire to take you as His adopted child?[14] He has a plan for your life, to give you a future and a hope. Why else would He have already prepared wonderful things for you to do as you live out His destiny for you?[15] He will never leave you or desert you, but will be with you and guide you every step of the way. Why else would He send His Holy Spirit to dwell in you?[16] According to Jesus, eternal life is to know God the Father, the only true God, and Jesus Christ whom the Father has sent.[17]

Knowing Him is not simply knowing about Him. It requires more than simply reading Scripture, or hearing what someone else says about God. It requires developing an intimate relationship with Him. That will not happen by passively waiting for Him to get our attention. We must seek Him, and we will find Him when we search for Him with our heart.[18] To do so we must spend time with him in prayer, not just to ask Him to supply the needs of ourselves and others, but to hear from Him as to His desires and to seek His direction and guidance. It requires worshiping and praising Him and honoring Him for who He is and for all He has done. It also requires submitting to His authority and lordship. James 4:7-8 instructs us: "[S]ubmit to God. Resist the devil and he will flee from you. Draw near to God and He will draw near to you."

You and I are here for a purpose. God has a plan for each of our lives. It is our destinies. All of the days fashioned or planned for each of us were written in God's book before we were born.[19] God has given us glimpses of personal destinies. The LORD told Jeremiah, "Before I formed you in the womb I knew you; before you were born I sanctified you; I ordained you a prophet to the nations."[20] This does not mean that Jeremiah existed before God formed him in the womb. It means that God, through His foreknowledge, had a purpose and plan for Jeremiah's life before he was even born. Long before Cyrus was born and about 150 years before he began ruling Persia, God said about Cyrus, "*He is* My shepherd, and he shall perform all My pleasure, saying to Jerusalem, 'You shall be built,' and to the temple, 'Your foundation shall be laid.' "[21] Before Cyrus could be in a position to issue those edicts, he had to conquer Babylon, which was obviously God's plan. Paul, writing by the inspiration of the Holy Spirit, wrote that God had separated him from his mother's womb and called him to preach Jesus among the Gentiles.[22] The calling to do the work of an apostle did not occur until Paul was an adult.[23]

In describing our relationship with Jesus, Scripture uses the analogy that believers are His body and He is the head.[24] A person's head cannot do anything without a body. That analogy shows that God has an important role for each of us to play as part of the body of Christ. He wants to work through each of us to accomplish His purposes. That includes you and me. You have something to contribute. You have a part to play. You are significant in God's eyes.

It does not matter what one has done in the past, or one's nationality, or one's station in life. The persons whom God chose to be in the genealogy of Jesus through Mary, His earthly mother, included a child born out of wedlock (Perez), a prostitute (Rahab), a poor widow from Moab who was not a Jew (Ruth), an adulteress (Bathsheba, the wife of Uriah, a soldier), and an adulterer and murderer (King David). Even though they had not lived perfect lives, Rahab was praised in Scripture for her faith,[25] and King David was described by God as *"a man after My own heart*, who will do all My will."[26]

Sometimes, people equate destiny with position, power, fame, or fortune. If they are leading what they view as ordinary lives, they feel they have no destiny. Our destinies are more than things that are merely temporal. All of these things are described in Scripture as wood, hay, and straw that will be burned up.[27] As we walk out our destinies, it may include God putting us in positions of significance or power or bestowing upon us fame or fortune, but that is simply to enable us to do what He has planned for us to do.

We cannot judge a person's destiny by secular standards. The focus of each of our destinies is our relationship with God and doing what He asks, not what we gain in the eyes of the world. The most significant part of our destinies, the only part of eternal significance, is the role we play in God's plan. Look at Jesus. When He walked the earth, He had no secular position or power. He did not occupy a position of authority or prestige in either the religious structure or the government. He was not wealthy. In fact, as an adult He did not even have a home.[28] He was not accepted or revered except by a few. Jesus was rejected by His generation and by those who knew Him in his home town,[29] and His own brothers did not believe in Him.[30] In fact, many of the people said that Jesus had a demon and was mad.[31] Yet, He certainly had a destiny and fulfilled it!

Our destinies include all aspects of our lives. We cannot separate our lives into the secular and the spiritual. God's plan for our lives is all encompassing. It includes family, friends, and career. We are to bear fruit to God[32] in all that we do.

In *The Seven Mountain Prophecy*,[33] Johnny Enlow identifies seven culture-shaping areas—the media, government, education, economy, religion, celebration (arts and entertainment), and the family. He refers to these seven foundations of culture or areas of influence as "mountains." When considering your destiny, it may be useful to think about what mountain you are on. What is your primary area of influence? What gifts and talents has God given you? What passion and desires has He placed in your heart? Where has he placed you? How can Christ use you to influence others for Him? We are each to be a Christlike influence where we are assigned. In this life, we will probably never know the positive impacts we have had on the lives of others.

When the Israelites were ready to cross the Jordan River and take possession of the Promised Land, God told Joshua, "Every place that the sole of your foot will tread upon I have given you, as I said to Moses. . . . No man shall *be able to* stand before you all the days of your life . . . . I will not leave you nor forsake you. Be strong and of good courage . . . ."[34]

Likewise, walking out our destinies will be a battle, but it will be God's battle. After all, it is His plan for your life. He wants you to succeed! He will go with you each step of the way. As God told Joshua, "Have I not commanded you? Be strong and of good courage; do not be afraid, or be dismayed, for the LORD your God *is* with you wherever you go."[35]

Because our destinies are God's plan for our lives and He is all-knowing, all-powerful, and present at all places at all times, nobody or nothing can keep us from fulfilling our destinies except ourselves. Only you can keep you from doing and being all that God has planned for your life. The focus of the battle will be our hearts—our minds, our wills, and our emotions. That is the primary battlefield. Our enemy will do all that he can to keep us from doing God's will by seeking to influence our minds, our wills, and our emotions. The enemy's goal is to cause us to derail our destinies.

Our thought-lives will be the front line in this battle. God brought the great flood in the time of Noah because "the LORD saw that the wickedness of man *was* great in the earth, and *that* every intent of the thoughts of his heart *was* only evil continually."[36] As Jesus said, "For from within, out of the heart of men, proceed evil thoughts, adulteries, fornications, murders, thefts, covetousness, wickedness, deceit, lewdness, an evil eye, blasphemy, pride, foolishness."[37] Having an improper thought is not sin, but it can certainly lead to sin if we continue to entertain it. As explained in James 1:14-15: "[E]ach one is tempted [by evil] when he is drawn away by his own desires and enticed. Then, when desire has conceived, it gives birth to sin; and sin, when it is full-grown, brings forth death." That is why we are to bring "every thought into captivity to the obedience of Christ."[38]

Christianity is first and foremost a relationship with God. "[T]he people who know their God shall be strong, and carry out *great exploits*."[39] Satan will do all he can to keep us from knowing our God. I believe that is why he tempted Adam and Eve in the garden, because he sought to destroy their relationship with God by causing them to sin. He thought that introducing sin into the world would destroy not only Adam's and Eve's relationships with God, but also that of their descendants. Later, I will discuss Satan's primary strategies for doing so. However, he did not anticipate that the relationship would be restored by the sacrifice of Jesus on the cross. In Christ, we are holy and without blame before God.[40] When we come to God through Jesus Christ, we become God's adopted children and can draw near to him, crying out, "Abba, Father."[41]

Our hearts must be fully devoted to God. Each of us must *"love the LORD your God with all your heart, with all your soul, and with all your mind."*[42] Our heart's desire must be as stated in Psalm 27:4:

> One *thing* I have desired of the LORD,
> That will I seek;
> That I may dwell in the house of the LORD
> All the days of my life,
> To behold the beauty of the LORD,
> And to inquire in His temple.

He created each of us for His glory.[43] Our attitudes must simply be, God, I am Yours; use me as You wish. "A man's heart plans his way, but the LORD directs his steps."[44] Because fulfilling your destiny will be a battle, to prevail you must have the heart of a warrior!

---

[1] Hebrews 11:28.
[2] 1 Corinthians 5:7. Jesus is also the "Lamb of God who takes away the sin of the world" (John 1:29) and "a lamb without blemish and without spot" who redeemed us with His precious blood (1 Peter 1:18-19).
[3] Exodus 12:1-42.

[4] 1 Corinthians 10:1-4.
[5] Genesis 15:7; 28:4; Exodus 23:30.
[6] Exodus 3:8; Leviticus 20:24.
[7] Deuteronomy 6:10-11.
[8] Joshua 1:2-3.
[9] Isaiah 43:7, 21.
[10] Genesis 17:7-8; Exodus 6:2-8; 29:45-46; 34:10-16; Leviticus 20:22-26; 25:38; 26:11-12.
[11] Isaiah 59:2.
[12] Jeremiah 31:34; Ezekiel 36:26-28.
[13] 1 John 4:9-10.
[14] Romans 8:15-17.
[15] Ephesians 2:10.
[16] John 16:13; Romans 5:5.
[17] John 17:3.
[18] Jeremiah 29:13.
[19] Psalm 139:16.
[20] Jeremiah 1:4-5.
[21] Isaiah 44:28.
[22] Galatians 1:15-16.
[23] Acts 13:2; Romans 1:1.
[24] 1 Corinthians 12:27; Ephesians 4:12-16; Colossians 1:24.
[25] Hebrews 11:31.
[26] Acts 13:22.
[27] 1 Corinthians 3:12-15.
[28] Matthew 8:20.
[29] Matthew 11:16-19; 13:55-57.
[30] John 7:5.
[31] John 10:20.
[32] Romans 7:4.
[33] Charisma House, 2008.
[34] Joshua 1:3-6.
[35] Joshua 1:9.
[36] Genesis 6:5.
[37] Mark 7:21-22.
[38] 2 Corinthians 10:5.
[39] Daniel 11:32.
[40] Ephesians 1:4.
[41] Romans 8:15-16.
[42] Matthew 22:37.
[43] Isaiah 43:7; Matthew 5:16.
[44] Proverbs 16:9.

Freedom Is Your Destiny!

5

CREATURE COMFORTS

You therefore must endure hardship as a good soldier in Jesus Christ.

2 Timothy 2:3

On September 27, 1967, I took the oath of office to become a soldier in the United States Army. As soon as I did so, my life was no longer my own. I literally became the property of the United States Army. In fact, I read about a soldier in Vietnam who was threatened with being court-martialed for damaging military property because he had allowed his leg to become infected by not seeking prompt medical care for a shrapnel wound.

I knew that by joining the Army, I would have to give up things of civilian life. My first meal in the Army was a breakfast of powdered eggs, two extremely well-done link sausages, and a glass of very strong grapefruit juice. You will not find powdered eggs on anyone's list of favorite foods. Once we had eaten, we were transported to a barber shop where I got an Army regulation haircut, which is simply cutting off all of your hair. I even had to pay the barber 90¢. We were then taken to a supply building where we were issued uniforms, underwear, socks, boots, hats, and other items and had to relinquish all items of civilian clothing, which were then shipped back to our homes. After the first day, the only things I owned were my wristwatch, my wallet, and some money. Everything else I had was Army issue.

I had to give up the comforts of civilian life throughout the time I was in the military, not just in boot camp. When I arrived in Ft. Eustis, Virginia, for helicopter maintenance school, my first barracks was an uninsulated, two-story, wooden building that we were told had previously been condemned. The walls were simply 2x4 studs with wooden siding nailed to the outside. There were holes in the walls where the siding had warped and pulled away from the studs. Even though it was winter and there was snow on the ground, we had to keep the windows wide open so that large floor fans could blow away the coal smoke that came up through the heat vents. My two Army blankets were none too warm. Every morning, my nose was black from breathing the coal smoke during the night. Fortunately, we only had to stay in that barracks building for a couple of weeks until a more modern one became available.

In Soc Trang, our drinking water was yellow in color, and it had a strong, bitter flavor. I once tried in vain to cover the taste by dumping a whole packet of Kool-Aid into one cup of water, but I could still taste the water. I therefore always gulped down the water in order to shorten the time I had to taste it. To avoid drinking the water, I drank whatever liquid I could buy at the small PX (post exchange) on our base, but sometimes that was not much. One month, the only thing I could buy to drink was warm root beer. I could count on one hand the number of root beers I have drunk since then.

During my entire second year in Vietnam, the Army usually provided me with only one meal a day—a box of C-rations. We in the gunship platoon typically took off in the morning before the first shift of cooks had breakfast prepared in the mess hall, and we usually returned after the second shift of cooks had left for the day and the mess hall was closed. One morning when I arrived at the mess hall to pick up my box of C-rations, one of the aircrew members asked the sergeant in charge, "Can't you give us something for breakfast?" The sergeant looked around for a few minutes and then gave each of us one slice of white bread, saying, "This is all we have ready." We got the message. Do not expect anything on the days we flew except a box of C-rations for lunch. I flew almost every day.

Each box of C-rations contained a canned meat item, a canned fruit item, a can of bread or crackers, and a small disc of chocolate. The meals with crackers also had peanut butter or cheese spread, and the chocolate was formulated not to melt as easily in the tropical heat. There were twelve different meal selections, each containing about 1200 calories. To me, the worst meal was ham and lima beans, and my favorite was beans and wieners, what I called "beanie weanies."

At first I tried to make the C-rations more appetizing by heating them and adding hot sauce. I heated them in two ways. One was using C-4, a plastic explosive that burned very hot. I would tear off a small piece and light it to heat my can of food. The other was by using JP-4, the jet fuel used in my helicopter. If I had a can of white bread, I would mash it down in the opened can, pour jet fuel into it, and light it to heat another can of C-rations. After a while, I simply ate my C-rations cold. We usually did not have time to heat them and would just eat them cold while flying.

If I wanted more than one meal on the days I flew, I went to the Enlisted Men's Club after I returned from flying and purchased what they passed off as a hamburger and

French fries. The French fries were not made from fresh potatoes. They appeared to be instant potatoes to which they added enough water to make into a paste and then used something to form it into French fry shapes, which were deep fat fried. The ketchup was tomato paste to which they added enough water to make it runny. The buns were okay, but I never asked what the meat was.

There are two things that stand out in my memory regarding the times I did eat in the mess hall. I got milk, if I could find some that had not turned sour. There were quart cartons of milk sitting on a table, and I would go from carton to carton, opening it and smelling the contents until I found one that had not turned sour. I usually had to open several before finding one I could drink. When we did make it back from flying before the mess hall had closed, everyone else had already eaten. By then, there were no more forks or spoons left, so I had to eat with a case knife, which was challenging for some foods like peas. If I could have had my choice of C-ration meals, I would have preferred eating them rather than eating in the mess hall.

Needless to say, food was a high priority when I was in Vietnam. For a few months I was stationed at a larger base named Vihn Long, which was located about 45 miles north of Soc Trang. I had a nonflying job, and so I ate in the mess hall every day. At every meal, there was a long line of soldiers waiting to enter the mess hall. Once inside, we picked up our trays and slid them down the chow line so that cooks could dole out the food onto our trays. One time the soldier in front of me complained that the cook was not putting enough food on the soldier's tray. The cook answered: "We're not trying to fatten you up. We're just trying to keep you alive." Once we had our tray of food, we had to find a place to sit, which was often difficult because the eating area was always crowded. It was also very noisy with several hundred men talking at once.

One morning, just as we were getting up, we had a mortar attack. Everyone else ran to the bunkers for safety. I ran to the mess hall. When I arrived, there was no line. I just walked right in. The cooks were gone, so I could serve myself. I had just the right amount of scrambled eggs, three strips of bacon instead of two, and I did not drown my pancake in syrup. I had no problem finding a place to sit. The room was empty. I selected a table in the middle of the mess hall, sat down, and had a nice, quiet, leisurely breakfast, followed by a cup of coffee. By the time I was done, the mortar attack was over, so I slipped out and returned to my barracks. That was the best meal I had in Vietnam!

One day when I was stationed in Soc Trang, we were returning to base from a mission when I looked down and saw a watermelon patch. I told the pilot, and he landed the helicopter so I could grab a few watermelons. That may have been the first helicopter gunship watermelon raid in history.

Although it was very hot and humid in Vietnam, our hootches (barracks) were not air conditioned. We had no television. Obviously, we had no computers, internet, cell phones, or even regular telephones that we could use. There were only two radio stations we could listen to—Armed Forces Radio and Radio Hanoi (propaganda and music broadcast from North Vietnam). For entertainment, we had an outdoor theater where we, and the mosquitoes, could watch movies during the evenings on weekends.

The living conditions of foot soldiers were worse. Being assigned to a helicopter company meant that I had a dry bed to sleep in each night; I did not have to slog through mud, rice paddies, and leech-infested streams; I did not have to carry anything on my back; and while flying

I had a form of air conditioning (the open door of the helicopter). I also had a fan blowing on me when I slept at night to keep the mosquitoes off. We were to take malaria tablets regularly, but they were distributed with meals in the mess hall. Since I rarely ate there after I began flying, I did not take those tablets during most of my time in Vietnam. After I returned to the United States, I went through a short period of sudden high fevers and chills, which may have been a mild case of malaria.

Living without many of the conveniences to which we have grown accustomed is simply the life of a soldier, especially in combat. We were there to fight, not to relax and enjoy sunny Southeast Asia as if on vacation. We had to make do with what we had.

As Christians, we are not our own. We have been bought at a price.[1] We have been redeemed and purchased "with the precious blood of Christ, as a lamb without blemish and without spot."[2] Since we are members of the spiritual army, we must put the things of civilian life behind us. We "must endure hardship as a good soldier of Jesus Christ. No one engaged in warfare entangles himself with the affairs of *this* life, that he may please him who enlisted him as a soldier."[3]

That does not mean that we must withdraw from anything that is not "religious" or "spiritual." Some wrongly believe that Christians should not become involved in politics or government, or that they should not even vote. God calls His servants to all areas of life, including politics and government (Joseph and Daniel). Compartmentalizing life into the religious and the secular is not Biblical. We must keep the affairs of this life in proper perspective, keeping in mind what is of eternal significance and what is not.[4] "[O]ur citizenship is in heaven,"[5] and we must therefore set our minds on things above, not on things on the earth.[6] Our identity must be as a soldier of Christ, and our desire must be to please our Commander, the Lord Jesus Christ.

As obedient soldiers, we may be called to do things that entail giving up some of the comforts of this world. When I answered God's call to become a judge, it resulted in about a 40% cut in income. "[O]ne's life does not consist in the abundance of the things he possesses."[7] We can never find fulfillment in the things of the world. If we try, we will learn that we can never have enough money, power, sex, possessions, fame, or other things of the world. We will always want just a little more.

Before I became a believer in Christ Jesus, I knew that there was something missing from my life, but I did not know what it was. Not long after I married, my wife's brother invited us to church to hear him give his testimony about Christ. We went to be polite, but as soon as I entered the church, before the service had even begun, I knew what had been missing from my life. It was God! It is in Him that we find true fulfillment.

He has the right to "station" us wherever He wants and to assign us to whatever tasks He desires. Wherever we are stationed, whatever assignments we are given, our attitude must be as expressed by Paul.

> [F]or I have learned in whatever state I am, to be content: I know how to be abased, and I know how to abound. Everywhere and in all things I have learned both to be full and to be hungry, both to abound and to suffer need. I can do all things through Christ who strengthens me.[8]

There will be times when God will ask us to choose between obeying Him and enjoying the things of the world.

In the Parable of the Sower, Jesus warned what happens to those whose hearts are focused on the world, which He characterized as being like soil where thorns were growing. He said, "Now these are the ones sown among thorns; *they are* the ones who hear the word, and the cares of this world, the deceitfulness of riches, and the desires for other things entering in choke the word, and it becomes unfruitful."[9]

Our desire must be to be fruitful—to bear fruit to God that will last. After I graduated from law school, my plan was simply to become the best attorney I could. I had no desire to be a judge. When God called me into the judiciary, I obeyed, and I am glad that I did. The more I worked as a judge, the more I liked it. I have had a greater opportunity as a judge to impact others for Christ than I would have had I not obeyed.

---

[1] 1 Corinthians 6:19-20.
[2] 1 Peter 1:19.
[3] 2 Timothy 2:3-4.
[4] 1 John 2:15-17.
[5] Philippians 3:20.
[6] Colossians 3:2.
[7] Luke 12:15.
[8] Philippians 4:11-13.
[9] Mark 4:18-19.

6

THE PYRAMID SCHEME

"You know that the rulers of the Gentiles lord it over them, and those who are great exercise authority over them. Yet it shall not be so among you; but whoever desires to become great among you, let him be your servant."

Matthew 20:25-26

When I was in the Army, there was a hierarchy of authority from the Commander-in-Chief (the President); to the Secretary of Defense; to the Joint Chiefs of Staff; to the Commander in Chief of the Pacific Theater; to the Commander of the United States Military Assistance Command, Vietnam; to the Commander of the First Aviation Brigade; to the Commander of the 164th Combat Aviation Group; to the Commander of the 13th Combat Aviation Battalion; to the Commander of the 121st Assault Helicopter Company; to the gunship platoon leader; to the platoon sergeant; to me. At each level below the Joint Chiefs of Staff, there were multiple, parallel organizational groups. Thus, the organizational chart would look like a pyramid. At each level of the organizational hierarchy, there were officers and/or noncommissioned officers who assisted the commanders at those levels.

Authority was based on position (rank). Generally, I was subordinate to everyone who was higher in rank, particularly officers. The hierarchy was necessary because the President did not have the ability to communicate directly with each soldier, he did not know what each soldier was doing, and he did not have the experience and knowledge to know what each soldier needed to do. We were required to obey those who held higher positions of authority, regardless of their abilities.

For example, during the month that I was a door gunner on a slick (a troop-carrying helicopter), we were flying in formation one morning while it was still dark, headed for a staging area where we would pick up soldiers to insert into a landing zone. The pilot in the last helicopter in the formation had the responsibility of monitoring the formation. He radioed a Major, who was flying in the middle of the formation, and told him that he was about five rotor widths (a rotor width is about 86 feet) from the helicopter next to him and that he should close that distance to about two rotor widths. The Major immediately began screaming over the radio that he could not get any closer or they would all be killed. He was afraid that the rotor blades of his helicopter would overlap the rotor blades of the adjoining helicopter. I have seen that happen with two helicopters on the ground, and their main rotors simply disintegrated. If it happened in the air, both crews would be killed. However, getting to within about two rotor widths was not dangerous. It was standard when flying in formation, and all of the other pilots were maintaining that distance. Shortly after that, the Major was assigned to the desk job of being the company XO (executive officer).

As XO, the Major was second in command in the company. In 1968, around the beginning of the Vietnamese

Lunar New Year celebration (called "Tet"), the enemy in Vietnam had launched a major offensive in much of South Vietnam. The Major was certain that the enemy would do so again around Tet of 1969. Concerned that the Vietnamese who worked at the airfield may have installed booby traps, he walked around the company area with a pair of wire cutters, cutting any suspicious-looking wires. The wires he cut included the communication wires to the bunkers and an extension cord that ran from one officer's room to another's.

When there was no Tet offensive in 1969, the Major decided that we were not in a combat zone and that our company area needed to be beautified. There were dirt-filled rocket boxes (wooden boxes in which rockets were shipped) stacked about waist high around the hootches to provide some protection from flying shrapnel if a mortar round exploded near the hootch. The Major ordered that the unsightly rocket boxes be removed and that they be replaced with flowers. Even though his order made no sense, it was carried out because of his authority as XO. Shortly after some of the boxes had been removed, we had another mortar attack. Fortunately, nobody was injured due to the missing rocket boxes, but they were immediately returned to their original places. The Major was then nicknamed "Flowerpot Six." The "Six" designation in a radio call sign indicated the commanding officer. Thus, our company commander's call sign was "Tiger Six" (our company was called the "Tigers"). Shortly thereafter, the Major was transferred to battalion headquarters.

I mentioned above that I have seen what happens when the main rotors of two helicopters overlap. One day while I was flying in the slicks, my helicopter was in the middle of a single-file formation of helicopters that were all landing simultaneously along one side of the runway.

There was another helicopter in a revetment near the runway that was running at operational rpm's because they were tracking its tail rotor blades. Just as my helicopter touched down, the second helicopter in front of mine touched down too close to the helicopter in the revetment, and their rotor blades overlapped. There were immediately parts of helicopters flying everywhere.

I jumped out and began to run towards that helicopter to see if anyone was injured, but had to stop because there was still debris flying through the air and some of it severed a push-pull tube controlling the pitch on one of the main rotor blades of the helicopter immediately in front of mine. That helicopter began bouncing up and down and rotating clockwise, so that its tail boom blocked my path to the other helicopter. As I watched, the bouncing grew more violent until the helicopter's rotor blades flexed downward and sliced its tail boom in half.

I then ran to the helicopter ahead of it, and saw that nobody was injured. Its transmission had ripped through the back wall and ceiling of the cabin and was resting between the pilot's and copilot's seats.

The rotor blades of the helicopter in the revetment had simply disintegrated and its mast (the vertical steel pipe connecting the transmission and main rotor assembly) had snapped. The forces ripped the transmission from the helicopter, and the transmission flew towards the tail rotor, hitting the ground next to the crew chief, who was standing near the tail rotor. The mast of the helicopter that was landing snapped, and its main rotor blade assembly rocketed skyward. It went straight up, and then tilted to one side and flew across the runway, hitting the ground next to a bunker. Fortunately, nobody was injured.

Because of our limitations, hierarchical pyramids are necessary in order for us to organize people to accomplish a task. The person in charge is not omniscient, omnipresent, or omnipotent. There must be someone in authority at the top with others of lesser authority below to carry out orders. The larger the bureaucracy, the more levels of authority there are, and the more those at the top have to delegate decision making to those below. However, we must keep in mind that a hierarchy is an organizational structure that is necessary due to our limitations as created beings. It is not a structure necessary for God to accomplish His purposes. Although God can certainly use a hierarchy, He does not need one for His army.

As Jesus said, "My sheep hear My voice, and I know them, and they follow Me."[1] We simply must learn to discern His voice. We do not need intermediaries The only hierarchy needed is Jesus at the top and all of us under Him. As I mentioned above, the metaphor used in Scripture is Jesus is the head and we are all members of His body.[2] Just as your head can communicate directly to the various parts of your body, Jesus can communicate directly to each person who is part of the body of Christ—all believers. That does not mean that Christ will not speak to us through someone else. He can and will. But, we can also speak directly with Him. A go-between is not needed for us to communicate with Him. He hears our prayers, and we can learn to discern His voice.

In Christ's body there is diversity of function. Those who comprise His body have differing roles. The Lord has called and gifted each of us for how He has planned to work through us. God has set each one of us in the body as He pleased.[3] Each of us has a necessary part to play. You have a necessary part to play.

Unlike a physical army, in God's army authority does not come from holding a particular office or position. For example, when He walked the earth Jesus taught with authority,[4] but He did not hold an earthly office or position of authority. He was not a member of a religious or governmental hierarchy. In fact, it was those in positions of authority (the chief priests, who supported Roman rule so they could live in luxury; the Pharisees, who ruled through man-made religious obligations; and the elders) who opposed Jesus and sought to kill Him because He threatened their positions of power. Jesus's authority came from the fact that He was speaking as directed by God. As He said, "For I have not spoken on My own *authority*; but the Father who sent Me gave Me a command, what I should say and what I should speak."[5] Similarly, Paul's authority was based upon the fact that he was speaking, or writing, as directed by Jesus. As he wrote to the Church at Corinth, "[S]ince you seek proof of Christ speaking in me."[6] That is the only legitimate authority in which any believer can act, no matter what his or her title or position. A believer has authority to the extent that he or she is speaking or doing what Jesus, through the Holy Spirit, has commanded at that particular time.

That does not mean that there are no leaders in the body of Christ. Spiritual leadership simply differs from leadership based upon position or rank. Authority based upon position or rank is used to manage and control people in order to accomplish the purposes of those in positions of authority. True leaders do not manage or control people. They lead by example, and they build up and equip people in order to release them into their destinies. Leaders do not covet position, nor does their authority come from holding a position or rank. Their authority comes from their relationship and walk with God, and their anointing.

Kings Saul and David illustrate that difference. For King Saul, retaining his position of authority as king was more important than obeying the word of God. God told

Saul, through Samuel the Prophet, to go to Gilgal and wait seven days, when Samuel would come and offer burnt offerings, make sacrifices of peace offerings, and show Saul what to do.[7] Saul went to Gilgal and waited, but on the seventh day he took it upon himself to offer a burnt offering.[8] He did so, in disobedience to God's word, because the people were scattering from him out of fear of the Philistines.[9] If the people left him, he would lose his position of authority. That was more important to him than obeying the word of God. Saul again disobeyed God when he was told to destroy the Amalekites and all of their livestock.[10] Instead, he kept alive the Amalekite king and the best of the sheep and oxen, ostensibly to sacrifice to God.[11] Saul's excuse for his disobedience was that he "feared the people and obeyed their voice."[12] There is no indication that the people threatened harm to Saul. His only fear would have been that they would cease following him if he did not accede to their wishes. Again, his position of authority was more important to him than obeying the word of God. Ironically, because of his disobedience, he lost his position of authority.[13] Even after Samuel told Saul that God had rejected him as king, Saul's concern was maintaining the appearance of having God's approval. He begged Samuel to go with him to worship Samuel's God, so that Saul would be honored before the elders and the people.[14] He was more concerned with the disapproval of the people than the disapproval of God.

Saul also sought to kill David because, seeing that God was with David, Saul feared losing his kingdom—his position of authority.[15] He even killed the priests for assisting David, even though they did so innocently.[16] Leaders like Saul are threatened by others who are operating in God's favor and anointing because they fear the loss of their own positions of authority—that the people (congregation) will follow someone with a greater anointing. They therefore often attempt to destroy those people (such as through character assassination), drive them away (out of the church), or keep them from operating in their giftings (such as by placing restrictions on them or assigning them tasks where their giftings may not be apparent).

David did not place position above the word of God. After David had been anointed by Samuel as king and while Saul was seeking to kill him, David twice passed up an opportunity to kill Saul because doing so would have been disobedient to God.[17] He would not stretch out his hand against the LORD's anointed.[18] Had David desired the position of authority more than obedience to God, he would have rationalized that God had delivered Saul into his hand so he could kill Saul and assume his rightful place on the throne.

David shepherded the people "according to the integrity of his heart."[19] As David said, "The Rock of Israel spoke to me: 'He who rules over men must be just, ruling in the fear of God.' "[20]

The example given in the New Testament is that a local congregation would have elders, who are also called overseers or in some translations bishops. The elders were to shepherd (also translated pastor) the congregation by serving as Christlike examples, not as rulers. As stated in 1 Peter 5:3, elders are to shepherd the flock by serving as overseers, not "as being lords over those entrusted to you, but being examples to the flock." The Greek word translated "lords over" means "to exercise, or gain, dominion over."[21]

Likewise, the other ten Apostles became indignant toward James and John when their mother asked that they be given the places of highest honor and authority in

Jesus's kingdom (at His right hand and His left). In response, Jesus instructed the ten: "You know that the rulers of the Gentiles lord it over them, and those who are great exercise authority over them. Yet it shall not be so among you; but whoever desires to become great among you, let him be your servant."[22]

Leaders do not exercise dominion as lords; they are to lead by example. Leading by example is based upon Godly character, not position. Thus, when advising Timothy on leadership, Paul wrote, "Let no one despise your youth, but be an example to the believers in word, in conduct, in love, in spirit, in faith, in purity."[23] Similarly, he advised Titus, "Likewise exhort the young men to be sober-minded, in all things showing yourself *to be* a pattern of good works; in doctrine *showing* integrity, reverence, incorruptibility, sound speech that cannot be condemned, that one who is an opponent may be ashamed, having nothing evil to say of you."[24] Paul also exhorted others to follow the example he showed in living his life.[25] He wrote, "Imitate me, just as I also *imitate* Christ."[26]

Obviously, to lead by example we must be walking in fellowship with God according to His truth.[27] The focus is building His kingdom, not ours. Paul rebuked the church at Corinth because they were following men, not the Lord. He wrote, "Now, I say this, that each of you says, 'I am of Paul,' or 'I am of Apollos,' or 'I am of Cephas,' or 'I am of Christ.' Is Christ divided? Was Paul crucified for you? Or were you baptized in the name of Paul?"[28]

We cannot change people's hearts by exercising dominion over them. That change must come from within. Being a servant leader requires patience. As Paul advised Timothy, "Convince, rebuke, exhort, with all longsuffering and teaching."[29]

[1] John 10:27.
[2] Colossians 1:18; 2:19.
[3] 1 Corinthians 12:18.
[4] Matthew 7:28-29.
[5] John 12:49.
[6] 2 Corinthians 13:3.
[7] 1 Samuel 10:8.
[8] 1 Samuel 13:4-9.
[9] 1 Samuel 13:11-12.
[10] 1 Samuel 15:3.
[11] 1 Samuel 15:9, 15.
[12] 1 Samuel 15:24.
[13] 1 Samuel 13:14; 15:26.
[14] 1 Samuel 15:25-30.
[15] 1 Samuel 18:7-15.
[16] 1 Samuel 22:6-18.
[17] 1 Samuel 24:1-7; 26:1-12.
[18] 1 Samuel 24:6; 26:9.
[19] Psalm 78:72.
[20] 2 Samuel 23:3.
[21] W.E. Vine, "An Expository Dictionary of New Testament Words with their Precise Meanings for English Readers," *Vines Complete Expository Dictionary of Old and New Testament Words* (Nashville: Thomas Nelson Publishers, 1985), p. 325.
[22] Matthew 20:25-26.
[23] 1 Timothy 4:12.
[24] Titus 2:6-8.
[25] Philippians 3:17; 2 Thessalonians 3:7-9.
[26] 1 Corinthians 11:1.
[27] 1 John 1:6.
[28] 1 Corinthians 1:12-13.
[29] 2 Timothy 4:2.

7

AIMLESS RULES

"And in vain they worship Me,
Teaching as doctrines the
commandments of men."

Mark 7:7

When I was in basic training, I soon learned that my outward appearance was important. I was to look like a soldier. My uniform was to be clean and pressed, with every button buttoned. I was to keep my hair short, my face clean shaven, my hands out of my pockets, my hat on straight, my belt buckle polished, my pant legs bloused, and my boots spit shined. I spent many hours spit shining my boots. Once I was in combat, however, my outward appearance was no longer that important. In combat, you do not want the enemy to see the glint from a highly polished brass belt buckle, nor do you want to spend your time spit polishing your boots. Everything is reduced to what is really important for surviving and defeating the enemy. We did not care whether someone would look good on the parade field. We only cared about whether he could do his job under fire. It was performance, not appearance, that kept people alive and enabled us to prevail over the enemy.

Some of the Army's regulations actually hindered our combat effectiveness. For example, the Army had regulations as to how many spare parts we could have. Twice a year, inspectors arrived to check, among other things, whether we had too many spare parts. Prior to the arrival of the inspectors, extra spare parts were hidden, and those that could not be hidden were thrown away.

For a few months at the end of my first year in Vietnam, I was stationed at Vinh Long. It had large ponds along its runway where dirt had been excavated in order to build the runway. In preparation for a coming inspection, I was ordered to throw excess spare parts into the ponds. One of the parts I threw away was a 42-degree gear box, which was used where the tail rotor drive shaft along the top of the tail boom changed direction to go up the vertical fin. That small gear box, which I could easily hold in my hands, cost about the same as a brand new Chevrolet Nova.

My unit in Soc Trang had a helicopter (called the Wrecker) that was loaded with spare parts and would often fly to the airstrip from which we were operating in order to have the parts available to keep the helicopters running. One day we were operating out of Vinh Long, and the Wrecker was parked next to the ponds. While the pilot was waiting there, he decided to go fishing. As he was wading in the water, his foot struck something large. He obtained a crane and, upon lifting the object out of the water, discovered that it was a turbine engine shipping container which contained a brand new turbine engine for a Huey helicopter. He loaded it into the Wrecker and brought it back to our unit. The engine had probably been thrown into the pond to avoid discovery during an inspection.

I was told that the regulations as to the permissible inventory of spare parts had been drafted for when the helicopters were flying 70 to 75 hours per month (if my memory is correct) in peace time. Ours, at least the gunships, were flying about 200 hours per month, and parts were being damaged regularly by enemy fire. Thus, we needed more than the allotted amount of spare parts to keep the helicopters flying. It was not uncommon to have from one to four helicopters parked in front of the hangar so that they could be cannibalized (stripped of parts) in order to keep other helicopters flying. These regulations restricted the supply of necessary spare parts and hindered our operational effectiveness.

One thing we are very prone to do is to create doctrine and regulations—to create man-made religion. Christianity is not a religion, in that sense. It is a relationship with the living God. Neither performing religious rituals, nor belonging to a particular religious organization or group, nor submitting to the authority of any religious leader has anything to do with being saved, or with being effective in our spiritual battle.

In fact, many are deceived into believing that they can earn salvation, or God's love, or His acceptance, or His blessings, by following rules and performing good works. We can become so focused on our performance of rituals and works that we overlook developing a relationship with God and Christ. The rituals and works take the place of the relationship. They also appeal to our fleshly nature that wants to earn our salvation and blessing in order to show that we deserve it and how good or righteous we are.

A relationship with God is not built upon following rules and performing works. It must come from the heart. Obeying rules and regulations never changed anyone's heart.[1] As God told the Israelites, "[T]hese people draw near with their mouths and honor Me with their lips, but have removed their hearts from Me."[2] God said to them, "To what purpose *is* the multitude of your sacrifices to Me?

. . . Bring no more futile sacrifices; incense is an abomination to Me. The New Moons, the Sabbaths, and the calling of assemblies—I cannot endure iniquity and the sacred meeting."[3]

Because they were simply going through rituals but their hearts were not submitted to Him, God told them that He would not even hear their prayers.[4] Rather than perform meaningless rituals, He commanded them, "Cease to do evil, learn to do good; seek justice, rebuke the oppressor; defend the fatherless, plead for the widow."[5] He concluded by telling them, " 'If you are willing and obedient, you shall eat the good of the land; but if you refuse and rebel, you shall be devoured by the sword'; for the mouth of the LORD has spoken."[6]

When we focus on religious rituals and works, we can become very legalistic, looking down on others who do not measure up to the doctrines we have created and praising ourselves for how well we are doing and how righteous we have become. Our concern can become what others are doing wrong, not upon what they are doing right or what we can do for or learn from them. We can become critical and condemning, rather than seeking to edify others and build them up in Christ.

As Jesus said of the scribes and Pharisees, "Woe to you, scribes and Pharisees, hypocrites! For you cleanse the outside of the cup and dish, but inside they are full of extortion and self-indulgence. Blind Pharisee, first cleanse the inside of the cup and dish, that the outside of them may be clean also."[7] Likewise, He said, "Woe to you, scribes and Pharisees, hypocrites! For you pay tithe of mint and anise and cumin, and have neglected the weightier *matters* of the law: justice and mercy and faith. These you ought to have done, without leaving the others undone."[8] To exercise justice, mercy, and faith, our focus cannot be solely inward upon ourselves, to see how well we are obeying the rules. It must be outward to God and to others so we can serve Him and those He brings along our paths.

We need to keep in mind the admonition, "Beware lest anyone cheat you through philosophy and empty deceit, according to the tradition of men, according to the basic principles of the world, and not according to Christ."[9] Jesus said, "And this is eternal life, that they may know You, the only true God, and Jesus Christ whom You have sent."[10] Eternal life is knowing God and Jesus intimately, having a relationship with them, not performing religious rituals and attempting to earn their love and acceptance.

Manmade regulations can choke out the spiritual life of a congregation. When Jesus was in Bethsaida, they brought a blind man to Him to be healed.[11] Jesus could certainly have healed the man simply by touching his eyes, as He did at other times,[12] or even without touching him at all, as He did when He healed blind Bartimaeus.[13] However, when Jesus healed the blind man at Bethsaida, He "spit on his eyes and put His hands on him."[14] Another time when He healed a blind man, Jesus "spat on the ground and made clay with the saliva; and He anointed the eyes of the blind man with the clay."[15] If someone set about to heal a blind person in your congregation by either spitting on the blind person's eyes or anointing them with mud made of saliva and dirt, how would everyone react? Would that person be rebuked for doing things out of order?

David, wearing a linen ephod, "danced before the LORD with all *his* might" when the ark was brought into Jerusalem.[16] When his wife Michal looked out the window and saw him leaping and whirling before the LORD, she despised him in her heart and later rebuked him for his conduct.[17] David responded, "I will play *music* before the

LORD. And I will be even more undignified than this, and will be humble in my own sight."[18] As a result of her attitude, Michal was barren all the days of her life,[19] which symbolizes a lack of fruitfulness or blessing.[20] Because David was a type of Christ (aspects of his character, office, and function foreshadowed the Messiah),[21] Michal would be a type of the bride of Christ (the church). She typifies the person who is critical or judgmental of others because they do not follow manmade rules of decorum in their expressions of worship. I do not know of a single instance in Scripture where God rebuked someone for being too exuberant in worshiping Him.

The doctrines of man can also keep us from accomplishing what God has prepared for us to do. Had Peter followed the commandments of man, he would not have gone into a gentile's house, and he would not have preached the gospel to Cornelius and his household.[22] We must not allow manmade religious rules to keep us from going to certain places or from reaching out to certain people in order to tell them about Christ and show them His love.

We must keep in mind, "For *the* LORD *does* not *see* as man sees: for man looks at the outward appearance, but the LORD looks at the heart."[23] Jesus was the greatest spiritual warrior to walk the earth, and He did not allow Himself to be bound by manmade regulations.

---

[1] Romans 8:2-4.
[2] Isaiah 29:13.
[3] Isaiah 1:11, 13.
[4] Isaiah 1:15.
[5] Isaiah 1:16-17.
[6] Isaiah 1:19-20.

[7] Matthew 23:25-26.
[8] Matthew 23:23.
[9] Colossians 2:8.
[10] John 17:3.
[11] Mark 8:22.
[12] Matthew 9:28-30; 20:29-34.
[13] Mark 10:46-52.
[14] Mark 8:23.
[15] John 9:6.
[16] 2 Samuel 6:14.
[17] 2 Samuel 6:16 & 20.
[18] 2 Samuel 6:21-22.
[19] 2 Samuel 6:23.
[20] Genesis 1:28; Psalm 107:34; Hosea 9:16; Deuteronomy 7:14.
[21] Psalm 89:19-20; Ezekiel 37:24.
[22] Acts 10.
[23] 1 Samuel 16:7

.

Freedom Is Your Destiny!

8

ATTACK!

"[T]he kingdom of heaven suffers violence, and the violent take it by force."

Matthew 11:12

"I will build My church, and the gates of Hades shall not prevail against it."

Matthew 16:18

I was trained as a helicopter mechanic on Huey helicopters, which is the model of helicopter most associated with the Vietnam War. Its official designation was UH-1, with the "UH" standing for utility helicopter. The Army had originally designated it "HU-1" (helicopter, utility), hence the nickname "Huey."

The Huey was the first mass-produced helicopter powered by a jet turbine engine. It began service in the Army in 1959, primarily for evacuating wounded soldiers and for utility transport. The first Huey (UH-1A) could carry seven troops or three stretchers. In 1961 it was upgraded to the UH-1B, which had a larger engine. A major change was made in 1963 by increasing the size of the cabin and installing a larger engine and rotor blades. This new model, the UH-1D, could carry ten fully equipped soldiers and was used for transporting them into and out of landing zones, evacuating the wounded, carrying supplies, and as an aerial command post. With the development of the D-model, the UH-1B was used as a gunship. It was the Army's first helicopter gunship. Other models of Hueys were also produced for the Army, Air Force, and Marines. My company in Soc Trang had B-model gunships and D-model slicks. During my second year, the D-models may have been replaced with an upgraded version called the H-model.

Every 100 hours of flying time, the helicopters were brought into the hangar for a thorough inspection and replacement of worn or damaged parts. When I arrived in Soc Trang, I was assigned to a maintenance crew working in the hangar. When a helicopter was brought in a Technical Inspector (TI) would go over it, making a list of anything that needed to be fixed. A maintenance crew would then be assigned to the helicopter to complete the listed repairs. We generally worked from eight to five performing the scheduled and unscheduled maintenance on Hueys to keep them flying. After a couple of months, I was put in charge of a crew.

One day a new guy in country was assigned to my crew, and I decided to see whether he knew anything about helicopters. I wanted to have an idea of what work I could trust him to do. Each maintenance crew had a large, Army tool box full of various tools. The tool box contained the same tools regardless of whether it was to be used by helicopter mechanics or jeep mechanics. I grabbed the tire pressure gauge from the tool box, handed it to the new guy, and asked him to check the air pressure in the helicopter's skids. The skids were the Huey helicopter's landing gear, and they were simply aluminum tubes that bent upward in front, similar to the runners on a sled. The new guy spent about twenty minutes trying to find an air valve on the skids. He finally pressed the tire pressure gauge against the head of a large rivet and reported to me that the air pressure in the skids was 30 psi.

Working on a maintenance crew in the hangar was a safe assignment. The only contact I had with the enemy was being on the receiving end of the occasional mortar attacks. In the Vietnam War, soldiers were sent over to serve a one-year rotation. I could have served my year in Vietnam in the relative safety of the hangar. However, after several months I decided I would rather be in the air and requested a flight assignment.

The first available assignment was as a door gunner on a slick—a troop carrying helicopter. Each Huey, regardless of the model, had a crew of four men. There were two pilots (an aircraft commander and a copilot) and two enlisted men (a crew chief and a door gunner). The crew chief and door gunner each fired an M-60 machine gun. On the slicks, the machine guns were mounted on metal posts attached to the sides of the helicopter. Those posts were designed to limit the range of movement of the machine guns so that one could not accidently shoot the helicopter or its rotor blades. The crew chief was trained as a mechanic and was responsible for performing daily inspections and maintenance on the helicopter. The door gunner was responsible for cleaning and maintaining the machine guns. Sometimes, as in my case, mechanics served as door gunners simply because they wanted to fly and there were no available crew chief positions.

During my first month of flying on a slick, the enemy never shot at my helicopter. I fired my machine gun only once when, as we were approaching a landing zone, we were instructed to fire straight down to discourage enemy fire. One day towards the end of that month, after we had taken off from an LZ and had climbed to an altitude of 1000 feet, I looked down and saw two gunships weaving back and forth just above the ground. I decided that was where I wanted to be and requested a transfer to the gunship platoon. The other members of that platoon had to approve new members. I was soon voted in and assigned as a door gunner on a UH-1B gunship, and then as a crew chief as soon as there was an opening.

One time the company First Sergeant decided he would assign an enlisted man to our gunship platoon without the soldier having been voted in. Shortly thereafter, two of the largest (in size) crew chiefs the First Sergeant had ever seen dragged the soldier into the company headquarters, dropped him on the floor, and announced that he did not work out. That was the first and last time the First Sergeant attempted to assign someone to our gunship platoon.

After I joined the gunship platoon, one of the first things I did was go on a training exercise. There was a place not far from our base with an old, abandoned concrete structure that we used as an aerial target range. I would be shooting a hand-held, M-60 machine gun. Attached to its left side was a metal box which held about 200 rounds of ammunition. Because I am right handed, I would be holding the machine gun with the pistol grip in my right hand and my left hand grasping the plastic shroud around the rear portion of the barrel. When firing the machine gun, the shoulder stock (rear part of the machine gun) would be against my right side. Since I would be sitting on the left side of the helicopter, I would have to stand outside the helicopter on the rocket pod attached to its side in order to shoot toward the front. Before we took off, I was told how, with my left foot on the rocket pod and my right foot braced against the bottom of a vertical pole in front of my seat, I could stand far enough outside the helicopter to fire my machine gun towards the front while holding it against my right side.

The pole in front of my seat was called a "litter pole." One of the uses for which the B-model was originally designed was to evacuate wounded soldiers from the battlefield. When configured for that purpose, there was a vertical pole that ran from floor to ceiling near each cargo door. On each pole were three brackets that corresponded to brackets attached to the back wall. By hooking the handles of litters in those brackets, a vertical row of three litters with soldiers in them could be put in the helicopter. For our purposes, we removed the brackets. We attached a smoke grenade by its pin to a hook on the litter pole, so that when we received fire we could grab the smoke grenade, thereby pulling the pin, and flip it out to mark the spot. When standing outside the helicopter in combat with our outboard foot on the rocket pod, we also used the pole to keep from falling by bracing our inboard foot against the bottom of the inboard side of the pole.

When we arrived at the target range, we were at an altitude of about 1500 feet. The pilot put the helicopter into a dive towards the target on the ground, and I stood outside the helicopter with my left foot on the rocket pod and my right foot on the floor, braced against the bottom of the litter pole. As I was standing out there with the wind in my face and firing the machine gun in my hands, I knew that was where I wanted to be. The gunships would make me come alive. That was my destiny in Vietnam.

Living out our destinies is what will make us come alive—it is what will become our passion. Sometimes, however, we may not know what makes us come alive until we do it. When I was nearing the end of my second year in

Vietnam, I began thinking about what career I wanted to pursue. I eliminated everything I could think of except possibly practicing law. My father is a lawyer, and upon returning to America I began working in his law office doing legal research and other tasks during the summers and Christmas vacations as I was completing my undergraduate degree. The more I worked in the law, the more I liked it. I realized that being a lawyer would make me come alive; it would become my passion. I then decided to go to law school. I was able to write my first brief to the state supreme court before I started law school. After practicing law for ten years, God called me into the judiciary. Although that was not what I wanted to do at the time, the more I served as a judge, the more I enjoyed it, and it became my passion. Sometimes, we will discover our passion—our destiny—by first obeying God. After all, it is His plan, and He knows best.

As a crew chief, I was assigned to a particular helicopter. A crew chief views his helicopter much like a teenage boy views his first car. It became "my helicopter," the pilot was "my pilot," and the door gunner was "my door gunner." I never walked away from my helicopter without stopping, turning around, and looking it over from main rotor to skids and from nose to tail. My job was to perform daily inspections and maintenance on my helicopter and to be a door gunner while we were flying. During the time I was in Vietnam, I had several pilots and door gunners assigned to my helicopter.

By joining the gunship platoon, I was going on the offensive. I was entering the battle. I would be going out to find and attack the enemy. By joining the gunship platoon, I was also volunteering for an assignment that involved risk. Our job in the gunships was to find and engage the enemy. We did that in several contexts. Anytime we were called, day or night, seven days a week, we scrambled out to help ground troops who were being attacked. Before escorting the slicks into an LZ, we spent time scouting the area to see where the enemy was in order to locate a safe LZ. Once the troops were on the ground, we stayed overhead, trying to engage the enemy before they did. We also spent many days simply flying around in teams of two gunships seeking to locate and engage the enemy.

Our method of locating the enemy was quite simple. We had no high-tech equipment. Our most sophisticated electronics were the helicopter's two-way radios. In order to locate the enemy, we simply flew around, close to the ground, sometimes only three or four feet in the air, over and alongside suspected enemy positions, trying to be such an attractive target that the enemy would shoot at us. When they opened fire, we would know where they were and could take them on.

We were usually successful in getting the enemy to shoot at us. The enemy did not like to be found, but they did like to shoot down helicopters, especially gunships. The Army lost over one-half of its Huey gunships during the Vietnam War. It took only one bullet in the wrong place to bring down a Huey, and there were many wrong places. Both of the times my helicopter was shot down, it was hit by only one bullet— the first time by the largest bullet that was typically shot at us (.50 caliber from a Russian machine gun fire by a North Vietnamese soldier) and the second time by the smallest (.223 caliber from an American M-16 fired by a South Vietnamese soldier).

According to the History Channel, it was because of "the unacceptably high loss rate of Huey gunships" that the Army pushed for the development of the Cobra helicopter as an interim gunship to be used in Vietnam. After Vietnam, the Army adopted the Apache helicopter gunship, but the Marines kept the Cobra, although it has since been substantially upgraded to the Super Cobra.

In Vietnam, the Cobras operated at a higher altitude than we typically did. Their crew consisted of two pilots. For a few months I was stationed at another base where I was a crew chief on a Cobra, but did not like that assignment because a Cobra crew chief did not fly in it. A Marine who was a Gulf War veteran told me that during his training as a Cobra crew chief, he was told that the life expectancy of crew chiefs on Huey gunships in Vietnam was seven days. Other estimates I have read range from fourteen to ninety days.

Several years ago I met a man who had served as a Navy corpsman in Vietnam. He asked me what I had done in Vietnam, and I told him I was a door gunner on a Huey gunship (while flying, I was a door gunner and most people have no idea what a "crew chief" would do). He commented that I was fortunate to have made it home alive. He then asked when I was in Vietnam. I told him from May 1968 through April 1970. He responded, "God must really have protected you to have survived that long being a door gunner." He was right.

Our helicopters were not armor plated. Bullets came right through the walls and up through the floor. The pilot and copilot had armor plating on the bottoms, backs, and sides of their seats, but the crew chief and door gunner did not have that luxury. We sat in the doorways of the large, sliding cargo doors on the sides of the helicopter. Those doors were always open during combat. Our seats looked like camp stools. They were made of aluminum tubing with a piece of nylon fabric stretched across the top. They were attached to the floor and to the back wall, against which we sat facing forward. There was nothing around us that was designed to shield us from enemy fire.

There was a positive aspect to that. Since there was no cover, I never developed the conditioned response of ducking when the enemy opened fire. There was nothing to duck behind. One of the door gunners in the gunship platoon had served in the infantry. When he was home on leave, he and his girlfriend had gone to dinner with his parents to a nice restaurant (he was dressed in a suit). As they were walking out of the restaurant, a car backfired, and he immediately dove into the gutter. We also did not develop the hyper-alertness necessary to keep from being ambushed in ground combat. We were constantly trying to get the enemy to shoot at us, and they usually shot first. I did not care if they shot first, as long as I could shoot last.

Our main defense was simply the hope that the enemy could not hit a moving target. To do so, one must lead the target by shooting at a point the correct distance ahead so that the target and the bullets arrive at that point at the same time. Fortunately, the enemy missed us more than they hit us.

The vast majority of the bullets that struck my gunship hit in the cabin, in the area where the door gunner and I were sitting. I never had any bullets hit the tail boom. In fact, I had one door gunner transfer to another gunship because he thought mine was taking way too many rounds in the area where we sat, and he wanted to make it home alive.

When flying close to the ground, what we called "on the deck," we usually received fire from the side of the helicopter and from fairly close range. In that situation, I think the enemy fire was more likely to hit where the crew chief or door gunner was sitting for three reasons: (1) When one shoots at a target, the natural tendency is to shoot at the center of mass, which, for a Huey, is where the crew chief and door gunner were sitting; (2) The pilot and copilot had armor shields that slid into place on the outsides of their seats so that from the side one could only see their heads, while the crew chief and door gunner were fully exposed and therefore were easier to hit; and (3) Because the crew chief and door gunner each had a visible machine gun and could shoot to the sides, they were perceived as the greater immediate threat.

Our B-model gunships were armed with miniguns, rockets, and machine guns. There were two miniguns, one attached to a pylon on each side of the helicopter. They were six-barreled machine guns, similar to the Gatling gun used by the Army during the latter half of the 19th Century. The copilot fired the miniguns using a sight that swung down in front of his face. At the bottom of the sight there was a pistol-grip style handle with a trigger. As he moved the handle, the miniguns would point in unison up, down, left, or right. When he pulled the trigger, they would each fire 2000 rounds per minute. If he pointed them far enough to the left or right so that one of them hit its inboard stop to prevent shooting the helicopter, it would cease firing and the other would fire at 4000 rounds per minute. We carried 10,000 rounds of minigun ammunition on the helicopter in two rows of metal boxes located between the door gunner's and crew chief's seats. The boxes in one row fed the minigun on one side of the helicopter, and the boxes in the other row fed the minigun on the other side. Ammunition traveled from those boxes, through a flexible aluminum chute that went through the floor under the crew chief's or door gunner's seat, out the side of the helicopter, to the minigun. To conserve ammo, the miniguns were designed to fire in 3-second bursts. After a burst was fired, the copilot would have to pull the trigger again.

We had two rocket pods, one attached to the bottom

of the pylon on each side of the helicopter. Each pod held seven, 2.75-inch, folding-fin rockets. They were unguided rockets, not missiles, and were fired by the pilot using a trigger switch on the "stick" (the cyclic control located between the pilot's knees used for directional control of the helicopter). He had a sight that swung down in front of his face, and the sight had a reticle projected on a piece of glass positioned at a 45-degree angle. Most pilots would also make a mark on the windshield with a grease pencil to use in aiming the rockets.

The crew chief and door gunner each had an M-60 machine gun which fired about 550 rounds per minute. Mounted on the left side of each machine gun was a 200-round, metal ammo can with its lid removed. When ammunition arrived in those ammo cans, it was packed in two cardboard boxes with 100 rounds in each box. We took those boxes, cut their tops off, and taped them together with masking tape, covering the entire outside and inside in order to make them more durable. The result was one open-topped box with a divider in the middle formed by the short sides of the two boxes being joined together. That box would then fit into the metal ammo can attached to the machine gun. My door gunner and I each had ten of those fabricated cardboard boxes at our feet, each loaded with about a 200-round belt of machine gun ammunition. When we would expend the ammunition in one box, we would pull it out of the metal ammo can attached to the side of the machine gun, throw the box on the floor, pick up a loaded box, drop it into the ammo can, and resume firing. Our machine guns fired the same ammunition as did the miniguns (7.62 x 51 mm NATO, which is essentially the same as .308 Winchester), and so when we ran out of ammunition we could take some from the metal boxes of minigun ammunition.

I had the safety on my machine gun removed so that the only safety when we were in combat was my trigger finger. When we were not in combat, I would remove the barrel by flipping a lever. Because the barrel included the chamber, the machine gun could not fire with the barrel removed. I would then place the barrel in a rack attached to the inside front door frame of the cargo door and set the rest of the machine gun on the floor. We had an asbestos mitten to wear when removing hot barrels so that we did not burn our hands.

The aircraft commander (pilot) sat on the right side of the helicopter and the copilot sat on the left. The crew chief sat on the left side behind the copilot because there was a better view of the instrument panel from that location than from the right side. The door gunner then sat on the right side behind the pilot.

When I was firing my machine gun, I held it with the metal ammunition box attached to it resting on the top of my left forearm. I did that so that the brass and links would be ejected downward to keep them from hitting the tail rotor, which was on the left side of the tail boom. If the copilot needed an attitude adjustment, I would hold my machine gun so that the brass and links would be hitting the back of his helmet, with the occasional hot cartridge case slipping down the back of his neck.

For a while, we had one gunship armed with a belt-fed, 40-mm grenade launcher instead of miniguns. The grenade launcher was in a turret attached to the nose of the helicopter, and it had a rate of fire of about 220 rounds per minute. This gunship also had two, 19-shot rocket pods in place of the 7-shot pods on our other gunships. A gunship with this armament was called a "hog." The copilot fired the grenade launcher and the pilot fired the rockets.

After we had had the hog for a while, the copilot's

door began coming open when the helicopter lifted off the ground. The crew chief would wire it shut before taking off and then unwire it upon landing. When the helicopter went into the hangar for its scheduled maintenance, they discovered why the copilot's door was coming open. One of the two main I-beams that ran under the floor of the helicopter had cracked in two, probably due to metal fatigue from the vibration of the grenade launcher firing. When the helicopter lifted off the ground, the floor under the copilot's seat sagged enough for the door to come unlatched. That was the last hog we had, at least while I was in Vietnam.

Our gunships did not take off straight up as do helicopters in the movies. Because of the armor plating around the pilot's and copilot's seats and the weapons and munitions on board, they were loaded to about 500 to 1,000 pounds more than they were designed to carry. On a hot day, if the gunship's engine was worn, it strained just to get off the ground.

The Huey's engine, very simplistically, had three main sections. The first was the compressor, consisting of seven stages of turbine blades in the front of the engine that compressed air and forced it into the engine. Each stage was like a wheel with a row of angled blades protruding from the edge. Between each stage was a row of fixed blades (stators) to redirect the air into the next stage of turbine blades. The gap between the turbine blades and the stators was only a few thousandths of an inch, although I cannot now remember the exact distance. The second section, located behind the compressor, was the combustion chamber where the fuel was burned. The third section consisted of two stages of turbine blades at the rear which were turned by the hot gasses exiting the combustion chamber. Those two turbine blades were connected to a shaft that turned the compressor and that, through the transmission, turned the main rotor blades and the tail rotor.

When operating in an area like Vietnam, sand was often sucked into the engine when landing and taking off. Over time, the sand abraded the turbine blades so that they were less efficient in compressing air. Eighty percent of the air sucked into the air intake was used for cooling the engine. As the turbine blades in the compressor became less efficient, there was less air for cooling, and the engine would begin to overheat before it reached maximum power.

A helicopter can hover by its main rotor forcing air down against the earth so that it is basically resting on a cushion of air. For it to fly, it needs lift from air passing horizontally over the spinning main rotor, which acts as a wing (a rotary wing) just like the wing of an airplane (a fixed wing). The greater the speed of the air passing horizontally over the wing from front to back (forward air speed), the greater the lift. Forward air speed is a combination of the wind speed and the forward ground speed of the aircraft. That is why aircraft take off and land into the wind, when they can.

The hotter the air, the less dense it is, and the less lift it produces. Once the engine had become badly worn, it took quite a bit of runway for a fully loaded B-model Huey to take off on a hot day. The pilot would pull enough power to get the helicopter light on its skids and would then start sliding it down the runway. As the gunship picked up airspeed, it would be kind of bouncing down the runway until it hit "translational lift" at about 20 knots. Translational lift is lift from the air passing over the "wing" of the rotor blades as opposed to lift from the cushion of air being forced down against the ground by the rotor blades. Although technically there was some translational lift as soon as the Huey began moving forward, and it increased as we picked up forward air speed, what we called "hitting translational lift" was the point at which the helicopter had sufficient forward air speed that the main rotor was operating in undisturbed air.

You could feel the Huey straining as it neared that point and then shudder as it transitioned to flying. At that point we were flying, not very high or very fast, but flying nonetheless. The engine in one of our gunships became so weak that the crew chief and door gunner would get out while the pilot taxied from the reventment to the runway and then get in for the takeoff. The engine in mine never got that bad, but it did get worn enough that we had to lighten the load by carrying less ammunition. There were times when it was hot and my helicopter's engine was worn when I would be saying to myself, "Come on girl, come on girl," as she strained to get into the air.

For example, one day we landed at a small airstrip to refuel and rearm. It was typical of the ones we operated from while on a mission. There was a runway made of interlocking, perforated steel plates (PSP); a large rubber bladder of jet fuel lying on the ground near one side of the runway; a small, three-sided, wooden structure located a ways from the jet fuel in which were stored some boxes of machine gun ammunition and some rockets; and no buildings. After we refueled, the copilot was going to taxi to the small wooden structure so we could rearm. This airstrip had been constructed in a rice paddy, so there were ponds along each side of the runway as a result of having dirt excavated out of the rice paddy to build up the runway so it would be above the water level. Rather than taxi down the runway, the copilot decided to taxi over the pond along one side of the runway. It is much more difficult for the helicopter to hover over water than land, and as soon as we started over the water, I thought, "We're going to get wet." I could feel the copilot tense up as the helicopter strained to stay above the water. As we inched along, I kept saying to myself, "Come on girl, Come on girl," referring to my helicopter. When we finally made it to where we were going to rearm and were back over land, I think we all breathed a sigh of relief.

We typically flew in teams of two gunships: one flying lead and the other flying wing behind it. In combat we usually flew as close to the ground as feasible. Some pilots tended to fly higher than others. Whenever we got up to 100 feet above the ground, I would tell the pilot over the intercom, "I'm getting a nose bleed from the altitude."

More than once a pilot broke out the chin bubble (a small Plexiglas window down by the pilot's and copilot's foot pedals) on his helicopter by hitting tree branches. One pilot tore off the skids on his helicopter by hitting a grass hut. We had to stack sandbags next to the runway to provide a place on which the helicopter could land. That same pilot liked to initiate new copilots by flying close to the ground across a rice paddy toward a tree line that had a gap in the trees not quite as wide as the width of the helicopter's rotor blades. Just before going through the gap, he would turn the helicopter on its side, just to see the copilot's response.

When we were in combat, I sat part way outside the helicopter, with my left foot on the rocket pod attached to the side of the helicopter and my right foot on the floor, with the inside of my foot up against the bottom of the litter pole. When the pilot fired the rockets, the rocket exhaust would sometimes blast little bits of something into my lower leg causing it to bleed. However, I sat that way for two reasons. First, I wanted a panoramic view of everything on my side of the helicopter. By sitting partially outside, I could see to the front, side, and rear. Second, there were times when I would stand outside the helicopter on the rocket pod so that I would be entirely outside the helicopter except for my right foot braced against the bottom of the litter pole to keep me from falling. In some situations, enemy soldiers would wait until we flew overhead and then pop up and shoot at us from the rear. It is easier to hit a moving target when it is going directly away from or toward you. When my helicopter was flying wing and there was a risk of enemy soldiers shooting at us from behind, I would stand outside the helicopter on the rocket pod so that I could keep a lookout directly to the rear and could shoot directly to the rear in addition to the side and front. There was a floor switch near the litter pole, so I could key my microphone without using my hands while both sitting and standing.

To fulfill your destiny, you must go on the offensive. Our attitude must be like Isaiah's, "Here *am* I! Send me."[1] That does not mean we will be sent to some other country, although it could. However, that is the attitude we must have. Jesus said, "[O]n this rock [the declaration that Jesus is the Christ, the Son of the living God] I will build My church, and the gates of Hades shall not prevail against it."[2] The metaphor is going on the offense and attacking a walled enemy stronghold at its gates to liberate those who are inside. In both physical warfare and spiritual warfare, we must go on the offensive. We must attack.

Entering the battle, living out our destinies, will put us at risk. The Christian life is one of risk. God took a risk when He created us with a free will, knowing that we could turn away from Him, and that many would. We all take risks when we enter into relationships, knowing that we are making ourselves vulnerable to being hurt. Without risk, there is no reason to trust God. The enemy need not go after those who are not in the battle—who are not a threat. But the blessings we can receive by trusting our lives to God are more than we can ever imagine.

In the Parable of the Talents, the servant who was given one talent was afraid to risk it, so he buried it rather than use it for the benefit of his master. When his master returned, he called the servant "wicked" and "lazy," had the talent taken from him, and ordered "the unprofitable servant" cast into outer darkness.[3] We must use the talents and abilities God has given us for His glory and to advance His kingdom and not keep them hidden because we are afraid to risk.

We each must seek to discover our destiny and live it out. Psalm 37:4 says, "Delight yourself also in the LORD, and He shall give you the desires of your heart." As we delight ourselves in the Lord, our desires will become His desires, and He will show us what He would have us to do. We will have a passion to do what He has called us to do. Paul wrote, "[W]oe is me if I do not preach the gospel!"[4] Paul did not mean that he would be punished if he did not preach the gospel. Rather, preaching the gospel, particularly in places where Christ was not known, was his ambition. It was what made him come alive. It was his passion.

When we do live out our destinies, we can expect opposition from the enemy. He will do all he can to keep us from doing what God has called us to do. As Paul wrote concerning his ministry in Ephesus, "For a great and effective door has opened to me, and *there are* many adversaries."[5]

Our destinies will unfold throughout our lives. Psalm 119:105 states, "Your word *is* a lamp to my feet and a light to my path." The Hebrew word translated "word" refers primarily to the spoken word. God will guide us down the path. As Isaiah 30:21 says, "Your ears shall hear a word behind you, saying, 'This *is* the way, walk in it.' whenever you turn to the right hand or whenever you turn to the left." God's word is a lamp, not a searchlight. Living out our destinies will be like taking a walk in the forest where we cannot see around the bend up ahead in the trail. It will be an adventure.

There will be times when we may wonder whether we have a destiny. Our lives may seem routine, as if we are stuck on a plateau, or in a rut. Then, there will suddenly be an opportune time when things will change if we take the opportunity that God gives. For example, Galatians 6:9-10 says, "And let us not grow weary while doing good, for in due season we shall reap if we do not lose heart. Therefore, as we have opportunity, let us do good to all, especially to those who are of the household of faith." The Greek word translated "season" and "opportunity" is *kairós*, which means: "Season, opportune time. It is not merely as a succession of minutes, which is *chronós*, but a period of opportunity (though not necessity)."[6] There is no English equivalent for the word. Another place it appears is Romans 5:6, "For when we were still without strength, in due time [*kairós*] Christ died for the ungodly." The periods of our lives that seem like merely a succession of moments (*chronós*) are often times of preparation until a *kairós* moment when we have an opportunity to take another step in our destinies. We can be certain that God has a plan for our lives, and we must seize the opportunities He provides.

Living out our destinies will often require patience and endurance. We must be careful not to try to make it happen in our own strength and in our own way. For example, God promised Abram (later Abraham) that he would have more descendants than he could count.[7] For that to come true, Abram needed a son, but Sarai, his wife, appeared unable to bear children because she was past the child-bearing age.[8]   Therefore, she suggested that Abram have a child by her Egyptian maid, Hagar, in order to bring God's promise to fulfillment.[9]   Unfortunately, Abram agreed to do so rather than waiting for God to fulfill His promise, which He did about fifteen years later.[10]   Hagar's son, Ishmael, was a wild man; his hand was against every man and every man's hand was against him.[11]

In contrast, David was anointed as king over all of Israel long before he was able to assume that role.[12]   In the interim, he had to flee for his life from King Saul.   When presented with two opportunities to kill Saul, David's men viewed it as God delivering the King into David's hand so that David could slay him and become King.[13]   Rather than trying to secure his destiny in his own way and in his own strength, David did not kill King Saul or allow others to do so.[14]   Rather, he patiently waited and endured until God elevated him to the position of King.   Not every open door is one we should walk through.   Sometimes, it may be a test from God to see if we will obey and rely upon Him rather than taking matters into our own hands.

We must take risks to live out our destinies.   It may not involve physical risk, but it will require risk.   We may be called to a new job, career, or ministry where there is the risk of failure.   We may be asked to give a word to a stranger, a friend, or relative, and risk rejection.   We may be asked to stand for the truth, and risk ridicule.   Because Christianity is centered on relationships, we will have to open ourselves to others and risk being hurt.   It seems that God often calls us to do things we do not feel adequate to do.   That is because in those situations we must rely solely upon Him.

---

[1] Isaiah 6:8.

[2] Matthew 16:16-18.

[3] Matthew 25:24-30.

[4] 1 Corinthians 9:16.

[5] 1 Corinthians 16:9.

[6] Spiros Zodhiates, ed., *The Complete Word Study New Testament* (Chattanooga: AMG Publishers, 1991) p. 805.

[7] Genesis 15:4-5.

[8] Genesis 16:1; 17:15-17.

[9] Genesis 16:2-3.

[10] Genesis 16:16; 21:5.

[11] Genesis 16:12.

[12] 1 Samuel 16:1-13; 2 Samuel 2:1-7; 5:1-5.

[13] 1 Samuel 24:1-4; 26:6-8.

[14] 1 Samuel 24:6-7; 26:9-12.

Daniel T. Eismann

9

INVADING ENEMY TERRITORY

[T]he whole world lies under the sway of the wicked one.

1 John 5:19

In order to engage the enemy, we had to leave our airfield and go out into enemy territory. We could sit at our base and wait for them to attack, but then it would be at a time and under circumstances when the enemy thought they had the advantage. You can rarely succeed fighting solely a defensive battle. To go on the offensive, it is necessary to go out into enemy territory.

One afternoon, we received word that some enemy soldiers were congregating at a particular location. My gunship and another scrambled out, and when we arrived at that location, coming in low over the trees, we saw about forty enemy soldiers standing out in the open. They were all dressed in black, and, interestingly enough, were all carrying M-16 rifles. We swooped down and opened fire with our miniguns and machine guns, quickly expending all 10,000 rounds of our minigun ammunition. At 4,000 rounds a minute, it did not take long. My door gunner and I also fired almost all of our ammunition. As loud as our helicopters were, it always amazed me that we were able to catch the enemy by surprise out in the open, but we often did.

"[T]he whole world lies *under the sway of* the wicked one."[1] It is enemy territory. We cannot simply sit in military bases (churches) waiting for the enemy to attack, or for the wounded to straggle in. We must go out, into the world, into places where the unsaved and hurting are. In the power of the Holy Spirit[2] and under the authority of Jesus Christ,[3] we are to "[g]o into all the world and preach the gospel to every creature"[4] and "make disciples of all the nations, baptizing them in the name of the Father and of the Son and of the Holy Spirit, teaching them to observe all things that I [Jesus] have commanded you."[5] We must push back the darkness by demonstrating the power of God working through submitted vessels—His power over Satan and his fallen angels by casting them out, His power over creation through supernatural healings and miracles, and His power over sin by changed lives as we walk in love. Our goal is not to physically conquer the world, nor is it to exercise social or political dominion over it. The kingdom of God is within;[6] it is not imposed from without. To do so, however, we must go into enemy territory. Our attitude should be to gain victory, not just to avoid defeat. We must not overestimate our enemies. "He who is in you is greater than he who is in the world."[7]

To go out and engage the enemy, we must know his tactics. However, that does not mean that we should devote ourselves to learning the details of evil. We are to be "wise in what is good, and simple concerning evil."[8] Fortunately, the enemy's tactics have not changed over the millennia. He rebelled against God because he wanted to exalt himself and become equal with God. As described in Isaiah 14:12-14:

"How you are fallen from heaven,
O Lucifer, son of the morning!
How you are cut down to the ground,
You who weakened the nations!
For you have said in your heart:
'I will ascend into heaven,
I will exalt my throne above the stars of God;
I will also sit on the mount of the congregation
On the farthest sides of the north;
I will ascend above the heights of the clouds,
I will be like the Most High.'

His pride requires that he be worshiped. When the devil was tempting Jesus in the wilderness, he offered all the kingdoms of the world and their glory if Jesus would fall down and worship him.[9] That was Satan's best offer because being worshiped is what he wants the most. He would give anything to be worshiped. Jesus responded, "Away with you, Satan! For it is written, *'You shall worship the LORD your God, and Him only you shall serve.'* "[10] Those influenced by the enemy also want our worship. They want us following and bowing down to them rather than to God. Thus, Paul warned the Ephesian elders that from among themselves "men will rise up, speaking perverse things, to draw away the disciples after themselves."[11]

Jesus said that the devil "was a murderer from the beginning, and does not stand in the truth, because there is no truth in him. When he speaks a lie, he speaks from his own *resources*, for he is a liar and the father of it."[12] Therefore, the weapons of our warfare are "for pulling down strongholds, casting down arguments and every high thing that exalts itself against the knowledge of God."[13] We can go back to the beginning and see the tactics of deceit he used in the Garden of Eden.

He began by seeking to cast doubt on whether the prohibition that had been passed on to Eve was really God's word. He asked, "Has God indeed said, 'You shall not eat of every tree of the garden'?"[14] Before Eve had been created, God had commanded Adam, "Of every tree of the garden you may freely eat; but of the tree of the knowledge of good and evil you shall not eat, for in the day that you eat of it you shall surely die."[15] Adam then apparently passed that command on to Eve, adding the command that she was not even to touch it.[16] How would she know whether God really said they were not to eat of that tree? What if Adam was mistaken and had not accurately passed on God's word? The enemy tries the same tactic with us, seeking to get us to doubt whether the Bible is God's word, or whether it has been accurately preserved over the centuries, or whether it is accurately translated. He wants to get us to start questioning the accuracy of God's word.

The serpent then said, "You will not surely die."[17] Another of the enemy's deceits is to convince people that there is no consequence for sin. That deception can include that there is no hell, or that a loving God would not condemn people to eternal punishment in hell, or that one can escape hell if his or her good deeds outweigh the bad. For example, half of Americans believe that all persons are eventually saved or accepted by God no matter what they do.[18] Of course, if there is no consequence for sin, then we would not need Jesus as Savior because there would be nothing to save us from. Even believers can be deceived into thinking that because they are forgiven, their sin is overlooked.[19]

Jesus commended the church at Ephesus because they hated the deeds of the Nicolaitans.[20] He then rebuked the church at Pergamos because some in the church held to the doctrine of the Nicolaitans.[21] The Nicolaitans were a sect who believed that the body and the spirit were separate and that how they lived in the body had no effect on their souls or spiritual life. They led lives of unrestrained indulgence, pleasure, and lust. Jesus said that if they did not repent, He would fight against them with the sword of His mouth. Obviously, their conduct did not bring them into intimacy with God. A current version of that doctrine is the teaching that Jesus is our Savior, but He need not be our Lord. Persons espousing this doctrine focus exclusively upon the grace of God and ignore our responsibility, especially with respect to repentance from sin and obedience to God. "If we say that we have fellowship with Him, and walk in darkness, we lie and do not practice the truth."[22] To have fellowship with Him, we cannot be living a lifestyle of continual sin.

Next, the serpent said, "For God knows that in the day you eat of it your eyes will be opened, and you will be like God, knowing good and evil."[23] This contains two deceptions that often occur together. The serpent sought to humanize God (by attributing to Him an improper or selfish motive) and to deify man (by saying a human can be like God). We see deception that humanizes God by denying His omniscience or omnipotence or omnipresence. This deception often happens because we cannot understand why an omniscient, omnipotent, and omnipresent God would permit certain things to happen in this world—why He would permit bad things to happen to good people. Another deception that humanizes God attributes to Him human motivations or emotions, such as He must be appeased to avoid His wrath or He can be bribed or manipulated by our "good" conduct to gain His blessing. We see deception that deifies humans through teachings or doctrines that proclaim we can be the masters of our own destinies, such as through our faith or by reciting specific prayers.

The serpent stated that Eve would be like God, "knowing good and evil."[24] I do not think that the attraction of this statement was that Eve would know what God considered to be good and evil. She could have just asked Him if she was curious about that. In fact, when the serpent tempted her, she could have responded, "Let me inquire of God about this." I think the attraction was that if what the serpent said was true, Eve could be a free moral agent, deciding for herself what was good and evil. She could be morally autonomous, not being subject to God's authority. That deception today may be phrased in the assertions that there is no absolute truth; that moral or doctrinal truth is relative; that we can pick and choose the passages of Scripture we will accept; that Scripture does not apply to the reality of today; or that Biblical text has no single or true meaning, but only the meaning we each give it. Sixty-four percent of Americans now believe that moral truth is relative to the person and the person's situation.[25] As a result of this deception, declaring that something is sin has become the unforgivable sin.

The effect of the serpent's deception upon Eve was that she "saw that the tree *was* good for food, that it *was* pleasant to the eyes, and a tree desirable to make *one* wise, she took of its fruit and ate."[26] The fruit appealed to Eve's flesh. It appealed to her reasoning. Satan was trying to get her to reason for herself whether God's command seemed valid, and she decided that it did not. Her reasoning corresponds to 1 John 2:16, "For all that *is* in the world—the lust of the flesh, the lust of the eyes, and the pride of life—is not of the Father but is of the world." The enemy seeks to have us do the same—to decide based upon our own reasoning or understanding whether there is any validity to God's commands and prohibitions in Scripture.

He seeks to have us make decisions based upon our feelings or the desires of our flesh, rather than upon the truth of God's word. "There is a way *that* seems right to a man, but its end *is* the way of death."[27]

Adam apparently had told Eve that not only was she was not to eat the fruit of the tree, she was not even to touch it. He may have added the prohibition against touching the fruit in an abundance of caution to keep her from even coming close to violating God's command. However, when she reached out and touched the fruit, I wonder if she paused to see if anything happened. When it did not, she may have thought that the entire command was false.

Eve was deceived by the serpent's craftiness into eating the fruit,[28] but when she later gave the fruit to Adam, he ate without having been deceived.[29] He heeded her voice and ate.[30] I wonder if he knowingly and willingly violated God's command because of the power of Eve's beauty. One of the enemy's strategies is to use the lure of sex to lead us into sin. When the Israelites entered Moab, the Midianite women invited the people to the sacrifices of their gods. The people ate and bowed down to those gods, provoking God to anger, and thousands died from the ensuing plague.[31] When the Spirit of the LORD came on Samson, he had the strength to kill 1000 Philistines with the jawbone of a donkey,[32] but his weakness was Delilah, who finally convinced him to disclose the secret of his strength. After his head was shaved, the LORD departed from him, and he was captured by the Philistines, blinded, and turned into a grinder of grain in the prison.[33] Although David was a man after God's own heart who would do God's will,[34] after watching Bathsheba bathing on her rooftop, he summoned her to his house, committed adultery with her, and, when she became pregnant, had her husband killed in an attempt to cover up the sin.[35] When Solomon was old, his wives turned his heart to follow after other gods.[36] When Jehu arrived in Jezreel to kill Jezebel, she "put paint on her eyes and adorned her head, and looked through the window,"[37] obviously hoping to dissuade Jehu with her beauty. That allure did not work for her.

Why did the serpent seek to get Eve and Adam to sin? I think that he did so because he wanted to destroy their relationship with God. If he could do so, then they would worship him rather than God. When Adam and Even "heard the sound of the LORD God walking in the garden in the cool of the day, . . . Adam and his wife hid themselves from the presence of the LORD God among the trees of the garden."[38] The consciousness of their sin caused them to withdraw from God. That is a natural response. We may do the same thing out of shame, or thinking that God is angry and will not forgive us. The enemy uses condemnation as a way of trying to get us to withdraw from God. We always need to keep in mind, "*There is* therefore now no condemnation to those who are in Christ Jesus, who do not walk according to the flesh, but according to the Spirit."[39]

When Jesus said that Satan was the father of lying, He began by stating that Satan was "a murderer from the beginning." By Adam's sin, death entered the world.[40] That death consisted of both physical death and spiritual death, which is separation from God.

When Satan sinned, God cast him "as a profane thing out of the mountain of God,"[41] and God also cast down the angels who sinned.[42] They are "reserved in everlasting chains under darkness for the judgment of the great day."[43] This verse indicates that Satan and the fallen angels do not have an opportunity to repent and be redeemed. Colossians 1:13-14 states that the Father "has delivered us from the power of darkness and conveyed *us* into the kingdom of the Son of His love, in whom we have redemption through His blood, the forgiveness of sins." Likewise, Jesus sent Paul to the Gentiles "'to open their eyes, *in order* to turn *them* from darkness to light, and *from* the power of Satan to God, that they may receive forgiveness of sins and an inheritance among those who are sanctified by faith in Me.'"[44] Since being delivered from the power of darkness equates with redemption, being reserved in everlasting chains under darkness indicates that Satan and the fallen angels do not have an opportunity for redemption.

Satan and the fallen angels undoubtedly thought that if man sinned, he too would lose his relationship with God and have no opportunity for redemption. We would then worship Satan. They did not foresee God's plan of redemption through Jesus Christ. First Corinthians 2:7-8 states, "But we speak the wisdom of God in a mystery, the hidden *wisdom* which God ordained before the ages for our glory, which none of the rulers of this age knew; for had they known, they would not have crucified the Lord of glory." The phrase "the rulers of this age" does not refer to either the Romans or the Jewish leaders. Satan is "the god of this age," and some of the fallen angels are "the rulers of the darkness of this age."[45] There are only two ages mentioned in the New Testament, "this age" and the "age to come" when we have eternal life.[46] "This age" continues until the end of the world.[47]

Even though the plan of salvation was written in the Scriptures before Christ was crucified,[48] the enemy did not understand it. Indeed, "salvation," "the sufferings of Christ," and "the glories that would follow" are "things which the angels desire to look into."[49] The serpent certainly did not foresee God's plan of salvation when he deceived Eve. "[N]ow the manifold wisdom of God might be made known by the church to the principalities and powers in the heavenly *places*, according to the eternal purpose which He accomplished in Christ Jesus our Lord."[50]

The devil continues to use deception as his main weapon. He "transforms himself into an angel of light" and "his ministers also transform themselves into ministers of righteousness."[51] "[T]he Spirit expressly says that in latter times some will depart from the faith, giving heed to deceiving spirits and doctrines of demons."[52]

When deception does not work, the enemy tries to silence those who speak and stand for the truth, using tactics such as fear, intimidation, character assassination, and even murder. John the Baptist was in the wilderness, and ate locusts and wild honey.[53] He preached repentance and called those in positions of religious power, the Pharisees and Sadducees, a brood of vipers.[54] Jesus also preached repentance, called the religious leaders hypocrites, and ate with sinners and tax collectors.[55] The religious leaders tried to use character assassination against both of them. As described by Jesus: "For John came neither eating nor drinking, and they say, 'He has a demon.' The Son of Man came eating and drinking, and they say, 'Look, a glutton and a winebibber, a friend of tax collectors and sinners!' "[56] Ultimately, the chief priests and Pharisees plotted to kill Jesus because they were afraid of losing their positions of power. They had tried and failed to refute what He preached, so they later had false witnesses bring accusations against Him.[57]

The apostles were arrested and brought before the council and high priest for preaching the gospel of Jesus Christ. After beating the apostles, they commanded them not to speak in the name of Jesus and then let them go.[58] That tactic did not work because the apostles chose to obey

God rather than men.[59] Instead of being silenced, they did not cease teaching and preaching that Jesus was the Christ.[60] They knew that the truth will set people free.[61]

---

[1] 1 John 5:19.
[2] Acts 1:5.
[3] Matthew 28:18.
[4] Mark 16:15.
[5] Matthew 28:19-20.
[6] Luke 17:21.
[7] 1 John 4:4b.
[8] Romans 16:19.
[9] Matthew 4:8-9.
[10] Matthew 4:10.
[11] Acts 20:30.
[12] John 8:44.
[13] 2 Corinthians 10:4b-5a.
[14] Genesis 3:1.
[15] Genesis 2:16-23.
[16] Genesis 3.3.
[17] Genesis 3:4.
[18] www.Barna.org/faith-spirituality/543-top-trends-of-2011-changing-role-of-christianity (accessed March 16, 2013).
[19] Galatians 6:7-8.
[20] Revelation 2:6.
[21] Revelation 2:15-16.
[22] 1 John 1:6.
[23] Genesis 3:5.
[24] Genesis 3:5.
[25] www.barna.org/barna-update/article/5-barna-update/67-americans-are-most-likely-to-base-truth-on-feelings (accessed March 16, 2013).
[26] Genesis 3:6.
[27] Proverbs 14:12.
[28] 2 Corinthians 11:3.
[29] 1 Timothy 2:14.
[30] Genesis 3:17
[31] Numbers 25:2-3, 9; Psalm 106:28-29; Numbers 31:16.
[32] Judges 15:14-15.
[33] Judges 16:15-21.
[34] Acts 13:22.
[35] 2 Samuel 11:1-5, 14-17; 2 Samuel 2:7-13.
[36] 1 Kings 11:4 .
[37] 2 Kings 9:30.

[38] Genesis 3:8.

[39] Romans 8:1.

[40] Romans 5:12.

[41] Ezekiel 28:16.

[42] 2 Peter 2:4.

[43] Jude 6; see also 2 Peter 2:4.

[44] Acts 26:18.

[45] 2 Corinthians 4:4; Ephesians 6:12.

[46] Matthew 12:32; Mark 10:29-30; Luke 18:29-30.

[47] Matthew 13:40.

[48] Luke 24:44-47.

[49] 1 Peter 1:11-12.

[50] Ephesians 3:10-11.

[51] 2 Corinthians 11:14-15.

[52] 1 Timothy 4:1.

[53] Matthew 3:1-4.

[54] Matthew 3:3-7.

[55] Matthew 4:17; 6:2, 5, 16; 9:10-11.

[56] Matthew 11:18.

[57] Mark 14:55-59.

[58] Acts 5:40.

[59] Acts 5:29.

[60] Acts 5:42.

[61] John 8:31-32.

10

NO FEAR

The LORD is my light and my salvation;
Whom shall I fear?
The LORD is the strength of my life;
Of whom shall I be afraid?

Psalm 27:1

During the entire year and a half that I was in the gunship platoon, I was never afraid—not even when my pilot was yelling over the radio, "Mayday! Mayday! We're going down!" There were times I was even surprised by my lack of fear.

One night my gunship and another scrambled out to help an outpost that was being attacked. On our way out, the outpost radioed that the enemy had a .50-caliber machine gun (sometimes called a .51 caliber). The maximum effective range of the .50 caliber is over two miles. In order to take it out, we had to get well within its effective range, and I can tell you from experience that its 1/2-inch diameter bullets rip big holes in a helicopter.

The enemy usually attacked on dark, moonless nights. When we would arrive at night over an outpost under attack, we could not see anything on the ground except tracer rounds streaking towards each other from opposite directions. A tracer is a bullet that has a pyrotechnic material in a cavity in its base. When the bullet is fired, the material ignites and burns brightly. What your eyes see, even in daylight, is a bright red streak going through the air. Typically, every fifth round is a tracer. It allows the shooter to see where the bullets are going so he can adjust his aim accordingly in order to hit the target. We would usually have to circle overhead while in radio contact with the outpost to determine which tracers were from the good guys and which were from the enemy, so that we did not attack the wrong side. On this night we did not have to do so. We could immediately tell which side was the enemy because even from 1000 feet above the ground the tracers of the .50 caliber machine gun were noticeably larger than those of the other weapons.

We climbed to 1500 feet in elevation to begin the attack. We had one advantage. On a moonless night, you cannot see a blacked-out helicopter in the sky. However, because my helicopter was flying lead, its red rotating beacon was on so that our wing ship could tell where we were by the flashing red light. That rotating beacon also gave the enemy a target to shoot at.

My pilot put the helicopter into a dive flying directly toward the .50 caliber and began firing our rockets. We could not actually see the .50 caliber in the darkness; we could only see where its tracers were originating. Because our rockets were unguided, the pilot had to be flying directly toward the enemy gun, and it immediately began returning fire. Since we were flying directly toward him, the enemy did not have to lead us in order to hit us. He only had to shoot straight.

I sat there watching the .50 caliber tracers stream past the right side of my helicopter, missing us by several feet. They looked like a string of softball-sized fireballs zipping past, although some describe them as appearing to be the size of basketballs. As I was watching the tracers go by, my first thought was, "This looks neat. I wish I had my camera." I then thought, "Shouldn't I be afraid, or at least concerned?" but I was not. It was just as if I was watching a movie. We made three runs at the machine gun before it stopped shooting, and each time its tracers were streaming just past the side of my helicopter. Had the enemy shot just slightly to his right, we would have been shot down.

The reason that I was never afraid during the time I was in Vietnam is because of something that happened one afternoon as we were flying back to our base from a mission. When returning to base, we would normally fly at an altitude of 1000 feet because at that altitude there was little risk of being hit by enemy fire. That afternoon, it was raining hard. Due to the limited visibility, my pilot was flying at about 300 feet in order to make visual contact with a road so he could follow it back to our base. This was before GPS's; our only navigational instrument was a compass. You may have heard of IFR flying, which means flying in limited visibility situations by Instrument Flight Rules. In Vietnam, IFR flying meant "I Follow Roads."

Because it was raining, I had my door closed and was simply sitting there watching the scenery go by. I suddenly became very sleepy and could not stay awake. It was as if I had been drugged. One minute I was wide awake, and the next I could not stay awake. After fighting sleep for a while, I decided to take a nap and lie down sideways onto the "ammo trays" located next to my seat. Ammo trays were metal boxes that were about the same height as my seat, and they held a total of 10,000 rounds of ammunition that fed into the two miniguns mounted on the sides of the helicopter. I had just lain over sideways and closed my eyes, when I heard a loud noise and felt shards of Plexiglas hitting me. I immediately sat upright, and the first thing I saw was a large bullet hole in the window of my door. A .50 caliber round had come through the window and passed through the wall behind where my head had been less than two seconds earlier when I was sitting upright. Had I not lain down, that round would have hit me right in the Adam's apple. It would literally have blown my head off.

After tearing through the wall behind where my head had been, the bullet then burst through the transmission. That was not only the first time I was almost killed, it was also the first time my helicopter was shot down.

I pondered that event for a little while. Before then, being killed was an abstract possibility. Now, I realized that as long as I was flying in gunships there was a substantial risk that I would be killed. Perhaps what was most disconcerting was that the bullet came without any warning. It was literally like a bolt out of the blue. We were not even in a place where we were expecting enemy fire. There was absolutely nothing I could have done in my own ability to keep from being killed. I realized that I could be doing everything perfectly, and on any given day I could be killed by one bullet coming out of nowhere. I remember thinking that death could come even from someone firing a single-shot .22 (a small-caliber rifle that is often a youth's first firearm).

I concluded that I could either worry about dying and get ulcers, or simply choose not to worry about it. I chose the latter course. I simply accepted the fact that I had a good possibility of being killed, and did not worry about it. In a sense, I considered myself already dead. I accepted the fact of my death. Once you have accepted your death as a fact, you no longer fear it. That does not mean I wanted to die. I did not. I simply did not worry about it. I had no fear of death. Every day I flew, I knew I could die, but every day I flew, I believed I would live.

Being effective in combat requires two seemingly contradictory mind-sets. First, you must totally accept the fact that you are going to die, and not worry about it. You must consider yourself already dead. You cannot allow fear to hold you back from doing whatever needs to be done. Once you have accepted your death, you have nothing to fear. Second, you must totally believe that you are going to live, no matter how bleak the circumstances appear. You must desire life with all that is in you and never give up. The object is not to die for your country; it is to enable the enemy to die for his. You cannot passively allow the enemy to kill you. You must fight to live.

These same principles apply to spiritual warfare, as shown by Romans 6:1-14:

> What shall we say then? Shall we continue in sin that grace may abound? Certainly not! How shall we who died to sin live any longer in it? Or do you not know that as many of us as were baptized into Christ Jesus were baptized into His death? Therefore we were buried with Him through baptism into death, that just as Christ was raised from the dead by the glory of the Father, even so we also should walk in newness of life.
>
> For if we have been united together in the likeness of His death, certainly we also shall be *in the likeness* of *His* resurrection, knowing this, that our old man was crucified with *Him,* that the body of sin might be done away with, that we should no longer be slaves of sin. For he who has died has been freed from sin. Now if we died with Christ, we believe that we shall also live with Him, knowing that Christ, having been raised from the dead, dies no more. Death no longer has

dominion over Him. For *the death* that He died, He died to sin once for all; but *the life* that He lives, He lives to God. Likewise you also, reckon yourselves to be dead indeed to sin, but alive to God in Christ Jesus our Lord.

Therefore do not let sin reign in your mortal body, that you should obey it in its lusts. And do not present your members *as* instruments of unrighteousness to sin, but present yourselves to God as being alive from the dead, and your members *as* instruments of righteousness to God. For sin shall not have dominion over you, for you are not under law but under grace.

We must die to sin. "For he who has died has been freed from sin."[1] Jesus said: "He who loves his life will lose it, and he who hates his life in this world will keep it for eternal life. If anyone serves Me, let him follow Me; and where I am, there My servant will be also. If anyone serves Me, him *My* Father will honor."[2] To lose our lives we cannot cling to the things of this world. Jesus also said, "If anyone desires to come after Me, let him deny himself, and take up his cross daily, and follow Me."[3] Taking up the cross means denying oneself, crucifying the flesh, and obeying God no matter the cost. Denying ourselves may be the hardest part, but that we must do. If we are dead to those things, they will not hold any power over us. To die to them, we must totally submit to God's will in all areas of our lives. You cannot serve two masters.[4]

We must also not fear physical death. Revelation 12:11 states, "And they overcame him [Satan] by the blood of the Lamb and by the word of their testimony, and they did not love their lives to the death." To overcome, we must not love our lives to the death. In other words, we must be willing to serve Christ at any cost, even if it means our physical death. Because we know we will be raised from the dead, the fear of death should no longer have dominion over us.[5]

Fear is a choice. It is simply being afraid that we will lose, or fail to gain, something that we consider important. It may be wealth or lifestyle, prestige or power, affirmation or acceptance, love or companionship, or other things. Such fear holds us in bondage if we believe that we must comply with the world's principles in order to obtain or keep such things. If God is more important to you than anything else in your life, then there is nothing in this world to fear losing or not having. What is more important than a relationship with Him? What in this world is more important than living out the destiny God has planned for you?

God Himself has said, *"I will never leave you nor forsake you."*[6] Because He is faithful, we should be able to say boldly: *"The LORD is my helper; I will not fear. What can man do to me?"*[7] As Jesus said, "If they have called the master of the house Beelzebub, how much more *will they call* those of his household! Therefore, do not fear them."[8]

We must trust God completely in all circumstances. The first time I was almost killed in Vietnam illustrates something very significant about God. He began putting me to sleep so that I would move out of the path of the bullet before the bullet was even fired. He did not react to the problem. He had the solution before there even was a problem.

Nothing can happen to any of us that God does not foreknow and allow. As Jesus said, "Are not two sparrows sold for a copper coin? And not one of them falls to the ground apart from your Father's will. . . . Do not fear therefore; you are of more value than many sparrows."[9]

Romans 8:28 says, "And we know that all things

work together for good to those who love God, to those who are the called according to *His* purpose." This verse does not say all things we go through will seem good at the time. It says that all things will work together for good. This does not happen because God thinks quickly on His feet and is able to respond immediately to situations as they arise. It is because, as stated in Isaiah 46:9-10, "Remember the former things of old, for I *am* God, and *there is* no other; I *am* God, and *there is* none like Me, declaring the end from the beginning, and from ancient times *things* that are not *yet* done, saying, 'My counsel shall stand, and I will do all My pleasure.' "

We need never fear. He will never leave us nor forsake us.[10] Nothing can separate us from the love of God that is in Christ Jesus our Lord.[11] Fear, worry, and doubt are simply having more faith in the power of the enemy than in God's power, character, and love. We must trust God in all things, even with the lives of our loved ones.

There is a difference between fear and prudence. Fear keeps you from doing what God has called you to do. Prudence enables you to do it with wisdom. For example, while Paul was preaching in Damascus, the Jews plotted to kill him. Had he responded in fear, he would have stopped preaching and quit the ministry. Instead, one night he allowed the disciples to lower him through the wall in a basket so he could escape those trying to kill him. He then went to Jerusalem and continued preaching.[12]

We must not just die to the things of this world, but we must also earnestly desire the life we have in Christ. We must "walk in newness of life" and consider ourselves "alive to God in Christ Jesus."[13] Jesus said, "I have come that they may have life, and that they may have *it* more abundantly."[14]

When I was in my early thirties, a friend invited me

to church. I declined because I thought that the most exciting thing a Christian probably did was go to an ice-cream social. That belief came from my childhood experiences. My mother died when I was six years old, and my three sisters and I went to live with others for two years. When the older of my two sisters and I returned to live with our father, he hired a live-in housekeeper. She would take us to church on Sundays, and after church we would go to the home of one of her friends. While they talked, we had to sit in the living room and watch a musical variety show on the black-and-white television. The show was popular with the gray-haired generation, but rather boring to me. That went on for three years, and then the housekeeper moved away. My paternal grandmother who lived in a nearby city then wanted us confirmed in her church. We began spending weekends at her house so we could attend that church. I also went to classes at both churches. I never heard the gospel at either church. To me, church just seemed to consist of going through Sunday rituals and ceremonies that had no meaning. Once I was confirmed, I stopped going. The next time I went to church was one Sunday when I was in basic training, but the service was so dry it was boring. I assume it was designed so as not to offend the beliefs or practices of any denomination. I never went again.

In my late twenties and early thirties, I knew there was something missing from my life, but I did not know what it was. When I was 36 years old, one of my brothers-in-law invited my wife (his sister) and I to hear him give his testimony at the church he was attending. He had recently accepted Jesus as his Lord and Savior at a Billy Graham Crusade. We went to be polite, but as soon as I walked into the church, before the service even began, I knew what was missing from my life. It was God!

It is hard for me to describe that abundant life. But, it includes having a relationship with God; hearing from Him and having Him guide me and help me in walking out my destiny; having the peace that surpasses all understanding in difficult times; being used by Him to help others; and having the assurance of salvation and His unconditional love.

The life we live is to be lived unto God. It should be a life of righteousness, joy, peace, and hope in the Holy Spirit.[15] *"Eye has not seen, nor ear heard, nor have entered into the heart of man, the things which God has prepared for those who love Him."*[16] It will be an exciting life and a fulfilling one as we draw closer to God and develop a relationship with Him. As stated in Acts 2:28, "You have made known to me the ways of life; You will make me full of joy in Your presence." God has things for us to do, battles to fight, people to help, victories to enjoy!

---

[1] Romans 6:7.
[2] John 12:25-26.
[3] Luke 9:23.
[4] Matthew 6:24.
[5] Romans 6:9.
[6] Hebrews 13:5.
[7] Hebrews 13:6.
[8] Matthew 10:25b-26a.
[9] Matthew 10:29, 31.
[10] Hebrews 13:5-6.
[11] Romans 8:37-39.
[12] Acts 9:20-30.
[13] Romans 6:4, 11.
[14] John 10:10.
[15] Romans 14:17; 15:13
[16] 1 Corinthians 2:9.

11

RECEIVING FIRE

Do not marvel, my brethren, if the world hates you.

1 John 3:13

When I began flying in the gunships, guess what? The enemy shot at me! The first time someone tried to kill me, I thought, "I'm not such a bad guy." But I realized it was nothing personal. It was just because I was in an opposing army.

Typically, the enemy shot at my helicopter with AK-47's, with .30 caliber machine guns, and occasionally with .50 caliber machine guns. One time they shot at us with a 37 mm antiaircraft gun. We were flying low over heavy foliage on the islands in the Mekong River and had a MACV (Military Assistance Command Vietnam) advisor with us sitting on the metal ammunition boxes between my and my door gunner's seats. Suddenly, I heard a "whump," "whump," "whump" right below me. I immediately thought, "I don't know what that was, but it is the biggest thing they've ever shot at us with." The MACV advisor was wearing a headset, and he told us over the intercom, "I forgot to mention that intelligence says the enemy has a 37 mm antiaircraft gun in this area." Fortunately we were low enough that the enemy only got off three rounds.

Another time, according to the FAC (forward air control) pilot flying overhead, they shot at us with a B-40 rocket (a precursor to the RPG's used to shoot down the Black Hawk helicopters in Mogadishu). It was not close enough for us to notice.

One morning as we were sitting on the runway at an outpost, they shot at us with mortars. They were not just shooting at the outpost when we happened to land there. They began shooting at us after we landed. Our mission that day was to fly to various outposts to drop off and pick up manila envelopes containing some sort of information (I cannot now recall what). Just after we landed at the first outpost, we began hearing mortar rounds exploding behind us as we were sitting on the runway, and they did not sound very far away. Nobody was in sight at the outpost, and suddenly an officer came running from a bunker out to our helicopter. He gave my pilot a manila envelope and told us that the mortars were friendly fire. After talking with the officer for several minutes, my pilot pulled the helicopter into a hover, and we headed down the runway to take off. As we were doing so, it sounded as if the explosions were getting closer. Later that day, we returned to the same outpost. When the officer ran out to pick up a manila envelope, he told us that he had been mistaken and that the mortar rounds were enemy fire. Fortunately, in that area of the Mekong Delta there was no high ground from which the enemy could easily see where the mortar rounds were landing and adjust their aim accordingly.

If we were close enough to the enemy, I could hear the muzzle blast from his weapons as he opened fire. We could usually identify the weapon by the sound of the muzzle blast. I can tell you that there is a significant difference between the muzzle blast of an AK-47 and that of a 37-mm antiaircraft gun.

If we were too far from the enemy to hear the muzzle blast, I could hear the popping sound—mini sonic boom—made by bullets as they zipped past, although they had to be quite close for me to be able to hear them over the roar of the helicopter and while wearing a flight helmet. The cabin of the helicopter was very noisy, especially next to the transmission where I sat. When we had a passenger who was not wearing a flight helmet or headset and therefore could not talk over the intercom, I had to yell for him to hear me, and vice versa. I have seen tracers go past that appeared to be ten to fifteen feet away, and I could not hear them. Although I was unable to do any experimenting to determine precisely how close a bullet had to be in order for me to hear it go by, it seemed like it had to be within about ten feet or so. The loudness of the popping sound varied depending upon how close the bullets were. Those that were quite close were loud enough for everyone in the helicopter to hear. Those a little farther away were barely audible.

Sometimes we would immediately know when the helicopter was hit by enemy fire. For example, a .50 caliber tracer round going through the cabin did not go unnoticed. You not only heard it and saw the flash as it went by, but you could smell the burning tracer compound. One time we took a .30 caliber round from below that jarred the helicopter so much it felt just like we had hit a speed bump.

At other times, however, we did not even know we had been hit. One time a .30 caliber bullet hit about eighteen inches behind my head, causing structural damage to one of the I-beams upon which the transmission was mounted. The damage was significant enough that we could not fly the helicopter back to our base. I did not even hear or feel that bullet hit. I discovered the damage when we landed to refuel. The pilot simply shut the helicopter down and radioed for a larger helicopter, a Chinook. When it arrived, my helicopter was attached beneath it with straps, what we called a sling load, and it picked my helicopter up and transported it back to our base.

I soon got used to the popping sound of bullets going past, to hearing and feeling bullets hitting my helicopter, and even to bullets going through the cabin area, so that it was no big deal. It was all simply part of a day's work. One day we were flying on the deck when someone opened fire at us with an AK-47 from my door gunner's side of the helicopter. I immediately felt little pieces of something falling down into my eyes. I looked up at the ceiling, which was just a few inches above my head, and saw a bullet hole above my head in the quilted fabric that covered the ceiling. It was little pieces of the stuffing from inside that quilted fabric that were falling down into my eyes. I then looked to my right at the wall I was sitting against and saw another bullet hole a couple of inches to the right of my head, next to my ear. My reaction was simply a nonchalant, "You missed."

Another time, as we were flying about fifteen or twenty feet above the ground, a bullet went past my side of the helicopter that was barely close enough for me to hear a faint pop as it zipped by. I was the only one who heard it. I leaned outside the helicopter to look toward the front and saw a faint puff of smoke in the bushes directly in front of us. Although I would usually have told the pilot we were receiving fire at 12 o'clock, this time I did not. I thought: "We are flying right towards that guy so that he does not even have to lead us, and the bullet was barely close enough for me to hear it go by. If he cannot shoot any better than that, I am not going to worry about him."

We continued flying towards the bushes where he

was hiding, and just as we were over that area the pilot made a 180-degree, left-hand turn. When we made 180-degree turns on the deck, the pilot would gain enough altitude so that the rotor blades would clear the ground and then bank the helicopter about 90 degrees, turning it on its side. He would then bring it around in a hard turn. When he did so, our ground speed dropped significantly, making us more vulnerable to enemy fire. As we were about half way through the turn, with my side of the helicopter facing the ground, the guy in the bushes opened fire at us with his AK-47, emptying his 30-round magazine. This time, everybody in the helicopter heard the muzzle blast. He still missed us. My immediate thought was, "See, I knew he was a bad shot."

I became so used to being shot at that I do not even recall the incident in which I was awarded my first medal for heroism. The enemy fire must have been more intense than usual for us to have been awarded medals. However, whatever happened, it was not intense enough to etch the incident in my memory. The citation merely states that my door gunner and I "placed deadly accurate machine gun fire on heavily fortified enemy positions while receiving intense automatic weapons and small arms fire from an estimated company of enemy soldiers. With complete disregard for their own safety, they leaned far out of the aircraft numerous times exposing themselves to the enemy fire in their attempts to suppress and incapacitate the enemy." That description does not stand out as being significant, nor does it remind me of any particular day or occurrence. It is simply what we did on a regular basis.

In fact, there were times when we would try to get someone to shoot at us just to avoid boredom. Every night, one gunship from either our platoon or the other helicopter company at Soc Trang was assigned to fly "airfield security." It had to fly circles around the airfield all night long so that there would be at least one gunship in the air if we were attacked. In my opinion, flying airfield security was the worst assignment there was. Nothing ever happened. One of the times that my gunship was going to be flying airfield security, the assigned pilot was one who also liked a little excitement. As we were talking late in the afternoon, he suggested that we try to liven up the evening by flying to an area near our base where you could usually draw enemy fire. I readily agreed.

At dusk, the gunship assigned to fly airfield security and another would make a sweep of the countryside surrounding the airfield. When we made the sweep that evening, my gunship was flying lead, and we flew a little farther away than usual so that we passed over that enemy area. As we were doing so, about half a dozen tracers streaked past my door, coming from behind us. They missed us by about ten to fifteen feet. One of the ironies of war is the beauty that you sometimes see. The sight of those bright red tracers fading into the pink and pale blue evening sky was really quite lovely.

At about 10:00 p.m. that night, we returned to the enemy area. The pilot turned on the red rotating beacon, the navigational lights, and the landing light so that the enemy could see us in the darkness. Starting at an altitude of about 1000 feet, we began flying in a large, descending circle until the enemy would shoot at us. When he did, I would return fire with my machine gun until he stopped shooting. When he would no longer shoot at us, we would drop lower until he would shoot at us again. I would then return fire, and, when he stopped shooting, we would continue our descent until he shot at us again.

Eventually, we could no longer get the enemy to shoot at us. We kept dropping lower and lower trying to draw fire until we were flying just a few feet above the ground. This was before night vision goggles. We could only see because of the landing light, which, considering our speed, did not shine very far ahead. As we were flying past a grass hut, we were close enough to it and to the ground that by bending down slightly I was able to look into the doorway to see if there was anyone standing there with a gun who wanted to take us on. Although most of the interior was pitch black, the ambient light from our landing light enabled me to see if there was anyone near the doorway. Seeing nobody, I looked forward, and the only thing I could see out the front windshield was the trunk of a very large tree dead ahead. We were so low that I could not even see any branches. Fortunately, the pilot saw the tree at the same time and yanked back on the cyclic to pull up. We barely made it over the top of the tree. I wondered what the people in the grass hut thought to have a Huey gunship roar past their doorway in the middle of the night.

If you live out your destiny, if you take a stand for Christ, people will shoot at you, but not necessarily with bullets. It is usually with words and sometimes deeds. You should not be surprised by it. As stated in 1 Peter 4:12-14:

> Beloved, do not think it strange concerning the fiery trial which is to try you, as though some strange thing happened to you; but rejoice to the extent that you partake of Christ's sufferings, that when His glory is revealed, you may also be glad with exceeding joy. If you are reproached for the name of Christ, blessed *are you*, for the Spirit of glory and of God rests upon you. On their part He is blasphemed, but on your part He is glorified.

"[W]e do not wrestle against flesh and blood, but against principalities, against powers, against the rulers of the darkness of this age, against spiritual *hosts* of wickedness in the heavenly *places*."[1] In this spiritual battle, people are not our real enemy. Satan and his demons can work through and use people, and they can induce people to have wicked hearts. When people slander or verbally attack us, when they hate us without reason, we must always be aware of the spiritual battle that is raging, not losing sight of the real enemy. The attacks are really nothing personal. The spirit working through them simply does not like the Holy Spirit in us. We must not take the attacks personally. Do not take them to heart. It is simply because of who we are in Christ.

The attacks we experience may not even appear to be related to our faith. They can manifest in many ways. They are often personal attacks about our character, abilities, or appearance. They can occur at our work, in our home, or even at church. That does not mean they are not part of the spiritual battle. Our response is important. The person attacking you may one day be your brother or sister in Christ.

If I could become so used to being shot at in Vietnam that it was no big deal, you should not become overwhelmed when you are attacked with words. "[A]ll who desire to live godly in Christ Jesus will suffer persecution."[2] Persecution is simply part of the normal Christian life. If you are not being persecuted, you need to ask yourself, "Am I walking out my destiny?" "Am I living for God?" As Jesus said, "If the world hates you, you know that it hated Me before *it hated you*. If you were of the world, the world would love its own."[3]

Being attacked is a good sign. It means you must be doing something right. Otherwise, the enemy would not be trying to take you out. Indeed, Jesus said:

> Blessed are you when men hate you,
> And when they exclude you,
> And revile *you,* and cast out your name as evil,
> For the Son of Man's sake.
> Rejoice in that day and leap for joy!
> For indeed your reward *is* great in heaven,
> For in like manner their fathers did to the prophets.[4]

He also said, "Woe to you when all men speak well of you."[5] As you are following Him, you should not expect praise from others, particularly those who do not know Him. Rather, your desire should simply be to obtain the Lord's commendation.[6] At the present time, people who publically stand for Christ are often ridiculed and reviled, especially if they are public figures. That is just one of the enemy's tactics.

Part of the battle is how we respond to attacks that come through others. In Vietnam we had varying rules of engagement. Sometimes we could shoot the enemy on sight. Sometimes we had to wait until he shot at us first. Sometimes we could not even shoot back without first radioing for permission from higher ups.

In spiritual warfare, there are also rules of engagement. Do we respond in the flesh because our pride is hurt, or do we respond in the Spirit? 1 Corinthians 4:12b-13a states, "Being reviled, we bless; being persecuted, we endure; being defamed, we entreat." That is certainly easier said than done, but it is something we must do.

When I ran for election to the Idaho Supreme Court to unseat a liberal justice, a media person told me it was the most vicious attack by the media against a candidate that this person had ever seen. The media knew that I was a conservative and was pro-life, and it printed falsehoods and accusations. After the election, I heard second hand that a major media figure was confident that he could defeat me, and he certainly tried. Nevertheless, throughout the campaign I decided to trust God to take care of those attacks, and He gave the victory.

We are not to repay anyone evil for evil.[7] As Romans 12:19 says, "Beloved, do not avenge yourselves, but *rather give place to wrath; for it is written, 'Vengeance is Mine, I will repay,'* says the Lord." Seeking vengeance for ourselves is grounded in pride and in a lack of trust in God. It is pride that makes us desire to get even or avenge an insult or betrayal, and it is a lack of trust in God that makes us want to take the matter into our own hands. If it is possible, as much as it depends upon us, we are to live at peace with everyone.[8] Responding in anger or with personal insults or trying to get even is simply descending to the level of those who initiated the attack.

One of the enemy's favorite weapons is character assassination, by seeking to ridicule, belittle, insult, and disparage. That tactic is nothing new. We cannot stoop to that level. As I mentioned earlier, it was used against Jesus. As He said: "For John [the Baptist] came neither eating nor drinking, and they say, 'He has a demon.' The Son of Man came eating and drinking, and they say, 'Look, a glutton and a winebibber, a friend of the tax collectors and sinners!' But wisdom is justified by her children."[9] In my view, when the enemy uses character assassination as a tactic, it simply means that he cannot deal with the truth. My secretary, who is very protective, would become angry when the liberal media would make false accusations against me, and become frustrated when I would only laugh, saying, "It is just part of the spiritual battle."

Sometimes this is difficult, but it is part of the rules of engagement. When the battle heats up and the enemy fire becomes intense, we need to remember, " 'No weapon formed against you shall prosper, and every tongue *which* rises against you in judgment you shall condemn. This *is* the heritage of the servants of the LORD, and their righteousness *is* from Me,' says the LORD."[10] We simply must stand on the truth and let God take care of the rest.

We never know whether someone who is attacking us today will later become a brother or sister in the Lord. We are to just let our lights shine as we hold fast to the word of life.[11] If you respond at all, let it be as you are taught by the Holy Spirit.[12] I only responded to one false attack because, after praying, I felt I should. I did not respond with sarcasm or a personal attack. I simply recited the false allegations and then set forth the truth of what actually happened.

---

[1] Ephesians 6:12.
[2] 2 Timothy 3:12. See also John 15:18-21.
[3] John 15:18-19a.
[4] Luke 6:22-23.
[5] Luke 6:26.
[6] 2 Corinthians 10:18.
[7] Romans 12:17.
[8] Romans 12:18.
[9] Matthew 11:18-19.
[10] Isaiah 54:17.
[11] Matthew 5:13-16; Philippians 2:15.
[12] Luke 12:11.

Freedom Is Your Destiny!

12

FRIENDLY FIRE

But if you bite and devour one another,
beware lest you be consumed by one another!

Galatians 5:15

One night my helicopter and another scrambled out to help an outpost that was being attacked. When we arrived over the outpost, all we could see were tracers going towards each other from opposite directions. My helicopter was flying wing, which means it was blacked out. The lead helicopter had on its red rotating beacon so that we could see it, but the wing helicopter flew without lights. On a moonless night, you cannot see a blacked-out helicopter in the sky.

The lead helicopter began flying in a clockwise circle while the pilot was in radio contact with the ground trying to determine which side was the good guys and which side was the enemy. Once the pilot made that determination, the lead helicopter circled to the left and climbed to 1500 feet to begin its attack. The pilot of my helicopter lost sight of the lead helicopter and continued flying in the clockwise circle. As we were completing another lap of the circle, I could see out my door the rotating beacon of another helicopter above and behind us, and slightly to our left.

I was about to tell my pilot there was another helicopter out here, when the pilot radioed the lead helicopter asking where it was. The lead helicopter answered, and my pilot said, "Roger." By my pilot's answer, I thought he must be able to see the lead helicopter somewhere in front of us. Because the helicopter flies in a slightly nose-down attitude, the pilots could see farther out the front windshield than I could from my seat behind the copilot.

Suddenly, the helicopter I could see began firing rockets, and we were headed directly into the path of those rockets. It was the lead helicopter.

Not wanting to panic my pilot, I keyed my microphone and said in a normal voice, "Barry, break right." The copilot panicked, however, and began screaming over the radio, "Cease fire! Cease fire!" His words were so slurred by his hysteria that the pilot of our lead helicopter thought he was yelling, "Receiving fire," and he kept firing the rockets. The pilot of my helicopter froze, and we continued heading towards the path of the rockets.

The rockets we used in our gunships were unguided, 2.75-inch, folding-fin rockets. There is no doubt that they would do considerable damage to a Huey. During the late 1940's, similar rockets with six-pound warheads were developed for use by interceptors to shoot down heavy bombers. Our rockets had larger ten- and seventeen-pound warheads (we used both sizes). The rocket motors burned for slightly over one second, at which point the rockets with the ten-pound warheads would have reached a speed of about 2,525 feet per second and would have traveled about 1,280 feet. After the motors burned out, the rockets began to lose velocity, which hampered their accuracy from long range. Also, they were sensitive to the relative wind and would curve if the helicopter was not flying in trim. Some of our pilots learned how to make the rockets curve around obstacles to hit what was behind them.

Our gunships carried fourteen rockets, seven on each side. The pilots typically made either two runs, firing all seven rockets from one side on the first run and the seven from the other side on the second run, or four runs, firing three or four rockets each run. I began counting the rockets as they went by to see how many the pilot was going to fire.

We were heading into the path of the rockets at a fairly sharp angle (the lead helicopter was above, behind, and slightly to our left). I initially hoped that the pilot would fire them all before we crossed their path. When he fired the fifth one, I knew that would not happen. Each rocket was progressively closer to us than the one before. It seemed like the rockets were being "walked" towards us like artillery fire, but in reality we were heading into their paths. The fifth rocket was fairly close as it roared past about level with my waist. The sixth rocket cut that distance in half. I knew that the seventh one would hit us, probably right about where I was sitting.

Sometimes death comes without warning, but at other times you can see it approaching. After the sixth rocket roared past, I laid my machine gun on the floor; leaned over forward in my seat to try to become a smaller target; placed my left arm over the back of my neck hopefully to protect my brain stem; and waited for the explosion. The pilot had been firing the rockets at a set tempo, and when there was no explosion when there should have been, I turned and looked towards my door gunner. Just outside his door I saw hundreds of tracer rounds streaking past the right side of my helicopter. The copilot on the lead helicopter was now firing its miniguns at 4000 rounds per minute.

When the copilot fires the miniguns, it cuts off the

switch on the pilot's cyclic so that he cannot fire the rockets. I assume that is why the pilot did not fire that seventh rocket. Even though I had my head down waiting for the explosion, I know that he did not do so. By about the fifth rocket, the rocket motors were still burning as they roared past my helicopter, and they were close enough that I could hear them go by. I would have heard the seventh rocket go past had it been fired. I remember thinking at the time that it would have been very embarrassing to have been shot down by another gunship from our platoon. It would also undoubtedly have been fatal.

After returning to base, we learned that when the copilot began firing the miniguns, they were shooting below his point of aim. The initial burst from the miniguns would have gone right below us as we crossed the line of fire. By the time he adjusted his point of aim upwards, we had crossed the line of fire so that the bullets went past the right side of the helicopter.

Another time, my gunship was flying lead on the deck when it suddenly sounded like hundreds of bees were buzzing past my door, and I could see splashes where many bullets were hitting the water in the rice paddy directly in front of us. The copilot of our wing helicopter suddenly came on the radio saying, "Sorry about that." When we were flying on the deck, the gunship flying wing typically crossed back and forth from side to side while following the lead helicopter. As our wing ship was starting to cross from the left side of us to our right side, the copilot accidentally fired its miniguns, barely missing us.

We did not just receive accidental friendly fire. In addition to the enemy shooting at us, soldiers from the Army of the Republic of Vietnam (ARVN) also routinely shot at us with their M-16 rifles and M-79 grenade launchers. The M-79 fired a 40 mm, high-explosive, fragmentation round that had a range of about 400 meters and a "kill radius" of about 5 meters when it exploded. The kill radius meant it should kill 90% of the people who were within 5 meters of the explosion. The projectile traveled slowly enough that you could often see it going through the air.

Shortly after I began flying in the gunships, I noticed an ARVN soldier shoot at our command-and-control helicopter while the ARVN's were waiting to be picked up from an LZ. The helicopter was at 1500 feet, and I could tell the ARVN was not leading it enough to even come close. However, it caused me to watch them more carefully. Several days later we were providing cover for a group of ARVN soldiers that had been dropped off in a rice paddy and were approaching a large grove of coconut palm trees. We would fly on the deck between them and the palm trees, trying to draw fire from the enemy and engage him before the ARVN's got there so that we, rather than they, would take the brunt of any enemy fire. As the ARVN's were nearing the palm trees, they were shooting into the trees; what we called "reconning by fire." They were not returning enemy fire, but were merely shooting at the area in case the enemy was there. We happened to fly over the edge of the grove just above the tops of the trees, which were about thirty to forty feet tall, and I could hear the ARVN's bullets ripping through the leaves of the palm trees below me. Since the leaves are only at the tops of the palm trees, I thought, "They are either aiming at the ground and shooting way high or they are aiming at us and shooting a little low." After they had entered the grove and had been there some time, we again flew over it, and someone below us emptied his M-16 in our direction. All I could do was sit there and hope he missed.

Later, my gunship was one of three supporting a

group of ARVN soldiers who were walking across a rice paddy towards a line of trees and brush. My gunship was flying "at altitude" (at 1000 feet) while the other two gunships were flying on the deck. Three gunships operating together were called a "heavy team." The gunships on the deck would periodically fly between the ARVN's and the tree line, trying to draw enemy fire. From my position, I watched what happened when the gunships did so. The ARVN's would not be firing their M-79's until the gunships flew past. Then there would be M-79 rounds exploding all around the gunships. As soon as they were out of range, there would be no more M-79 rounds exploding until they flew by again.

As I continued observing the ARVN's while we were supporting and protecting them, there was no doubt that many of them were shooting at us on a regular basis. One of our slicks was hit by an M-79 round fired by an ARVN soldier. The slick had landed in an LZ and unloaded ARVN soldiers. One of them ran a ways away from the slick, turned, and fired his M-79 at it, hitting the helicopter just in front of the pilot.

One day, when the ARVN's were shooting at us more than usual, my pilot noticed an M-79 round fired by an ARVN soldier narrowly miss the nose of our helicopter. The pilot told my door gunner and me to shoot near the group of ARVN's to scare them so they would stop shooting at us. We did so. I walked a string of machine-gun bullets a couple of yards in front of the jagged line of ARVN soldiers, weaving the bullets in and out so they would hit a couple yards in front of each soldier, while being careful not to hit any of them.

There was one time when I was ready to shoot at an ARVN. One afternoon we were flying at about 1000 feet returning from a mission when we spotted an ARVN Bird

Dog approaching us from my side of the helicopter. A Bird Dog was a single-engine, high wing, two-seat, airplane used for Forward Air Control missions to mark targets for artillery and attack aircraft. It was armed with eight 2.75-inch rockets, four under each wing, and the rockets usually had white phosphorous warheads because the white smoke they produced was a highly visible target marker. The Bird Dog was flying straight and level directly towards us and appeared to be lining up on my helicopter, as if preparing to shoot a rocket at us. If it hit us with a white phosphorous rocket, we would probably have exploded in mid-air.

My pilot took evasive action, turning in a large circle to our right. However, the Bird Dog also circled around and, when we returned to our original heading, we again saw it on my side of the helicopter flying directly toward us. My pilot again took evasive action, but when we resumed our original direction the Bird Dog was again flying directly at us on my side of the helicopter. At that point, I picked up my machine gun from the floor at my feet, inserted the barrel, pointed it towards the Bird Dog, and told the pilot over the intercom, "Say the word and I will shoot it down." The Bird Dog suddenly banked to its left and flew away. Maybe the Bird Dog pilot saw that I had my machine gun in my hands, and it was pointing at him. He was close enough to have seen it. Being in a conflict where both sides were shooting at me helped prepare me to be a judge.

Unfortunately, one of the realities of war is that soldiers are often seriously wounded or killed by what is called "friendly fire"—fire from their fellow soldiers or from those who are supposed to be allies. When I was in the hospital, the soldier in the bed next to me had been wounded by an American artillery round that fell short.

Casualties can also be caused by other activities of those on your side. In Vietnam, our military used a defoliant called Agent Orange. It was sprayed on certain areas of heavy foliage in an attempt to deprive the enemy of cover from which to launch an ambush or attack. In the Mekong Delta where I was stationed, Agent Orange was usually sprayed in specific areas of dense cover along canals or rivers to try and protect against ambushes. There were several times when my helicopter was assigned to fly cover for the C-123's (twin engine cargo planes) spraying the Agent Orange. To do so, we flew below and behind the C-123's, which meant that my helicopter was flying in the midst of the Agent Orange, which was raining down so heavily that my pilot had to turn on the windshield wipers to see. Because the Plexiglas windshields of the Huey were easily scratched even by the wiper blades, the pilot turned them on only when absolutely necessary. My cargo door was also open because we were in combat, so I was breathing air filled with evaporated Agent Orange. We now know that Agent Orange is toxic to humans. I periodically received a pamphlet listing the various types of cancers and other diseases that, for the purpose of receiving veteran's benefits, would be conclusively presumed to have been caused by my exposure to Agent Orange if I ever contracted them. Thirty-eight years after returning from Vietnam, I was diagnosed with one of those cancers (non-Hodgkin's lymphoma). The aircrews spraying the Agent Orange and the commander who ordered us to fly cover for them had no idea that they were exposing us to a toxic chemical.

As you are following God, you will be attacked by fellow Christians. They may be blinded by the darkness, thinking they are only shooting at the enemy, as happened when our lead gunship almost shot us down. Chapter 10 of Acts tells us about Peter going to the house of Cornelius, a gentile, where he preached the gospel to Cornelius, his relatives, and close friends. They not only believed but were baptized with the Holy Spirit. When Peter returned to Jerusalem, certain Christian Jews verbally attacked him, saying, "You went in to uncircumcised men and ate with them!"[1] Those attacking Peter were blinded to God's plan to bring salvation to the gentiles.

They may not even be intending to attack at all, as when our wing gunship accidentally fired its miniguns, narrowly missing us. Well-meaning Christians will at times inadvertently say or do something that will hurt us.

There will be times when we will be deliberately attacked by other believers. We must keep in mind that Christians can be influenced by envy, jealousy, pride, self-centeredness, lust for power, and other weaknesses of the flesh. Emotional wounds can also make us very vulnerable to being used by the enemy to attack others, including fellow Christians.

When Christians attack us, we must remember who the real enemy is. We cannot retaliate in anger. Remember the admonition, "[A]bove all things have fervent love for one another, for *'love will cover a multitude of sins.'*"[2]

Another form of friendly fire is false doctrine. Just as many others and I were exposed to the toxic chemical Agent Orange by other members of our military, who were acting in good faith, there will be Christians who expose others to toxic doctrine. The Christians doing so may sincerely believe that what they are spreading is truth. Their sincere belief does not make it true, however.

We know that "the time will come when they will not endure sound doctrine, but according to their own desires, *because* they have itching ears, they will heap up for themselves teachers; and they will turn *their* ears away from the truth, and be turned aside to fables."[3] When people do not want to endure sound doctrine, there will be Christians willing to preach and teach what they want to hear. Paul warned the elders of the church at Ephesus that "from among yourselves men will rise up, speaking perverse things, to draw away the disciples after themselves."4

There are many false doctrines that appeal to itching ears. For example, Romans 4:17 declares that God "calls those things which do not exist as though they did." Some teach that we also have that same power so that we can proclaim what we want, and it will happen. Where in the Bible is there an example of Christians having that power? Obviously, through the gift of prophecy someone can proclaim something that later occurs, but his or her words do not make it happen. "[P]rophecy never came by the will of man, but holy men of God spoke *as they were* moved by the Holy Spirit."5 "Surely the Lord God does nothing, *unless* He reveals His secret to His servants the prophets."6 When a prophecy comes true, the person who prophesied did not make it happen. God did.

Another example is the teaching that if you have sufficient faith, you can create your circumstances so that you will be healthy, wealthy, and wise and nothing bad will happen to you. Those commended for their faith in Hebrews 11 included: "[O]thers [who] had trial of mockings and scourgings, yes, and of chains and imprisonment. They were stoned, they were sawn in two, were tempted, were slain with the sword. They wandered about in sheepskins and goatskins, being destitute, afflicted, tormented—of whom the world was not worthy."7 Obviously, their faith did not prevent adversity or make them healthy and wealthy, but regardless of the circumstances their faith did not fail.

Yet another asserts that our lives on earth should be like life in heaven and that we have the power or authority to bring heaven to earth. Proponents of that doctrine claim that because there is no sickness, pain, or lack in heaven, we should not experience any of those things on earth. Paul the Apostle was taught by revelation from the Lord.[8] The Lord apparently did not feel it necessary to teach Paul this doctrine because Paul suffered sickness, pain, and lack while preaching the gospel.[9] The other apostles also apparently missed this teaching when they walked with the Lord. There is likewise no death in heaven, but they all died.

Christians influenced by these doctrines may lose heart when they go through tribulation or do not receive what they desired even after mustering all the faith they can, confessing their sins, trying very hard to live righteously, repeatedly proclaiming what they want, and trying in vain to pull heaven down to the earth. They may even blame God when these techniques fail.

Because Satan "transforms himself into an angel of light" and "his ministers also transform themselves into ministers of righteousness,"[10] he can use Scripture and religion to deceive. For example, when tempting Christ, Satan set Him on the pinnacle of the temple, and said to Him, "If you are the Son of God, throw Yourself down. For it is written:

> *'He shall give His angels charge over you.'*
> *and*
> *'In their hands they shall bear you up,*
> *Lest you dash your foot against a stone.' "*[11]

If the enemy would try to deceive Christ with Scripture, he and his ministers will certainly use the same tactic against us. That is why it is important to read, study, and meditate upon God's word. There will be those who will preach another Jesus or a different gospel in order to deceive us.[12] We must know the whole teaching of God so that we are not deceived by Scriptures taken out of context. A passage of Scripture must be studied in the context in which it occurs and in the context of the entire Bible.

There is a subtle deception regarding our Commander that is typically phrased, "Jesus did not condemn . . . ." or "Jesus did not say anything about . . . ." or something similar. The subtle deception that can come from this is that there is a difference in attitude or nature between Jesus and the Father. Even though other parts of the Bible may forbid certain conduct, Jesus did not talk about it and so it must be acceptable now. Some view Jesus as the nice, gentle, forgiving God and the Father as the harsh, legalistic, angry God. Any such belief is wrong.

Jesus and the Father are one.[13] They are not in disagreement about anything. Jesus only did and said what the Father wanted Him to.[14] Nothing Jesus said or did conflicts with what the Father declared in the Law and the Prophets, or with what the authors of Scripture wrote as they were moved by the Holy Spirit.[15] We are to grow in Christlikeness,[16] but we must not be deceived by focusing only on certain aspects of Jesus's ministry. He is both the Lamb and the Lion,[17] the peacemaker and the warrior,[18] the Savior and the Judge.[19] He will judge according to the Father's will.[20]

Even the phrase, "What would Jesus do?" can be used to deceive. Jesus said: *"You shall love the LORD your God with all your heart, and with all your soul, and with all your mind.'* This is the first and greatest commandment. And the second *is* like it: *'You shall love your neighbor as yourself.'* "[21] If we seek to obey these commandments, whose meaning of "love" do we use? God's or our own? We can pour our own meaning into the word "love" to justify all sorts of conduct and beliefs. For example, some contend that love means supporting the government in taking money from some to give to others in order to make it fair. How does the government giving other people's money to the poor satisfy our Scriptural obligation to be charitable with our own money? Where is there Scriptural support for having the government redistribute wealth? As recorded in Luke 23:13-15, when a man asked Jesus to "tell my brother to divide the inheritance with me," Jesus answered, "Man, who made Me a judge or an arbitrator over you?" Jesus did not command the other brother to share the inheritance or to be fair.

Jesus explained what He meant by love. With respect to the commandments to love God and our neighbors, Jesus said, "On these two commandments hang all the Law and the Prophets."[22] If you want to know what Jesus meant by these two commandments, then you must study the Law (Genesis, Exodus, Leviticus, Numbers and Deuteronomy) and the Prophets (Joshua, Judges, 1 & 2 Samuel, 1 & 2 Kings, Isaiah, Jeremiah, Ezekiel, Hosea, Joel, Amos, Obadiah, Jonah, Micah, Nahum, Habakkuk, Zephaniah, Haggai, Zechariah, and Malachi). Likewise, the commandments proscribing adultery, murder, stealing, bearing false witness, covetousness, and any other commandment "are *all* summed up in this saying, namely, '*You shall love your neighbor as yourself.*' Love does no harm to a neighbor; therefore love *is* the fulfillment of the law."[23]

That is why "the weapons of our warfare *are* not carnal but mighty in God for pulling down strongholds [strong points or arguments in which one trusts], casting down arguments [reasoning that precedes and determines conduct] and every high thing [proud position] that exalts itself against the knowledge of God."[24] We are to increase in the knowledge of God.[25] We must know the truth as set forth in the Bible. Our desire must be to learn what God means, not what we wish He meant.

---

[1] Acts 11:1-4.
[2] 1 Peter 4:8.
[3] 2 Timothy 4:3-4.
[4] Acts 20:30.
[5] 2 Peter 1:21.
[6] Amos 3:7.
[7] Hebrews 11:36-38a.
[8] Ephesians 3:2-3; Galatians 1:11-12.
[9] Galatians 4:13; 2 Corinthians 11:24-27; 12:7-9; Philippians 4:12-13.
[10] 2 Corinthians 11:14-15.
[11] Matthew 4:6.
[12] 2 Corinthians 11:4.
[13] John 10:30.
[14] John 5:19-20, 30, 36; 8:28-29; 10:32, 37-38; 14:10-11.
[15] Matthew 5:17-18; 2 Timothy 3:16; 2 Peter 1:20-21.
[16] 1 Corinthians 11:1; Ephesians 4:15; 2 Peter 3:18.
[17] Revelation 5:12; 7:17; 5:5.
[18] John 14:27; Romans 5:1; Ephesians 2:14-18; Colossians 1:19-23; 2 Thessalonians 3:16; Matthew 10:34-36; Revelation 19:11-16.
[19] Philippians 3:20; 2 Timothy 1:10; Titus 2:13-14; John 5:30; Romans 2:16; 2 Timothy 4:1.
[20] John 5:30.
[21] Matthew 22:37-39.
[22] Matthew 22:40.
[23] Romans 13:9-10.
[24] 2 Corinthians 10:4-5.
[25] Colossians 1:9-10.

13

CASUALTIES OF WAR

For I consider that the sufferings of the present time are not worthy to be compared with the glory which shall be revealed in us.

Romans 8:18

One of the risks of helicopter combat is being shot down. A Huey could take quite a bit of damage and still fly. We had one D-model Huey that was hit by 125 rounds of enemy fire and was still flying. It had been rigged to lay down a smoke screen by spraying diesel fuel into its exhaust. One day while trying to lay down a smoke screen when there was a slight breeze, it had to keep flying back and forth in front of the enemy positions while receiving fire the entire time. Fortunately, nobody on board was injured, and it was not shot down. However, all it took was one bullet in the wrong place to bring a Huey down, and unfortunately there were many wrong places. My helicopter was shot down twice, and each time it was hit by only one bullet.

Even though being shot down was not an unexpected event, we were ill equipped to spend much time on the ground. We did not have canteens for water or iodine tablets for purifying water. We did not have any web gear to carry spare ammunition. I did not have a shoulder strap for my machine gun to make it easier to carry on the ground. For my battle rifle, I had a cloth bandolier with ten, open-topped pockets that held four, loaded, 20-round magazines and twelve ten-round stripper clips used to reload the magazines. After firing 80 rounds, not that many in a firefight, I would have to reload the magazines. We did not have hats to wear to keep the sun off or to provide some camouflage. If I wanted to take along my field dressing to use if I or someone else was wounded, I would have had to put it in my pocket. The assumption was that when we were shot down, another helicopter would be able to get in quickly to pick us up. It did not always work out that way. Before I arrived in Soc Trang, the crew of one Viking gunship that was shot down had to spend the night in the tall grass, fighting the enemy in hand-to-hand combat to stay alive.

I received two Purple Hearts for being wounded in combat. I received the first one a few months after I started flying in the gunships. One morning we were flying on the deck, and it suddenly felt like my right leg had been hit with a sledge hammer just above the ankle. My leg flew sideways, and the bones in my toes felt as if they were vibrating like a tuning fork. I looked down and, seeing that my foot was still there and in one piece, kept shooting. I later learned that a piece of shrapnel had torn into my lower leg and hit my tibia, chipping a small piece out of the bone.

About fifteen minutes later, I was bending down to grab a box of ammo to reload my machine gun when another small piece of shrapnel tore into my left side just below my ribs and lodged somewhere deep in my abdomen. I did not tell the pilot of either wound because to me it would simply have been complaining. There was nothing that anybody in the helicopter could do for me; I did not need any first aid. Since I was not incapacitated and was still able to shoot, I did not see any need to terminate our mission in order to return to the base for medical care. Therefore, to me there was no valid reason to say anything; doing so would simply have been complaining.

Later that night, after we had returned to base and I had completed the daily maintenance on my helicopter, I went to the medical unit, thinking I probably needed an antibiotic. After x-raying my abdomen, the doctor ordered me to lie down and not move. The next morning, I was flown to a nearby field hospital. The crew chief on the medevac helicopter later told me that he was surprised to see me walking out to get in. He expected to see me being brought out on a stretcher. I walked into the triage area and sat down in a chair along the wall of the tent. Eventually someone came over and asked, "May I help you?" I answered, "I have shrapnel wounds in my leg and my side." He told me to get on the table, which was located in the middle of the room. When I walked over and climbed onto the table, the nurse in charge exclaimed, "You walked in here with a shrapnel wound in your side!" I responded, "I'm sorry ma'am, my foot hurt too much to run." The trauma to my lower leg had caused my foot to swell up and it was pretty sore. I spent two weeks in the hospital, and then I was back flying the day after I was released.

My physician at the hospital ultimately left the shrapnel in my abdomen because he decided it was in too deep to remove. He said it would cause more damage to remove it than the shrapnel would probably cause if left where it was. I discovered years later that it is lodged a fraction of an inch in front of my spine. Another crew chief in my platoon was hit in the neck by a piece of shrapnel that lodged under his jugular vein. He was told they could not remove it because nobody in Vietnam had the expertise to do so. When he protested that it could cut his jugular vein if it dislodged, he was simply told to be careful. He continued flying as a crew chief on a Huey gunship.

I received the second Purple Heart during my second year in Vietnam. One day we were flying on the deck in combat when it suddenly felt like I had been hit in the forehead by a hammer. Immediately, there was so much blood pouring down that I could not see out of my left eye. I paused from firing my machine gun to assess how badly I was hit, whether all of my systems still seemed to be functioning. The pilot looked back to see why I was not shooting, and his eyes got as big as saucers. He radioed our wing ship that I had been hit in the head and then headed for a nearby field hospital. Upon concluding that my skull was probably intact (my first thought was, "What if my helmet was holding my head together?"), I removed my helmet so I could try to stop the bleeding. My door gunner came over and tied a field dressing (a thick, 4-inch by 7-inch gauze bandage with long cloth tails) around my head. I think he was a little shaken because when that field dressing immediately filled with blood, he tied on a second one over the top of it. Once we arrived at the field hospital, an x-ray confirmed that I had been hit by a piece of shrapnel, but it had not penetrated my thick skull. It hit me about 1½ inches above my left eye. As sometimes happens when a projectile hits one's head, the shrapnel merely followed the circumference of my skull and came to rest under the skin on the top of my head. I had a headache the rest of the day, but was otherwise fine.

Being wounded is simply one of the risks of war. You cannot enter into the war unless you are willing to take a risk, and sometimes you will be shot down or wounded.

By saying that, I am not in any way minimizing the grievous wounds suffered by some, particularly those who were horribly disfigured, paralyzed, or have lost hands, feet, arms, and/or legs. I am also not minimizing the loss to family and friends when a soldier is killed.

God spared my life many times when I was in Vietnam, and He kept me from any crippling injury. Others died or were severely injured. The fact that He did not intervene to protect them, or that He did to protect Me, does not mean that He loved them less or me more, or that I deserved His favor.

We tend to look at suffering and death from our perspective on the earth because we enjoy life here. When compared to eternity, however, the time spent here will be less than the blink of an eye. "Precious in the sight of the LORD *is* the death of His saints."[1] When we die, we go to be with Him.[2] We will never fully know the good that can come from a death or from a life of adversity lived in obedience to God.

For example, let's look at Jesus. The plan of salvation had Him being born in human form as God's only son so that He could die for our sins. The death of an only son was the most grievous loss you could suffer in the Jewish culture. As Jeremiah 6:26 says, "Make mourning *as for* an only son, most bitter lamentation." Zechariah 12:10 states, "Yes, they will mourn for Him as one mourns for *his* only *son*, and grieve for Him as one grieves for a firstborn." The Father loved the Son and was well pleased with Him.[3] Nevertheless, Jesus had to suffer a terrible death in order to provide salvation for us. Crucifixion was designed to bring a very slow, extremely painful death. He was totally innocent of any wrongdoing. He did not deserve to suffer and die as He did. From our perspective it was not fair, but it was necessary for our sins to be forgiven. It is by His death that we can have salvation.

All of the days ordained for each of us were decided before we were born.[4] We each have a part to play in God's larger plan. That some must endure suffering or the death of loved ones does not mean that God loves them less. God does not show partiality.[5] We simply are unable to understand why He causes or allows what we consider bad things to happen. We often cannot see how specific events fit into God's larger plan. However, we can be confident that "[t]he LORD *is* righteous in all His ways."[6] We also must realize that "His ways [are] past finding out."[7] If we could understand why He does or allows bad things to happen, we would be God. Job thought that God owed him an explanation for why Job was going through suffering,[8] but God's response was, "Shall the one who contends with the Almighty correct *Him*? He who rebukes God, let him answer it."[9] If God owed us an explanation, it would mean that we have the right to judge the merits of or reasons for His decisions. Demanding to know why is simply not trusting God.

There are many instances in the Bible when people suffered tribulations, sickness, and death because of their sins. However, we must be careful not to assume that God is displeased with those who are suffering or going through difficult times. Job suffered because of his righteousness. God described him as "My servant Job, that *there is* none like him on the earth, a blameless and upright man, one who fears God and shuns evil."[10] John the Baptist baptized Jesus and declared him to be the "Lamb of God who takes away the sin of the world."[11] Later, Herod imprisoned John because he had rebuked Herod for taking his brother's wife.[12] While he was in prison, John sent his disciples to ask Jesus if He was really the Messiah.[13] It may be that John was thinking that if Jesus, his cousin, was really the Messiah,

He would surely have sprung John from prison. John remained in prison until he was beheaded. Jesus prophesied regarding the death that Peter would suffer in order to bring glory to God.[14] Stephen was a man full of faith and the Holy Spirit, yet Jesus stood by and watched Stephen be stoned for proclaiming truth.[15] After Paul's conversion on the road to Damascus, Jesus told Ananias to go to Paul because "he is a chosen vessel of Mine to bear My name before Gentiles, kings, and the children of Israel. For I will show him how many things he must suffer for My name's sake."[16] Paul was a "chosen vessel" of our Lord's and was used mightily by Him, but Paul still suffered. Paul summarized what he had to endure as follows:

> From the Jews five times I received forty *stripes* minus one. Three times I was beaten with rods; once I was stoned; three times I was shipwrecked; a night and a day I have been in the deep; *in* journeys often, *in* perils of water, *in* perils of robbers, *in* perils of *my own* countrymen, *in* perils of the Gentiles, *in* perils in the city, *in* perils in the wilderness, *in* perils in the sea, *in* perils among false brethren; in weariness and toil, in sleeplessness often, in hunger and thirst, in fastings often, in cold and nakedness.[17]

Although people disagree as to what was Paul's "thorn in the flesh" (the "messenger [or angel] of Satan" that buffeted him) one thing is clear: It caused him sufficient distress that he pleaded with the Lord three times that it might depart from him.[18] It was not given to him as punishment, but to keep him from becoming arrogant because of the abundance of divine revelations he had received.[19] God miraculously delivered Paul from prison early in his ministry,[20] but Paul spent some of his later years in prison, and he was ultimately martyred.

1 Peter 4:13 says, "[R]ejoice to the extent that you partake of Christ's sufferings, that when His glory is revealed, you may also be glad with exceeding joy." The "fellowship of His sufferings"[21] is something that our flesh wants to avoid, but it is often part of our destinies. We cannot expect this spiritual battle to be a walk in the park. Scripture does not promise us an easy victory. We are "heirs of God and joint heirs with Christ, if indeed we suffer with *Him*, that we may also be glorified together."[22] We also cannot allow the wounds to take us out of the battle for good. After the Jews stoned the Apostle Paul and drug him out of the city, believing he was dead, Paul rose up and went back into the city.[23]

Scripture shows us some of the attacks of the enemy that can cause us loss and pain. Satan's first assault against Job consisted of a raid by the Sabeans who stole Job's oxen and donkeys and killed his servants who were tending them; of fire from heaven that burned up Job's sheep and his servants who were tending them; of a raid by the Chaldeans who stole Job's camels and killed his servants who were tending them; and of a great wind that destroyed the house of Job's oldest son, killing Job's sons and daughters who were inside.[24] Satan's second assault against Job consisted of afflicting him with painful boils from the soles of his feet to the crown of his head.[25] Job's less than empathetic wife told him, "Curse God and die!"[26] Then, Job's friends arrived and "comforted" him by saying he was simply receiving just punishment for some undisclosed sin. The enemy may incite others to attack us or incite us to sin against God; he may attack our health, family, relationships, or possessions; and he may use natural or supernatural forces (e.g., great wind or fire from heaven).

Many times, the most painful wounds will be emotional ones from those we love. Our family members may turn against or ridicule us. As Jesus said:

> "Do not think that I came to bring peace on earth. I did not come to bring peace but a sword. For I have come to 'set a man against his father, a daughter against her mother, and a daughter-in-law against her mother-in-law,' and 'a man's foes will be those of his own household.' He who loves father or mother more than Me is not worthy of Me. And he who loves son or daughter more than Me is not worthy of Me."[27]

Likewise, our Christian friends may hurt us. As Paul wrote, "This you know, that all those in Asia have turned away from me, among whom are Phygellus and Hermogenes," "Demas has forsaken me," and "[a]t my first defense no one stood with me, but all forsook me."[28]

Unfortunately, our most grievous wounds can sometimes come from our earthly fathers. Children, both boys and girls, want affirmation, acceptance, and love from their fathers. A father who is absent physically or emotionally, or who devotes too much time working, or who has difficulty communicating acceptance, can inflict wounds that cause his child to constantly seek affirmation or acceptance. Both sons and daughters can seek that affirmation or acceptance through sex or conforming to the conduct of their peers. A father who is critical and demanding can inflict wounds that cause his child to seek love through perfectionism, workaholism, or absolute obedience. It can also cause the child not to try things for fear of not being able to be perfect. A father who calls his child derogatory names during times of anger or frustration can inflict wounds that result in his child accepting those derogatory names as his or her identity and living down to that identity. Worst of all, wounds inflicted by our earthly fathers can color how we view our Heavenly Father.

Wounds can be inflicted by another's words or conduct, or by how we perceive another's wounds or conduct. The Israelites accused God of not being fair.[29] The people in Nazareth were offended at Jesus's teaching because they did not think Him worthy to teach them.[30] The scribes and Pharisees were offended when Jesus truthfully called them hypocrites.[31] Neither God nor Jesus sinned, nor were They unjust in their conduct, and yet others were "wounded" because of their own sinful natures. Sometimes we may be "wounded" not because someone else did anything wrong, but because they simply did not do what we wanted them to or other similar reasons.

Part of us wants to be accepted and respected by others, particularly our family and Christian friends. We must always remember, however, that it is God to whom we must give account. He is the One from Whom we must seek validation and affirmation. It is He Who we want to say at the end of our lives, "Well done my good and faithful servant." When obeying Him, particularly if you have a public position of authority, you will be cursed and spitefully attacked. That is to be expected. "A disciple is not above *his* teacher, nor a servant above his master. It is enough for a disciple that he be like his teacher, and a servant like his master. If they have called the master of the house Beelzebub [Satan], how much more *will they call* those of his household!"[32]

When we are wounded, we must neither deny the wounds nor dwell on them. We must ask and allow God to heal them. The LORD "heals the brokenhearted and binds up their wounds."[33] Emotional wounds that are not healed make us vulnerable to the enemy. The fear of being hurt again can cause us to yield to temptations and influences that are not from God. We may seek to control others so that they cannot hurt us. We may close our hearts to relationships, including our relationship with God. We may become judgmental, condemning others to make ourselves feel better. We can become so self-focused upon avoiding hurt, that we do not see how we are hurting others. We may also seek to assuage the pain by destructive activities, such as becoming intoxicated with drugs or alcohol or seeking love through sexual promiscuity. Emotional pain also makes us very vulnerable to deception. We may even allow the enemy to define who we are, rather than standing on who we are in Christ, and accept the enemy's characterization of us rather than our heavenly Father's.

There are times when we need to take a rest for healing, but we must always return to the battle. We can be assured that the enemy cannot do anything to us unless God allows it,[34] and that God also limits the extent of the enemy's attack.[35] If we have been hurt by another, it is imperative that we also forgive the person who wounded us, so that no root of bitterness rises up. Forgiving those who hurt us is for our benefit, not theirs. Jesus said, " 'For if you forgive men their trespasses, your heavenly Father will also forgive you. But if you do not forgive men their trespasses, neither will your Father forgive your trespasses."[36] He also commanded, " 'I say to you, love your enemies, bless those who curse you, do good to those who hate you, and pray for those who spitefully use you and persecute you, that you may be sons of your Father in heaven . . . .' "[37] We may have to force ourselves to do it, but we must pray for those who have hurt us. That will bring about our own healing.

One day after refueling at one of the small airstrips we used to rearm and refuel, the engine fuel filter on my helicopter became clogged because there had been dirt in the fuel. We had to land at another small airstrip so I could change the filter. When we returned to base, I looked as best as I could through the filler opening down into the fuel cell (rubber fuel tank), and there appeared to be chunks of dirt at the bottom. I decided to drain the fuel cells and refill them with fuel from our base to make sure the fuel filter did not become clogged again. There was a valve at the bottom of the helicopter for draining fuel out of the fuel cells. What I did not know at the time was that it would literally take hours to drain the fuel cells using that valve. In fact, it took all night. At the time, I was upset at that turn of events. I was wondering why my helicopter got the bad fuel and why they did not design the helicopter so that you could drain the fuel faster. I finished draining the fuel and refilling the helicopter about thirty minutes before we were scheduled to take off. However, because I had stayed up all night, the platoon sergeant would not let me fly that morning. He had another crew chief fly in my place, and he was shot and very badly wounded. But for the bad fuel, it would have been me who was shot.

We often do not know why things happen that change our plans. In recounting this event, I am in no way suggesting that the other crew chief deserved to be shot or that God loved him less. Many things are beyond our understanding.

Sometimes we wonder why God allows us to go through adversity. We know some reasons from Scripture, which include the following: Paul was given a thorn in the flesh so that he would not be exalted above measure.[38] Adversity will help us mature as Christians because "tribulation produces perseverance; and perseverance, character; and character, hope," and it can also produce patience.[39] Adversity can also demonstrate our patience and faith to show that we are worthy of the kingdom of God.[40] We may suffer adversity so that we can be glorified with Christ.[41] When we receive the Father's comfort while going through adversity, we are better able to comfort others in their adversity.[42] When God delivers us from adversity, it can teach us to trust in Him and not ourselves, and going through adversity can show us that we "can do all things through Christ who strengthens [us]."[43] We may suffer adversity simply for doing good, and for living a godly life in Christ Jesus.[44] We may also suffer for doing evil,[45] or as chastening in order to produce "the peaceable fruit of righteousness to those who have been trained by it."[46] Adversity can also rearrange our priorities so that we do not live "in the flesh for the lusts of men, but for the will of God."[47] God brought adversity upon the Israelites, which caused them to cry out to Him.[48] We may suffer adversity for Christ's glory,[49] or for preaching and teaching the gospel to the unsaved.[50] In fact, our adversity may be part of God's plan to spread the gospel. For example, the persecution that arose in Jerusalem over Stephen when he was martyred caused believers to flee to Phoenicia, Cyprus, and Antioch, where they preached the word;[51] Paul preached the gospel in Galatia because he stopped there due to physical infirmity;[52] and he was taken in chains to Rome to spread the gospel.[53] We may also suffer adversity to reveal the works of God, such as the man born blind and the man born lame, both of whom God miraculously healed.[54] Lazarus became sick and died for the glory of God when he was raised from the dead.[55]

Our inability to understand why there is suffering should not cause us to question God's love and kindness. I cannot answer for God as to why He allows bad things to happen (He does not consult me regarding these matters). However, I will offer this possibility. When the plague came upon Israel because King David sinned by numbering the people, Gad, the prophet, told David to erect an altar to the LORD on the threshing floor of Araunah the Jebusite. When David went to the threshing floor and asked to buy it, Araunah offered to give it to him. David responded, "No, but I will surely buy *it* from you for a price; nor will I offer burnt offerings to the LORD my God with that which costs me nothing."[56]

We are to be living sacrifices to God.[57] Maybe being a living sacrifice means there will be a cost. The risk we are willing to take and the cost we are willing to bear is a measure of the value we place upon what we are fighting for. How much do you value your relationship with God? What cost are you willing to pay for that relationship? What are you willing to do to save another? How important is it to live out your God-ordained destiny? We should be able to say, "For I consider that the sufferings of this present time are not worthy *to be compared* with the glory that will be revealed in us."[58]

This is not a war between equal forces. We know who God is and, from Scripture, how this war ends. We also know what is at stake. We are "heirs of God and joint heirs with Christ, if indeed we suffer with *Him*, that we may also be glorified together."[59]

---

[1] Psalm 116:15.
[2] 2 Corinthians 5:6-8.
[3] John 5:20; Matthew 3:17; 17:5.
[4] Psalm 139:16.
[5] Deuteronomy 10:17; Romans 2:11.
[6] Psalm 145:17.
[7] Romans 11:33.
[8] Job 23:3-7; 31:35b.
[9] Job 40:2.
[10] Job 1:8-12.

[11] John 1:29.
[12] Mark 6:17-18.
[13] Luke 7:18-20.
[14] John 21:18-19.
[15] Acts 6:5; 7:1-60.
[16] Acts 9:15-16.
[17] 2 Corinthians 11:24-27.
[18] 2 Corinthians 12:8.
[19] 2 Corinthians 12:7.
[20] Acts 16:25-26.
[21] Philippians 3:10.
[22] Romans 8:17.
[23] Acts 14:19-20.
[24] Job 1:12-19.
[25] Job 2:6-7.
[26] Job 2:9
[27] Matthew 10:34-37.
[28] 2 Timothy 1:15; 4:10; 4:16.
[29] Ezekiel 18:25-29; 33:17-20.
[30] Matthew 13:53-58.
[31] Matthew 15:1-12.
[32] Matthew 10:24-25.
[33] Psalm 147:3; also Luke 4:18.
[34] Luke 22:31.
[35] Job 1:12; 2:6; 1 Corinthians 10:13.
[36] Matthew 6:14-15.
[37] Matthew 5:44-45.
[38] 2 Corinthians 12:7.
[39] Romans 5:3-4; James 1:2-3.
[40] 2 Thessalonians 1:3-5.
[41] Romans 8:16-18.
[42] 2 Corinthians 1:3-5.
[43] 2 Corinthians 1:8-10; Philippians 4:12-13.
[44] 1 Peter 3:17; 2 Timothy 3:12.
[45] 1 Peter 3:17, 4:15
[46] Hebrews 12:7-11.
[47] 1 Peter 4:1-2.
[48] Judges 3:7-10, 12-15; 4:1-3.
[49] 1 Peter 4:14.
[50] 2 Timothy 1:11-12.
[51] Acts 11:19.
[52] Galatians 4:13.
[53] Philippians 1:12-13.
[54] John 9:1-7; Acts 3:1-10.
[55] John 11:4.
[56] 2 Samuel 24:24.

57 Romans 12:1.
58 Romans 8:18.
59 Romans 8:17.

14

PICKING A FIGHT

"Do not think that I came to bring peace on earth. I did not come to bring peace but a sword."

Matthew 10:34

My favorite C-ration meal was beans and franks (beanie weanies), pound cake, and peaches. After eating the beans, I would combine the pound cake and peaches for dessert. The beans and pound cake came in the same C-ration meal, but the peaches came in another meal. When I got a can of peaches, I would save it until I could get the meal with the beanie weanies and pound cake in it. Unfortunately, there was only one such meal in each case of C-rations. Every morning we flew, we would go to the mess hall where they had various boxes of C-rations on a table just inside the door. Because the beanie weanies was also others' favorite, I would usually try to get to the mess hall early to get it. During one week I was unable to find any beanie weanies. The only C-rations available were the meals that were leftovers from prior days because nobody had wanted them. As a result, I had accumulated two cans of peaches that I saved in a storage compartment in my helicopter. Those two cans of peaches saved me from serious injury or death.

Late one afternoon during that week, my gunship

and another were sent out to locate a North Vietnamese Army (NVA) battalion, which would consist of about 500 enemy soldiers. My gunship was flying lead, and when we arrived at the area where the NVA battalion was supposed to be, we dropped down to an altitude of about fifteen feet above the ground and began flying around trying to get someone to shoot at us so that we could discover where they were. After a short while, we flew across a large rice paddy and came to a banana tree plantation that ran along the side of the rice paddy. The banana trees were about ten feet tall, with slender stalks and long, wide leaves radiating out in all directions from the tops of the stalks. There were thousands of banana trees that were planted close together, and the large leaves, and the shadows cast by those leaves, made it very difficult to see down into the trees from the air.

As we turned and started to fly straight and level down the center of the banana tree plantation, just above the tops of the banana trees, it looked to me like a pretty good place for enemy soldiers to be hiding. The banana trees provided good cover, and there was a rice paddy on one side and dense forest on the other. I thought, "We've been out here for about fifteen minutes now and nobody has shot at us. Let me see if I can stir something up." I decided to shoot at random down into the banana trees, hoping that if the enemy was there he would shoot back, letting us know he was there.

Although the enemy usually liked to shoot down helicopters, some enemy troops were trained not to shoot at helicopters because that would reveal their location. A man who had been a crew chief on a Huey gunship in a company located north of Saigon told me that the enemy almost never shot at them. The area where they operated was thick jungle. They enemy had learned that they could not be seen from helicopters flying overhead and that by shooting at the helicopters they simply revealed their location. I thought I may have to pick a fight in order for the enemy to disclose his location.

I fired down into the banana trees, and, sure enough, the enemy returned fire, riddling my helicopter with bullets. My pilot did not take any evasive action, but continued flying straight and level. The enemy stopped shooting, and I thought, "That seemed to work. Let me try it again." We were looking for a battalion, so I wanted to see if there were more than just a few enemy soldiers in the trees.

I again fired at random down into the banana trees. As I was doing so while looking down at the trees, I felt the sting of something hitting my right cheek just below my eye. I looked up and first noticed a large hole in the copilot's windshield (I sat behind him) that had been made by a burst of AK-47 fire. I then saw, at about eye level in front of my face, a hole where a bullet had exited the doorframe of my cargo door. I assumed that the bullet is what had hit me in the face, and I wiped my cheek with my right hand to see if I was bleeding. I was not, but briefly wondered why the bullet had not caused serious injury.

Although my pilot did not take evasive action, the enemy stopped shooting. I again fired at random down into the banana trees. This time the return fire came from below and slightly behind us, again riddling my helicopter with bullets. A warning light lit up on the console between the pilot's and copilot's seats. The pilot immediately glanced down at it, and then said, "The left fuel pump is not working." It was located in the fuel cell (rubber fuel tank) behind my seat. The lower two thirds of the fuel cell was self-sealing, but not the fiberglass plate on which the fuel pump was mounted. I knew that if a bullet had hit the pump, it went through that plate. I told the pilot, "We are leaking fuel out the bottom of the helicopter." My concern was that the pilot should keep an eye on the fuel gauge because we would be running low on fuel sooner than expected. Both fuel cells were connected by a tube, and so as the left one drained it would also drain the right one. He decided, however, that we should call it a day.

Even though we were shot up and forced to leave, we had done what we had been asked to do. We had located the enemy battalion. By picking a fight, I had caused them to reveal where they were.

We flew back to the staging area. Because I did not want to leave my helicopter there, the pilot and I decided to try and fly it back to our base, which would normally have been about a 1½-hour flight. My door gunner stripped the miniguns, rockets, machine guns, and ammunition from my helicopter, and I removed all but one radio. The pilot and I were going to be flying back alone, and so if we did not make it we did not want the enemy to get those items. We took off into the darkness and stopped every place we could along the way to refuel. We made it back without incident.

The next morning, I began going over my helicopter to locate all of the bullet damage and commenced repairing those things that I could. I discovered that when the burst of AK-47 fire had made a large hole in the copilot's windshield, one bullet had gone past the copilot's door, had torn into the fuselage where it bulges outward just behind the door, went through both cans of peaches, and then exited the doorframe. It was probably because of the two cans of peaches that what was left of the bullet only stung when it hit me in the cheek. The liquid in the cans of peaches would have absorbed a lot of the bullet's energy, as did the door frame of the cargo door. But for the two cans of peaches, I would probably have been seriously wounded or killed. That was the only time I had two cans of peaches in that storage compartment. There is no limit to the ways in which God can intervene in a situation.

As I continued going over my helicopter, I then discovered that we had literally come within ½ inch of being shot down. The Huey helicopter has a turbine engine located on top of the fuselage just aft of the main rotor mast. If a piece of metal is sucked into the engine, the damage to the turbine blades causes the engine to fail. Air enters the engine through an air chamber called a plenum chamber located on top of the fuselage between the main rotor mast and the front of the engine. The plenum chamber has wire mesh over its top to let air in while keeping out objects that could damage the engine and sponge-like filters in its bottom half to trap sand. A steel-cored bullet had come up through the bottom of the helicopter, had ripped all the way through the fuselage, and had entered the plenum chamber, tearing through one of the filters and stopping 1/2-inch from coming out the top of the filter. Had it gone slightly farther, it would have been sucked into the engine, our engine would have failed, and we would have crashed in the midst of that NVA battalion. It probably would have ruined the rest of our day. I still have the bullet as a souvenir.

In combat you sometimes have to pick a fight with the enemy so that they will reveal themselves. Did Jesus ever pick a fight? He certainly did, as described in Mark 3:1-6:

> And He entered the synagogue again, and a man was there who had a withered hand. So they watched Him closely, whether He would heal him on the Sabbath, so that they might accuse Him. And He said to the man

159

who had the withered hand, "Step forward."
Then He said to them, "Is it lawful on the
Sabbath to do good or to do evil, to save life
or to kill?" But they kept silent. And when
He had looked around at them with anger,
being grieved by the hardness of their
hearts, He said to the man, "Stretch out your
hand." And he stretched *it* out, and his hand
was restored as whole as the other. Then the
Pharisees went out and immediately plotted
with the Herodians against Him, how they
might destroy Him.

Had Jesus been someone who did not want to make
waves, cause any controversy, or offend anyone, He would
not have healed the man's hand on the Sabbath. He would
have told the man to return the next day. Instead, He did
what He knew would offend the Pharisees.

Jesus did not pick a fight simply to antagonize the
Pharisees. He was not simply trying to push their buttons.
He did so to demonstrate an important truth to the others
present. One of the Ten Commandments given by God was:
"Remember the Sabbath day, to keep it holy. Six days you
shall labor and do all your work, but the seventh day *is* the
Sabbath of the LORD your God. *In it* you shall do no work . .
. ."[1] Over the years, the religious leaders had created a
myriad of rules regarding what did and did not constitute
doing "work" on the Sabbath. The legalism under which
they operated had so hardened their hearts that they
considered keeping the Sabbath according to their rules as
more important than the crippled man being healed. In
their eyes, the Law was more important than man. By
healing the crippled man on the Sabbath, Jesus was
demonstrating that in God's eyes, man is more important
than the Law.[2] "The Sabbath was made for man, and not
man for the Sabbath."[3] Jesus also picked a fight when He

pointed out the hypocrisy of the scribes and Pharisees.[4]

In picking a fight, Jesus was demonstrating truth. God's Law was made for man's benefit, not vice versa. The Law was to show us our need for a savior and to bring us to Christ. Otherwise, the Father would not have sent His only begotten Son to earth to die for our sins.[5] He would not have provided a means of salvation apart from the Law through faith in Jesus Christ.[6] If the Law was more important than man, God would not have provided a means of salvation that did not require obedience to the Law. "[T]he law was our tutor *to bring us* to Christ, that we might be justified by faith."[7] The futility of trying to keep the Law perfectly, something none of us can do, shows us that salvation can only be by faith in Jesus Christ.

Also, obedience to God's Law is for our benefit. The focus of Christianity is having healthy relationships with God and with our neighbors. Murdering, committing adultery, stealing, bearing false witness about someone, or coveting another's spouse or possessions does not foster a healthy relationship with others, or with God. Showing love to both God and our neighbors does promote healthy relationships.

Even though salvation is by faith, God's moral Law remains. Jesus came to complete our understanding of the Law and the Prophets to show us how to live a righteous life. If our conduct did not matter under the New Covenant, there would be no commandments. On the night before His crucifixion, Jesus said, "A new commandment I give to you, that you love one another; as I have loved you, that you also love one another."[8] The commandment to love one another sums up what we call the Ten Commandments.[9] As John wrote, "This is love, that we walk according to His commandments. This is the commandment, that as you have heard from the beginning, you should walk in it."[10] Even under the New Covenant, we are to be holy. "[A]s He who called you *is* holy, you also be holy in all *your* conduct, because it is written, *'Be holy, for I am holy.'* "[11]

There have been those who assert that Christians should not do or say anything that would offend anyone, that we should not be confrontational, that we should simply be quiet and keep our faith and beliefs to ourselves. The enemy routinely tries to intimidate Christians to do just that. That is not how Jesus lived His life on earth.

There are times when strong words are appropriate. For example, Jesus called the scribes and Pharisees hypocrites, blind guides, fools, serpents, and a brood of vipers.[12] However, He did not use that language when addressing other sinners, such as the Samaritan woman at the well who had had five husbands and was living with a man out of wedlock;[13] or Zacchaeus, the chief tax collector;[14] or the woman caught in adultery.[15] The scribes and Pharisees were trained in the written word of God, and they had a greater knowledge of the truth than many others. They simply did not practice what they preached.[16]

Sometimes we must pick a fight by standing for holiness, for God's moral law, or for His truth. When we do that, we will be attacked. We will have picked a fight. We must follow the leading of the Holy Spirit as to when and how we pick fights. The purpose is not simply to pick fights or to antagonize those who disagree with us. Rather, there are times when we must stand for the truth or confront others with it. We must always remember that we are to speak the truth in love.[17]

We must not allow legalism to justify picking a fight when it is unnecessary. Paul preached the gospel to Greeks in the Areopagus, where there were objects of pagan worship. He did not refuse to enter the area because of those objects, nor did he rebuke those present for being pagans. Rather, he tried to use their altar "To the Unknown God" as a lead-in to tell them about the true God.[18] Rebuking or insulting those who are misled is not the way to bring them to Christ.

Do not be afraid to pick a fight when necessary. Jesus was not a milquetoast. But when we do pick a fight, we must not do so out of self-righteousness or legalism. Paul was an example when he wrote:

> For though I am free from all *men*, I have made myself a servant to all, that I might win the more; and to the Jews I became as a Jew, that I might win Jews; to those *who are* under the law, as under the law, that I might win those *who* are under the law; to those *who are* without law, as without law (not being without law toward God, but under law toward Christ), that I might win those *who are* without law; to the weak I became as weak, that I might win the weak. I have become all things to all *men*, that I might by all means save some. Now this I do for the gospel's sake, that I may be partaker of it with you.[19]

---

[1] Exodus 20:8-10a.
[2] Mark 2:23-26.
[3] Mark 2:27.
[4] Matthew 23:1-36; 26:1-4.
[5] John 3:16-18.
[6] Romans 3:21-26.
[7] Galatians 3:24.
[8] John 13:34.

[9] Romans 13:9.
[10] 2 John: 6.
[11] 1 Peter 1:15-16.
[12] Matthew 23:1-33.
[13] John 4:1-26.
[14] Luke 19:1-10.
[15] John 8:1-12.
[16] Matthew 23:1-2.
[17] Ephesians 4:15.
[18] Acts 17:22-33.
[19] 1 Corinthians 9:19-23.

15

THE STILL SMALL VOICE

And behold, the LORD passed by, and a great and strong wind tore into the mountains and broke the rocks in pieces before the LORD, but the LORD was not in the wind; and after the wind an earthquake, but the LORD was not in the earthquake; and after the earthquake a fire, but the LORD was not in the fire; and after the fire a still small voice.

1 Kings 19:11-12

One afternoon we were flying over a rice paddy that was ready for harvest. It would have been similar to flying over a field of ripe wheat. We were three or four feet above the ground, with the helicopter's skids just above the tops of the rice stalks, and flying parallel to a paddy dike that was about thirty yards away on my side of the helicopter. There was brush along the top of the paddy dike, and someone from that brush opened fire with an AK-47. I kept a smoke grenade hanging by its pin on the litter pole in front of my seat. When we received fire from my side of the helicopter, I typically reached up with my left hand, grabbed the smoke grenade, and tossed it out before returning fire. I did that to mark the area so that we could circle back and re-engage the enemy. This time, as I started reaching for the smoke grenade, a voice in my head, which was as clear as an audible voice, said, "Don't worry about the smoke grenade." Just as I pulled my hand back to grab my machine gun, the smoke grenade was shot off the pole.

At that same instant, we flew over someone who must have been lying in the rice, and he fired up through the bottom of the helicopter, exploding a can of hydraulic fluid that I had sitting on the floor. Hydraulic fluid is bright red in color, and when the pilots saw the red fluid splattered over the inside of the windshield, they thought that it was blood and that either my door gunner or I had been shot. The smoke grenade that was shot off my litter pole landed near the feet of my door gunner and began to burn, spewing out smoke. When the pilot of our wing helicopter saw the smoke pouring out of my door gunner's door, he thought we were on fire. My door gunner was temporarily blinded by the hydraulic fluid that had splattered into his eyes, so I had to direct him over the intercom so he could locate the burning smoke grenade and kick it out his door.

After we returned to our base, I began checking the damage to my helicopter. The bullets that came up through the floor were close enough together to leave a three-inch-long hole that ran laterally. When I removed that section of the floor, I saw something that amazed me. There are two, inch-wide aluminum push-pull tubes that run under the floor from the pilot's cyclic stick to the hydraulics located behind the rear cabin wall. These two push-pull tubes control the rotor head, with one controlling the fore-and-aft movement and one controlling the lateral movement. When I removed the floor section with the bullet hole in it, I saw a corresponding three-inch-long hole in the bottom skin of the helicopter. The push-pull tube that controls the lateral movement of the rotor was exactly centered in that three-inch long hole, but the tube was undamaged. Had that tube been severed, the pilot would have lost lateral control of the helicopter while we were flying at about 60-70 knots about three to four feet above the ground, and we would have crashed.

In trying to find out how the bullets could have missed the tube, I moved the pilot's cyclic (control stick) every way I could and discovered that when I pushed it all the way forward and to the right, the linkage mechanism caused the aluminum tube to move sideways just enough for the bullets to have missed it. However, the pilot would not have had the control stick in that position. We were flying straight and level, not diving or turning to the right. If the control stick had been pushed all the way forward, we would have flown into the ground. If it had been moved all the way to the right, we would have been in a hard right turn and, being only three or four feet above the ground, the helicopter's rotor blades would have hit the earth causing us to crash. I have no explanation for the bullets missing the push-pull tube, except the hand of God.

Although I did not realize it at the time, it was the Holy Spirit who warned me not to grab the smoke grenade. Had I not instantly obeyed that warning, I would have been shot in the hand. God speaks to us in many ways. Obviously, He speaks to us through His written word. "All Scripture *is* given by inspiration of God, and *is* profitable for doctrine, for reproof, for correction, for instruction in righteousness."[1] However, that is not the only way He speaks to us. Isaiah 30:21 states, "Your ears shall hear a word behind you, saying, 'This *is* the way, walk in it,' whenever you turn to the right hand or whenever you turn to the left." The Hebrew word translated "way" means the path that is traveled, the journey. Fulfilling our destinies is a journey down a pathway foreordained by God. Finding and staying on that pathway will require that we learn to hear from God—that we become able to discern between the flesh, the enemy, and the Spirit.

Learning to do so can take years of trial and error. At times, we may do something, thinking it is in response to the Spirit's direction, and later find out it was really our flesh or the enemy. Likewise, at times we will not do something, thinking it is our flesh or the enemy, and later find out that it was really the Spirit. The important thing is that our heart's desire be to learn to discern the difference and obey, and that we do not give up. God wants us to learn to discern His voice.

The apostles and the elders of the church at Jerusalem met to decide whether Gentile believers had to be circumcised and to keep the law of Moses. After considering the matter, they wrote a letter to Christian Gentiles in Antioch, Syria, and Cilicia. In their letter, they wrote, "For it seemed good to the Holy Spirit, and to *us*, to lay upon you no greater burden than these necessary things."[2] To me, it is significant that they wrote "it **seemed** good to the Holy Spirit" rather than "the Holy Spirit said." The use of the word translated "seemed" expressed their subjective mental estimate or opinion. They may not have been absolutely certain that they were hearing correctly from the Holy Spirit. If they were not always absolutely certain that they were hearing accurately from the Holy Spirit, we should not become discouraged if we do not always hear accurately.

Unfortunately, there are not three, or ten, or even twenty easy steps to discerning between the Spirit and the flesh. It is "by reason of use" that we have our "senses exercised [trained] to discern both good and evil."[3] One thing that complicates discerning between the Spirit and the flesh is that God communicates with us in many different ways. He does not speak to each of us in the same ways. For example, not all of us will have visions or hear an audible voice from heaven. In addition, He does not speak to each of us in the same way every time. He may speak to us in a dream one time and by a word of knowledge the next time. The ways in which God may speak to us include, but are not limited to, the following:

Dreams: The magi were "divinely warned in a dream that they should not return to Herod."[4] Joseph was "warned by God in a dream" not to go to Judea with Jesus and Mary, and he instead went to the region of Galilee.[5] Not every dream we have, however, is from God. Also, dreams often have to be interpreted, and the interpretation must come from the Holy Spirit.[6]

Visions: A person can see a vision with his or her eyes wide open. Examples include Moses seeing the burning bush;[7] Cornelius seeing the angel who told him where Peter was and to contact him;[8] Peter seeing the sheet filled with animals descending from heaven and hearing the voice telling him to rise and eat;[9] Paul seeing the Lord who told him to leave Jerusalem because the Lord was sending him to the Gentiles;[10] and Paul seeing a vision at night of a man of Macedonia pleading for Paul to come and help them.[11] Daniel had a vision in a dream.[12] Visions also often have to be interpreted.[13]

An audible voice. On the road to Damascus, the Lord spoke audibly to Paul, and those who were journeying with Paul heard the voice.[14] When Jesus was transfigured in the presence of Peter, James, and John, a voice came from the bright cloud overshadowing them, saying, "This is is my beloved Son, in whom I am well pleased."[15] Peter,

James, and John heard the voice.[16]

A voice in your mind or thoughts. Jesus told his disciples, "Now when they bring you to the synagogues and magistrates and authorities, do not worry about how or what you should answer, or what you should say. For the Holy Spirit will teach you in that very hour what you ought to say."[17] The word translated "teach" means to instruct by word of mouth. When Peter and John were arrested and brought before the Sanhedrin, the following occurred:

> Then Peter, filled with the Holy Spirit, said to them, "Rulers of the people and elders of Israel: If we this day are judged for a good deed *done* to a helpless man, by what means he has been made well, let it be known to you all, and to all the people of Israel, that by the name of Jesus Christ of Nazareth, whom you crucified, whom God raised from the dead, by Him this man stands here before you whole. This is the '*stone which was rejected by you builders, which has become the chief cornerstone.*' Nor is there salvation in any other, for there is no other name under heaven given among men by which we must be saved."[18]

The Holy Spirit told Peter what to say, but it was obviously not with a voice audible to the others. While Peter thought about his vision of the sheet filled with animals descending from heaven, "the Spirit said to him, 'Behold, three men are seeking you. Arise therefore, go down and go with them, doubting nothing; for I have sent them.'"[19] Peter obeyed, and Cornelius and his household became believers.

Something you just know. The Holy Spirit situationally gives us a word of knowledge.[20] When Jesus told the paralytic that his sins were forgiven, some of the scribes were reasoning in their hearts that Jesus spoke blasphemies. "But immediately, when Jesus perceived in His spirit that they reasoned thus within themselves, He said to them, 'Why do you reason about these things in your hearts?' "[21] God reveals things to us by His Spirit.[22] When Peter declared that Jesus was the Christ, the Son of the living God, Jesus answered, "Blessed are you, Simon Bar-Jonah, for flesh and blood has not revealed this to you, but My Father who is in heaven."[23] When Paul was in Lystra, he saw a man who was a cripple from his mother's womb. "*This* man heard Paul speaking. Paul, observing him intently and seeing that he had faith to be healed, said with a loud voice, 'Stand up straight on your feet!' And he leaped and walked."[24] There is no indication that the man had done or said anything indicating that he had faith to be healed. But Paul, "seeing" that he had faith told him to stand up. The meaning of the word translated "seeing" includes intuitively knowing because it has been revealed by God. Some truths we receive by revelation.[25] "[T]he natural man does not receive the things of the Spirit of God, for they are foolishness to him; nor can he know *them*, because they are spiritually discerned."[26]

A prompting or stirring to do or say something. Closely related to knowledge or under-standing from the Spirit is being prompted or urged to do or say something, without necessarily knowing why. Nehemiah wrote that "my God put it into my heart to gather the nobles, the rulers, and the people, that they might be registered by genealogy."[27] Paul said he was "bound in the spirit to Jerusalem, not knowing the things that will happen to me there."[28] In that context, the phrase "bound in the spirit" means "impelled in mind or compelled." "When Silas and Timothy had come from Macedonia, Paul was compelled by the Spirit, and testified to the Jews *that* Jesus *is* the Christ."[29] There are many things we may be prompted to do without knowing why. For example, we may be prompted to give someone money, not knowing why, and later find out that it was exactly the amount he or she needed for some purpose. As another example, I was invited to attend a ceremony for women graduating from a Christian transitional housing program that was primarily for women on parole or probation. The people attending the graduation were all sitting at round tables in a large room. One of the speakers was a young lady who had graduated a few years earlier. She told about being placed by the state in a group home for troubled youth when she was a teenager and being sexually molested by one of the male staff. The state later agreed to let that man and his wife have custody of her, so he continued molesting her in his home. After she and two other girls reported the abuse, she was then placed in foster care, which was not a positive experience. At age eighteen, she was released on her own, began using drugs, and was found unconscious under a bridge. When she awoke in the hospital, a nurse sitting on the edge of her bed told her about the transitional housing program. As the young lady began her story, I realized that I was the judge who presided over the trial of the man who molested her in the group home. After she finished speaking and returned to her table, the woman who ran the program told everyone, "Turn to the person next to you and say, 'Thank you, you are amazing.' " I was immediately prompted by the Holy

Spirit to say that to the young lady. I got up, walked to her table, knelt beside her, looked up into her eyes, and said, "Thank you, you are amazing." She looked at me quizzically, and I told her I was the judge. She gave me a polite hug, and I returned to my table. At the end of the ceremony, I was standing at my table when I felt someone poke me in the middle of my back. I turned around, and she was standing there. She asked if I would give her a hug, and of course I did. The woman in charge of the program later told me that the young lady said she had been struggling with that part of her life, and when I hugged her it felt like a huge weight was lifted off her. You never know what will happen when you follow the prompting of the Holy Spirit.

Peace. One of the reasons Jesus came to earth was "[t]o guide our feet into the way of peace."[30] We are to "let the peace of God rule in [our] hearts,"[31] "[f]or He will speak peace to His people and to His saints."[32] The meaning of *shalom*, the Hebrew word translated peace, includes tranquility, as does the meaning of the equivalent Greek word (*eirne*). His peace is not based upon our circumstances. We can have peace in tribulation.[33] There will be times when we will seek direction from God about a decision or situation, and He will give us nothing other than a sense of peace. By the peace He gives us, or the lack of peace, He will give us direction.

A check in our spirits. There are other times when we will feel a strong check in our spirits about a matter. When we consider or begin doing something, suddenly we get a strong feeling or sense that we are not to do it. When Paul was on his first missionary journey, the Holy Spirit did not permit Paul, Silas, and Timothy to go into Bithynia.[34] Scripture does not say how the Holy Spirit did so, but it may have simply been a check in their spirits, or in Paul's spirit. There have been times when I wanted to pray for someone who was very ill, but when I tried to do so there was such a strong check in my spirit that I could not get any words out. For some reason, God did not want me praying for that person.

A word or counsel from others. The Holy Spirit may give someone a prophecy, which includes a tongue and interpretation, a word of wisdom, or a word of knowledge.[35] At times the Spirit will give someone else a word of wisdom, a word of knowledge, or a prophecy for us. In that circumstance, God is using someone else to communicate to us. For example, the Holy Spirit gave Agabus a prophecy about the coming famine, which prompted the disciples in Antioch to send aid to the brethren dwelling in Judea.[36] There may be times also when something someone else says confirms what God has been telling us. However, we must use discernment when someone says they have a word for us from God. Someone claiming to have a word from God for us may be lying.[37] For example, 1 Kings 13:11-24 recounts an incident in which an old prophet lied to a young prophet, convincing him to disobey God by telling him he had a message from an angel, and the young prophet was then killed for not doing what God had commanded. Also, someone claiming to have a word from God may not have accurately discerned what God was saying, or the word may actually have been for himself or herself rather than for others.

Coincidences or divine appointments. The Ethiopian eunuch had a divine appointment as he was returning home from Jerusalem. An angel of the Lord told

Philip, "Arise and go toward the south along the road which goes down from Jerusalem to Gaza."[38] As Philip went down the road, he came upon an Ethiopian eunuch who was a man of great authority under the Ethiopian queen and had charge of her treasury. As a result, Philip was able to lead the Ethiopian man into belief in Jesus as the Messiah, and the man was baptized. There are times when God will bring us in contact with people for a particular reason, maybe for our benefit, for theirs, or for both our benefits. He does so for a purpose, and we must discern His purpose.

Songs. God had Moses write down a song and teach it to the Israelites as a witness or testimony to them and their descendants.[39] Colossians 3:16 says that we are to teach and admonish one another "in psalms and hymns and spiritual songs, singing with grace in your hearts to the Lord." God may speak to us at times through a song being sung or by quickening a song in our hearts. God may put a song in our spirits to speak to us, or we may hear the lyrics of a song that suddenly grip our spirits.

A passage of Scripture. "All Scripture *is* given by inspiration of God, and *is* profitable for doctrine, for reproof, for correction, for instruction in righteousness, that the man of God may be complete, thoroughly equipped for every good work."[40] The Scriptures can give us hope,[41] and admonition.[42] When King Josiah heard the words of the law, he repented and had the words read to the Israelites, who also repented.[43] As we hear or read a passage of Scripture, sometimes the Holy Spirit will have it grip our spirits, and we will know that the passage has particular significance for us.

Signs along the way. Jonah had some signs along

the way indicating that he should not refuse to do what God had commanded him. As Jonah was fleeing on a ship, God caused a storm to arise that was about to break the ship apart. The sailors cast lots, and God caused the lot to fall on Jonah.[44] The sailors then threw him overboard, and a great fish prepared by God swallowed him. After three days and three nights in the fish, Jonah got the message.[45] When the king of Tyre sent David messengers, cedar trees, masons, and carpenters to build him a house, "David knew that the LORD had established him as king over Israel, for his kingdom was highly exalted for the sake of His people Israel."[46] The LORD told Gideon to go and he would save Israel from the hand of the Midianites.[47] When the Midianites and the Amalekites later crossed the Jordan River and encamped in the Valley of Jezreel, Gideon asked for and received two signs confirming that God would do as He had said.[48] He received further confirmation when he snuck down to the enemy camp and overheard an enemy soldier recount a dream.[49] When we embark on a path that we may believe, but not be certain, that God wants us to go, He may give us signs along the way to confirm that we are on the right path.

Open and closed doors. Paul wrote, "For a great and effective door has opened to me [in Ephesus], and there are many adversaries,"[50] and "when I came to Troas to *preach* Christ's gospel, and a door was opened to me by the Lord."[51] He also asked for prayer "that God would open to us a door for the word, to speak the mystery of Christ."[52] The word translated "door" is used metaphorically to mean access or opportunity. At times, God will arrange circumstances to give us an opportunity. Sometimes, the way in which He opens the door may seem strange to us. Paul was "bound in the spirit to Jerusalem," not knowing what would happen to him there.[53] While on his way, a prophet warned him that he would be bound and delivered into the hands of the Gentiles.[54] After Paul had arrived in Jerusalem, he was taken into Roman custody. Jesus appeared to him and said, "Be of good cheer, Paul; for as you have testified for Me in Jerusalem, so you must also bear witness at Rome."[55] After Paul was eventually taken to Rome and placed in chains, he wrote, "But I want you to know, brethren, that the things *which happened* to me have actually turned out for the furtherance of the gospel."[56]

At other times, however, God will close doors. For example, the Holy Spirit closed the door and prevented Paul from going to Asia and Bithynia.[57] Obviously, when God opens the door, we should walk through it, and when He closes the door, we must not try to force it open. When He opens a door, we must expect opposition from the enemy. Open doors can be to preach the gospel, to do good, or to take the next step in our destinies.

A sudden memory. As Jesus was celebrating Passover with His disciples on the night He was betrayed, Jesus told them that the Holy Spirit "will teach you all things, and bring to your remembrance all things that I said to you."[58] When Peter was defending himself for going into Cornelius's house, he said, "And as I began to speak, the Holy Spirit fell upon them, as upon us at the beginning. Then I remembered the word of the Lord, how He said, 'John indeed baptized with water, but you shall be baptized with the Holy Spirit.' "[59] God may speak to us by suddenly bringing to our remembrance a passage of Scripture, a word we had previously received, a prior prophecy, or something else that will be applicable to our current situation. When Peter suddenly remembered what Jesus had said about being baptized with the Holy Spirit, he understood the significance of what had occurred in Cornelius's house and could counter, "If therefore God gave them the same gift as *He gave* us when we believed on the Lord Jesus Christ, who was I that I could withstand God?"[60]

A sign or a wonder—supernatural events. A nobleman, and his whole household, believed because Jesus healed the nobleman's son.[61] Others did not believe in Jesus in spite of the many signs He performed.[62] When Paul tried to give the word of God to the proconsul at the island of Paphos, a sorcerer who was with the proconsul tried to turn him away from the faith. Paul, filled with the Holy Spirit, looked at the sorcerer and proclaimed that the hand of the Lord was upon him and that he would be blind for a time. The sorcerer immediately was, and when the proconsul saw what happened, he believed.[63] When Paul and Barnabas were at Iconium, the Lord "was bearing witness to the word of His grace, granting signs and wonders to be done by their hands."[64] In order to make the Gentiles obedient to the gospel, the Lord accomplished through Paul "mighty signs and wonders, by the power of the Spirit of God, so that from Jerusalem and round about to Illyricum [Paul had] fully preached the gospel of Christ."[65] The writer of Hebrews wrote that God had born witness to the message of salvation "both with signs and wonders, with various miracles, and gifts of the Holy Spirit, according to His own will."[66]

We must be careful, however. Signs and wonders are intended to bear witness to God and His message, not the messenger. He works through imperfect people. The fact that someone performs signs and wonders does not necessarily validate the person's character, spiritual maturity, or doctrine. We must also keep in mind that "[t]he coming of the *lawless one* is according to the working of Satan, with all power, signs, and lying wonders."[67]

Prophetic acts. God may have someone perform acts that are intended to convey a message to us. For example, as a sign to the house of Israel to warn of the coming siege, God had Ezekiel portray the city of Jerusalem on a clay tablet and build a siege wall against it. He then had Ezekiel place an iron plate between himself and the clay tablet, as a sign that God would not intervene on behalf of Jerusalem when it occurred.[68] God had Hosea marry Gomer, a harlot, to portray the fact that the house of Israel had committed harlotry by departing from the Lord.[69]

* * * * * * * *

God said, "I will instruct you and teach you in the way you should go; I will guide you with My eye."[70] For Him to guide us with His "eye," we must be in His presence, in communion with Him, attentively waiting for His direction, seeking His face.

In response to a vision, Cornelius, a centurion of the Italian Regiment, sent two of his servants and a soldier to Joppa in search of Simon Peter. When they arrived at the house where Peter was staying and asked for him, "the Spirit said to him, 'Behold, three men are seeking you. Arise therefore, go down and go with them, doubting nothing; for I have sent them.'"[71] Peter did as the Holy Spirit directed, and as a result Cornelius, his family, and his close friends were saved.[72] As Zechariah 4:6 states, "'Not by might nor by power, but by My Spirit,' says the LORD of hosts." We must be guided by the Holy Spirit to be effective in this spiritual battle, and there are times when it is essential that we respond promptly to His leading. Often, we will have no idea why He wants us to do what He is prompting us to do.

There are several things that can hinder our being able to correctly discern the still small voice. Discernment is through our spirits because they are in communication with the Holy Spirit; it is not through our understanding or reasoning. Sometimes, trying to reason or understand why the Holy Spirit would be telling us to do a specific thing will interfere with discernment because we cannot always know why He would have us do something. I was at a drug court graduation when I felt that I should tell a prior graduate who was there to get off drugs. I was not sure it was from the Holy Spirit, and had no reason to believe he was using drugs, so I did not tell him. Two days later he was arrested for using drugs.

If we cling to sin, it can harden our hearts so that we do not hear His voice.[73] We can be deceived by false voices that appeal to our flesh. A non-exhaustive list of the works of the flesh is: "adultery, fornication [any sexual sin], uncleanness [immorality], lewdness [insatiable desire for pleasure], idolatry, sorcery [the occult or illicit drugs], hatred, contentions, jealousies, outbursts of wrath, selfish ambitions, dissensions, heresies, envy, murders, drunkenness, revelries, and the like."[74] A voice appealing to the flesh is not the Holy Spirit.

Sometimes that deception can be subtle. An appeal to our flesh can be couched in terms of how much good we could do for others if we give into it. "If I only had wealth, position, or power, think of all the good I could do for others." "If I had a particular anointing, think of how many I could evangelize or heal." We may have to ask ourselves: "Is this going to glorify Jesus in me, or me? Is the appeal that it will advance His kingdom, or mine? Will this bring me to a state of greater surrender to Jesus, or make me independent of Him? Is my desire that others follow Jesus, or that they follow me?"

The Holy Spirit will not contradict Scripture. We need to make sure that what we are being asked to do or believe would not violate any precepts of Scripture. That is one way to help us discern whether it is the Holy Spirit, our fleshly nature, or the enemy. The Holy Spirit will never tell you something that will violate Scripture. The word of God can divide between soul and spirit and discern or judge the thoughts and intents of our hearts.[75]

We are warned by 1 John 4:1, "Beloved, do not believe every spirit, but test the spirits, whether they are of God; because many false prophets have gone out into the world." John goes on to write one of the ways of testing a spirit is whether it confesses that Jesus has come in the flesh. "By this you know the Spirit of God: Every spirit that confesses that Jesus Christ has come in the flesh is of God, and every spirit that does not confess that Jesus Christ has come in the flesh is not of God."[76] There may also be times when we need to pray for confirmation.

On June 21, 2004, a friend telephoned me with the news that his father was in a care center dying of cancer. He called to ask whether I would perform the graveside service because none of his family attended a church. I felt an immediate prompt that I must go there that day and give the gospel to his father, whom I barely knew. I told my friend I would like to visit his father that afternoon, and he said that I could. I went home and picked up my wife, and we went to the care center. My friend's father was on morphine, but he would occasionally awaken for a few minutes. During the next seven hours, I sat next to his bed waiting for him to awaken. He did briefly three times. With my wife praying in the Spirit and me talking to him when he awakened, I was able to give him the gospel, and he accepted Christ as his Lord and Savior. That day, they put him on a morphine patch so that he had a constant supply of morphine. Had I waited and not responded immediately to the Holy Spirit's leading, it may have been too late. As in the parable of the workers in the vineyard, he entered the vineyard at about the eleventh hour.[77]

---

[1] 2 Timothy 3:16.
[2] Acts 15:28.
[3] Hebrews 5:14.
[4] Matthew 2:12.
[5] Matthew 2:22.
[6] Genesis 40:8; Daniel 4:18.
[7] Exodus 3:1-6, Acts 7:35.
[8] Acts 10:3-6.
[9] Acts 10:9-16.
[10] Acts 22:17-21.
[11] Acts 16:9.
[12] Daniel 7:1-8.
[13] Daniel 8:14-27.
[14] Acts 9:3-7.
[15] Matthew 17:5.
[16] 2 Peter 1:17-18.
[17] Luke 12:11-12.
[18] Acts 4:8-12.
[19] Acts 10:19-20.
[20] 1 Corinthians 12:8.
[21] Mark 2:8.
[22] 1 Corinthians 2:10.
[23] Matthew 16:17.
[24] Acts 14:9-10.
[25] Galatians 1:12.
[26] 1 Corinthians 2:14.
[27] Nehemiah 7:5.
[28] Acts 20:22.
[29] Acts 18:5.
[30] Luke 1:79b.
[31] Colossians 3:15a.
[32] Psalm 85:8b.
[33] John 16:33.
[34] Acts 16:7.
[35] 1 Corinthians 12:7-11.
[36] Acts 11:27-30.
[37] Ezekiel 13:1-7.

[38] Acts 8:26.
[39] Deuteronomy 31:16-21.
[40] 2 Timothy 3:16-17.
[41] Romans 15:4.
[42] 1 Corinthians 10:1-13.
[43] 2 Chronicles 34:18-33.
[44] Proverbs 16:33.
[45] Jonah 1:1 to 2:1.
[46] 1 Chronicles 14:2.
[47] Judges 6:14.
[48] Judges 6:36-40.
[49] Judges 7:9-15.
[50] 1 Corinthians 16:8-9.
[51] 2 Corinthians 2:12.
[52] Colossians 4:3.
[53] Acts 20:22.
[54] Acts 21:10-11.
[55] Acts 23:11.
[56] Philippians 1:12.
[57] Acts 16:6-7.
[58] John 14.26.
[59] Acts 11:15-16.
[60] Acts 11:17.
[61] John 4:46-54.
[62] John 12:37.
[63] Acts 13:4-12.
[64] Acts 14:3.
[65] Romans 15:19.
[66] Hebrews 2:4.
[67] 2 Thessalonians 2:9.
[68] Ezekiel 4:1-3.
[69] Hosea 1:2.
[70] Psalm 32:8.
[71] Acts 10:19-20.
[72] Acts 10:21-48.
[73] Hebrews 3:12-15.
[74] Galatians 5:19-21a.
[75] Hebrews 4:12.
[76] 1 John 4:2-3.
[77] Matthew 20:1-16.

Freedom Is Your Destiny!

16

ON THE JOB TRAINING

Blessed be the LORD *my Rock,*
Who trains my hands for war,
And my fingers for battle—

Psalm 144:1

One evening I got a late start on the daily maintenance of my helicopter. It had been dark for some time when I opened the cowling on the left side of my helicopter and climbed atop it to begin my work. My helicopter was parked facing north and parallel to the western edge of the runway. Across the runway were some revetments where the slicks were parked, and beyond that were the perimeter bunkers and fence. Behind me were the company buildings, including the pilots' hootches. I was standing on the left side of my helicopter facing the runway with my back to our company buildings. Suddenly I heard a mortar fire some distance in front of me, the whooshing sound made by the mortar round as it passed overhead, and then the explosion as it impacted somewhere behind me. I immediately turned around toward the company area, yelled "Incoming" three times as loud as I could, and then jumped down, closed the cowling on my helicopter, unhooked the rotor blade, and waited for the rest of the crew so we could take off to go in search of the mortar tubes.

A pilot soon came running out, jumped into the right seat, and began starting my helicopter, which took a few minutes. When the pilot hit the starter, an electric motor began turning the compressor in the turbine engine, and the igniters in the combustion chamber began popping as they were emitting sparks to ignite the jet fuel. You could hear a whoosh as the fuel ignited, and as the turbines within the engine picked up speed, the sound would gradually go from a low-pitched whine to a high-pitched roar. Once the engine was turning at sufficient rpm's, the transmission would engage and begin turning the main rotor and tail rotor, slowly at first but gradually increasing in speed until they were finally running at operational rpm's.

My door gunner arrived immediately after the pilot and, after closing the pilot's door, climbed into the helicopter and sat in his seat. When the helicopter was finally running at operational rpm's, I was still standing at the copilot's door waiting for a copilot so that I could help him get in and we could take off. The mortar rounds were still falling, and the pilot yelled at me, "Get in." I climbed into the copilot's seat, and, just after I strapped in, the copilot came running out and jumped into my seat. The pilot pulled the helicopter into a hover, taxied out onto the runway, and we headed down the runway to gain sufficient airspeed to take off.

Just as we started climbing, the pilot told me over the intercom, "You take it." I had not been trained to fly a helicopter, and I had never flown the helicopter in combat before. I grabbed the cyclic with my right hand and the collective with my left, put my feet on the tail rotor pedals, and said, "I've got it." I then continued to climb, maintaining an airspeed of 70 knots and a 500-feet-per-minute rate of climb. When I reached about 1000 feet, I pulled into formation behind the lead gunship and followed it as we went in search of the mortar tubes.

Unfortunately, the enemy stopped firing, and we were unable to locate them, so I did not have an opportunity to fire the miniguns. After flying around for about twenty minutes, we headed back to the base. As I was approaching the end of the runway on short final, the pilot asked me if I wanted to try to land the helicopter. Not being entirely crazy, I declined, and he took back the controls. Landing is one of the most difficult skills to learn in flying a helicopter, and I did not want to risk damaging my helicopter. However, I was disappointed that I did not get to fire the miniguns.

One of our company's helicopters took a .50 caliber round through a main rotor blade, which caused such a violent up-and-down vibration that the pilot's helmet kept sliding down onto the bridge of his nose. He landed at a staging area (a small runway where we could rearm and refuel). The door gunner of one of our gunships that was there had been a prop and rotor mechanic before he was a door gunner. The pilot asked him if the helicopter could be flown back to our base. After examining the blade, the door gunner said that it could be. The pilot then stated that he was not sure he could fly it back because of the violent vibration, and the door gunner responded, "Give me your 45." The pilot handed his pistol to the door gunner, who walked over to the undamaged rotor blade and fired a bullet through it. Having bullet holes in both blades eliminated most of the vibration, and the pilot was able to fly the helicopter back to our base.

In combat, you must improvise. You will rarely be trained for every situation that may occur. You cannot hold back simply because you have not been formally trained for the particular operation. Much of combat is on-the-job training. Basically, all of my training for combat was on the job, from learning how to fire my machine gun accurately, to learning how to spot the enemy, to learning some of the enemy's tactics. You cannot allow fear of failure to keep you from doing what needs to be done.

There is no indication that Gideon was trained in combat before the pre-incarnate Christ called him a "mighty man of valor."[1] In fact, Gideon was at the time threshing wheat in a winepress in order to hide from the Midianites. According to him, his clan was the weakest in Manasseh, and he was the least in his father's house. However, Christ told Gideon: "Go in this might of yours, and you shall save Israel from the hand of the Midianites. Have I not sent you?"[2] Gideon had only to go in obedience in his own strength, and God would take care of the rest.

The only question is, "Has God sent you?" As Joshua and Caleb said when the Israelites were afraid to enter the Promised Land, "If the LORD delights in us, then He will bring us into this land and give it to us, 'a land which flows with milk and honey.' "[3] Similarly, Jonathan told his armor bearer: "Come, let us go over to the garrison of these uncircumcised; it may be that the LORD will work for us. For nothing restrains the LORD from saving by many or by few."[4] When the Philistines' response showed Jonathan that the LORD was with him, he and his armor bearer went up and killed twenty Philistines.[5]

We must always be available to be used by God. That often requires being attentive to what is happening around us spiritually, to the needs of others, and to the leading of the Holy Spirit. When God assigns us a mission, we need not fear that we have not yet been trained to do what He has called us to do. When He calls us to do something, we simply need to obey, even if we do not feel qualified. That is part of trusting Him, responding in obedience with the confidence that He will supply whatever is lacking. He qualifies those He calls; He does not call the qualified. As stated in Psalm 144:1, "Blessed *be* the LORD my Rock, Who trains my hands for war, *and* my fingers for battle."

My wife and I learned of a young man who had been badly beaten and was in a coma in a nearby hospital. We did not know him, but he was the brother of a friend of one of our family members. We had not been trained for a "hospital ministry," but both felt we needed to go see him. We had never before met the young man or any of his family. We arrived at the hospital in the evening, and some of the family members were in the intensive care waiting room. They told us the young man's room number.

We walked through the double doors into intensive care, and were able to go directly to his room. I thought it was strange that we could just walk right into his room in intensive care. When our daughter was in intensive care about fifteen years earlier, we could not go back to her room without first calling for permission. Either the rules for intensive care had changed, or God opened the way. When we walked into intensive care, we did not see any medical personnel. We walked past the nurses' station and into his room.

His wife and mother were in the room. They told us the young man had been involved in an altercation in which he had been knocked down a small flight of stairs and then kicked several times in the head as he lay motionless on the ground. As a result, he had three skull fractures and was still in a coma. The doctor had to cut away part of the young man's frontal lobe because it was rendered "hamburger" during the beating. To do so, the doctor had removed a part of the young man's skull, which was inserted into his abdomen until it was ready to be replaced. We also learned that the young man had developed blood clots in his legs and arms.

I anointed him with oil, and my wife and I prayed that God would heal him, that he would come out of his coma, and that the blood clots would be removed. A couple of days later I returned and learned that the young man had awakened from his coma and had spoken a few words. His wife also told me that the morning after we prayed for him the doctors examined him and found that the blood clots were gone. However, she said that a high resolution MRI revealed an infection in the young man's brain and that the doctor was going to operate the next morning. I again prayed for him and rebuked the infection. When they operated the next morning, there was no infection.

We later saw the young man in the therapy section of the hospital. He was very conversant and told us the doctors were amazed at how well he was doing. God will do great works through us if we make ourselves available. We just have to be obedient and trust Him to do the rest. We cannot worry about not having done the task before or not having been officially trained to do it. We simply have to do what He asks, and He will do the rest.

---

[1] Judges 6:12.
[2] Judges 6:14.
[3] Numbers 14:8.
[4] 1 Samuel 14:6.
[5] 1 Samuel 14:7-14.

17

PRIDE GOES BEFORE A FALL

Pride goes before destruction,
And a haughty spirit before a fall.

Proverbs 16:18

The Army's AH-64D Apache Longbow is the most advanced attack helicopter in the world. It has a cruising speed of about 165 m.p.h. and can perform loops and rolls. The Longbow can be armed with a variety of weapons including Hellfire air-to-surface guided missiles, several varieties of air-to-air guided missiles, rockets, and a 30 mm chain gun. It has a sophisticated, targeting radar that allows it to determine the location, speed, and direction of travel of up to 256 separate targets. During Operation Iraqi Freedom, the Army wanted to show off the capabilities of the Longbow.

On March 24, 2003, it sent thirty-four Apache Longbows against the Medina Division of the Republican Guard near Karbala, fifty miles south of Baghdad, without first having the Air Force A-10 Warthogs soften up the enemy positions. The Apaches were to be the stars of the show. To defend against the Apaches, the Iraqis simply sent a barrage of AK-47 and other small arms fire into the air. The intense ground fire caused the Apaches to abort their mission. Upon their return to base, twenty-seven of the Apaches were not flyable because of bullet damage, and one had been shot down. Helicopters, no matter how advanced, are susceptible to small arms fire because an armor-plated helicopter would be too heavy to fly. An AK-47 could be purchased for $75 to $150 on the street in Iraq, and it could bring down a $24 million aircraft. Pride in the abilities of the Apaches did not make them bullet proof; it simply made them vulnerable. In combat, pride will simply get you or others killed.

Uzziah was sixteen years old when he became king of Judah, and he reigned fifty-two years.[1] He did what was right in the sight of the LORD; and as long as he sought the LORD, God made him prosper.[2] God helped him in war, and he became exceedingly strong with a mighty army.[3] He became proud, and he transgressed against the Lord by entering the temple to burn incense on the altar of incense.[4] God had only authorized the priests to do so. When Uzziah became angry at the priests who tried to stop him, the LORD struck him with leprosy.[5] He lost his throne to his son and lived as a leper in isolation until he died.[6] Uzziah was a king and a mighty warrior who the LORD prospered, but he was brought down because of his pride. Even King David succumbed to pride, both when he had Uriah the Hittite killed in order to protect his own reputation and when he numbered Israel.

Pride can make one very vulnerable to the enemy's schemes. That is why Satan tried to appeal to Jesus's pride during the temptation in the wilderness. In the first attempt, Satan said, "If You are the Son of God, command that these stones become bread."[7] In other words, "Prove that you are the Son of God by exercising supernatural power." Jesus had just finished fasting forty days and forty nights, and He was hungry.[8] Satan undoubtedly thought that Jesus's hunger made him vulnerable to that temptation. Likewise, as Jesus hung on the cross, passersby taunted Him saying: "You who destroy the temple and build *it* in three days, save Yourself! If You are the Son of God, come down from the cross."[9] Such words did not cause Jesus to sin because He did not perform miraculous works out of pride to show how great or spiritual He was, nor did He need to prove to anyone who He was to satisfy His ego.

In Satan's second attempt, he took Jesus to the pinnacle of the temple and said: "If You are the Son of God, throw Yourself down. For it is written: *'He shall give His angels charge over you,'* and, *'In their hands they shall bear you up, Lest you dash your foot against a stone.' "*[10] Again, he sought to appeal to pride, but this time with respect to Jesus's relationship with the Father. In other words, "Prove that the Father loves You so much He will save you from injury." Similar words were hurled at Jesus as He hung on the cross. "He trusted in God; let Him deliver Him now if He will have Him; for He said, 'I am the Son of God.' "[11] Such words were ineffective because Jesus was confident in His relationship with the Father and in the Father's love, even while hanging on the cross.

Finally, Satan took Jesus up on a high mountain, showed Him all the kingdoms of the world and their glory, and said, "All these things I will give You if You will fall down and worship me."[12] All of the kingdoms of the world would represent power and wealth, and the word translated "power" means favorable human opinion. Jesus was offered wealth, power, and fame. Because He was not proud, He did not crave those things and could not be enticed by them. His relationship with the Father was more important than anything the world had to offer.

God formed each of us in the womb,[13] creating our innate talents and abilities. He gives us wisdom and the power to get wealth.[14] He has set before us our individual destinies, and He will empower us to fulfill them. Reveling in pride about our accomplishments is taking credit for what God has done. It is simply trying to take the glory for ourselves, rather than giving God the glory. God created us for His glory.[15] He will not give His glory to another.[16]

The root of pride is failing to accept and appreciate the love of the Father. As a result, we seek affirmation by trying to exalt ourselves, usually in the eyes of other people. We try to perform or achieve in a way that will bring us glory, or that will enable us to believe that we are superior to others. When we glory in such affirmation or begin to believe in our superiority, we become proud. True affirmation can come only through our relationship with the Father. He gives it freely because He has chosen to love us and, through Christ, to accept us as His adopted children.[17]

Likewise, we must examine ourselves whenever we think, "I deserve." Is that simply pride? As stated in Hebrews 13:5: "*Let your* conduct *be* without covetousness; *be* content with such things as you have. For He Himself has said, '*I will never leave you nor forsake you.*' " Covetousness and envy are grounded in pride.

God's attitude towards pride is clear. "Yes, all of *you* be submissive to one another, and be clothed with humility, for '*God resists the proud, but gives grace to the humble.*' Therefore, humble yourselves under the mighty hand of God, that He may exalt you in due time."[18] As stated at Jeremiah 9:23-24:

> Thus says the LORD:
> "Let not the wise *man* glory in his wisdom,
> Let not the mighty *man* glory in his might,
> Nor the rich *man* glory in his riches;
> But let him who glories glory in this,

That he understands and knows Me,
That I *am* the LORD, exercising
lovingkindness, judgment, and
righteousness on earth.
For in these I delight," says the LORD.

Living in humility is so important that Paul was given "a thorn in the flesh" to keep him from becoming exalted above measure, and, although he pleaded with the Lord three times, He refused to make it depart.[19] As Paul wrote, "But God forbid that I should boast except in the cross of our Lord Jesus Christ, by whom the world has been crucified to me, and I to the world."[20]

We must never become so proud as to think that God will overlook our disobedience because we have become indispensable in His plan. I suspect that some well-known Christian leaders who have fallen began believing that they had done so much for God and were so important in His plan and His kingdom that He would overlook a little disobedience. The good they did would certainly outweigh a little bit of sin. Unfortunately, such disobedience tends to continue to grow until God must respond. God disciplines His children.[21] He does so for our good so that we may be partakers in His holiness.[22]

We must keep in mind the admonition, "Pride *goes* before destruction, and a haughty spirit before a fall."[23] "*Let* nothing *be done* through selfish ambition or conceit, but in lowliness of mind let each esteem others better than himself."[24] Pride simply makes us vulnerable to the schemes of the enemy. We can become blinded by selfish ambition and not see the traps and snares of the enemy. We can be deceived by it.[25] It also creates strife,[26] destroying the unity that we are to have as believers. Our attitude must be like Christ's, who, although He was equal with God, humbled Himself, came in the likeness of men, and was obedient even to the point of death on a cross.[27] Therefore, God exalted Him.[28]

We have a choice. We can seek to exalt ourselves, or we can humble ourselves and allow God to exalt us in His time.[29] Which is better?

We must not, however, confuse pride or arrogance with confidence. When I was in the gunship platoon in Vietnam, I was confident we could accomplish any mission we were given. We could take on anybody, anyplace, anytime. We simply altered our tactics when necessary to give us the advantage or lessen the enemy's advantage. Being confident of the abilities of the pilots and crew in my platoon is not the same as pride. We are to be confident in the Lord. He who is in us is greater than he who is in the world.[30] As stated in Psalm 27:1-5:

> The LORD *is* my light and my salvation;
> Whom shall I fear?
> The LORD *is* the strength of my life;
> Of whom shall I be afraid?
> When the wicked came against me
> To eat my flesh,
> My enemies and foes,
> They stumbled and fell.
> Though an army may encamp against me,
> My heart shall not fear;
> Though war may rise against me,
> In this I *will be* confident.
> One *thing* I have desired of the LORD,
> That will I seek:
> That I may dwell in the house of the LORD
> All the days of my life,
> To behold the beauty of the LORD,
> And to inquire in His temple.
> For in the time of trouble
> He shall hide me in His pavilion;
> In the secret place of His tabernacle

He shall hide me;
He shall set me high upon a rock.

"If God *is* for us, who *can be* against us?"[31]

"Though the LORD *is* on high, Yet He regards the lowly; But the proud He knows from afar.[32] Do you want God to know you from afar, or do you want a close relationship with Him? We must seek to bring glory to Him, not to ourselves.

---

[1] 2 Chronicles 26:3.
[2] 2 Chronicles 26:4-6.
[3] 2 Chronicles 26:7-15.
[4] 2 Chronicles 26:16.
[5] 2 Chronicles 26:17-20.
[6] 2 Chronicles 26:21.
[7] Matthew 4:3.
[8] Matthew 4:2
[9] Matthew 27:40.
[10] Matthew 4:6.
[11] Matthew 27:43.
[12] Matthew 4:9.
[13] Psalm 139:14-15.
[14] James 1:5, Deuteronomy 8:18,
[15] Isaiah 43:7.
[16] Isaiah 42:8.
[17] Romans 8:14-16; Galatians 4:4-7.
[18] 1 Peter 5:5-6.
[19] 2 Corinthians 12:7-9.
[20] Galatians 6:14.
[21] Hebrews 12:5-7.
[22] Hebrews 12:10.
[23] Proverbs 16:18.
[24] Philippians 2:3.
[25] Obadiah 1:3.
[26] James 4:1-6.
[27] Philippians 2:5-8.
[28] Philippians 2:9.
[29] 1 Peter 5:6.

[30] 1 John 4:4.
[31] Romans 8:31.
[32] Psalm 138:6.

18

BLESSED ARE THE MERCIFUL

"Blessed are the merciful,
For they shall obtain mercy."

Matthew 5:7

One group of warriors not usually directly engaged in offensive combat operations, although many are on or near the battlefield and come under enemy fire, are the medical personnel. It was because of them that soldiers who were seriously wounded in battle in Vietnam had a better survival rate than those individuals who were seriously wounded in motor vehicle accidents on California freeways. I think the trauma of war had a greater impact on them than on those engaging the enemy. One invests much more emotion in trying to save lives than in trying to end them.

The person who had the greatest impact upon me while I was in Vietnam was not someone who was on the battlefield. She was the nurse who cared for me during the two weeks I was in the hospital recovering from shrapnel wounds. Her first name was Annie, and she was from Pittsburgh. She was in charge of a ward containing about forty soldiers lying in beds arranged side-by-side in two long rows. The mercy and love she demonstrated to the soldiers under her care was truly amazing. They were not the easiest group of patients.

One soldier was paralyzed from the waist down. He had been on patrol, and they had sat down to rest. When he heard shooting, he stood up to see what was going on, and the enemy shot him, severing his spinal cord. He reminded everyone within earshot numerous times a day that he was paralyzed. Another had been burned severely on his side and was very vocal about his pain whenever she had to attend to his injury. Another had some prior medical training and would at times loudly critique her care, such as when she sutured a wound on another soldier's chest. (He approved of her suturing ability.) I could not stand listening to it all, and as soon as I was able I would limp down the hall to the library and spend much of my days there.

However, Annie cared for each soldier, never showing any impatience or exasperation and always showing compassion and mercy. Her care did not end with her shift. During the evenings, she took some of her patients to the movies, those she had to push in a wheel chair because they were not ambulatory. From their perspective, her taking them to the movies was a priceless gift. They looked forward to it almost as much as they looked forward to their flight home from Vietnam.

On the day of my discharge, as I stood in the hallway thanking her and saying goodbye, I wanted more than anything to give her a kiss on the cheek. However, I did not ask her if I could because she was an officer and I was an enlisted man.

Even though Annie was not on the battlefield, she was in the battle. She was truly an exceptional warrior.

In many ways, I believe the horror of war was hardest on the nurses, who had to spend long hours comforting the injured and dying. Because of their kind smiles, their gentle touch, their soft words, their boundless compassion, and their unselfish love, their memories remain etched in the hearts of those of us who were wounded.

A true warrior will show mercy. Jesus was certainly an exceptional warrior. However, He was also full of mercy. "The LORD *is* gracious and full of compassion, slow to anger and great in mercy."[1] Jesus healed and fed the multitudes because He had compassion for them.[2] God saved us according to His mercy.[3] All of us are to show mercy to others. God comforts us in all our tribulation "that we may be able to comfort those who are in any trouble, with the comfort with which we ourselves are comforted by God."[4] Part of the anointing of the Holy Spirit is to "heal the brokenhearted."[5] We are to "[r]ejoice with those who rejoice, and weep with those who weep."[6]

God has anointed certain people, however, with the motivational gift of mercy.[7] That anointing is different from natural human sympathy and normal Christian comfort. The Greek word translated "mercy" in Romans 12:8 "is the outward manifestation of pity; it assumes need on the part of him who receives it, and resources adequate to meet the need on the part of him who shows it."[8] Those who have mercy as a primary motivational gift are able to sense in others a wide range of emotional needs and then provide the comfort necessary to meet those needs and to help heal the wounds.

In battle, there will be soldiers who are wounded. In a spiritual battle, those wounds will often be emotional. Those with mercy as a primary motivational gift (whether male or female) are like medical personnel, empathizing with and effectively ministering to those with emotional wounds. In a spiritual battle, they are just as essential as are medical personnel in a physical battle. Sometimes those with a mercy motivation do not feel like they are "warriors" or that they are involved in spiritual warfare, but they are.

It is easy to give mercy to innocent victims or to those wounded in the battle against evil. It is just as easy to castigate those who have wrongfully harmed others. The more difficult task is granting mercy to those who, by their conduct, do not deserve it. That is because we cannot see perfectly into the human heart, nor do we know the future. Have they truly repented? Given another chance, will they turn their lives around?

Because it is so difficult to answer those questions, many people gravitate to one of two extremes. They either want to apply the letter of the law to everyone or they want to grant everyone mercy. Jesus chastised the scribes and Pharisees because they operated in the first extreme. They followed the law to the letter, even tithing from the spices grown in their gardens, but they "neglected the weightier *matters* of the law: justice and mercy and faith."9 Paul rebuked the church at Corinth for the latter extreme because they did nothing when a man in the congregation was having a sexual relationship with his stepmother.10

Only God knows when someone who deserves punishment should be granted mercy. As He said, "*I will have mercy on whomever I will have mercy, and I will have compassion on whomever I will have compassion.*"11 This is shown by how God dealt with Paul. Prior to his encounter with Jesus on the road to Damascus, Paul (then Saul) was a blasphemer of Jesus and a persecutor of the church. When Stephen was stoned to death, Paul was standing by, consenting to his death and guarding the clothes of those who were killing him.12 Yet, God knew Paul's heart; that he did it in ignorance and had a sincere, if misguided, love for God. God also knew that once Paul became a Christian, he would fulfill his destiny to be an apostle to the gentiles. He had mercy on Paul, even though Paul's actions deserved a harsh judgment.[13] Therefore, we must seek God's direction as to whether to show mercy in the situation where someone has wrongfully harmed another.

"Mercy triumphs over judgment."[14] God's mercy triumphed over the judgment we deserve for our sins. In addition, showing others mercy will triumph over being judgmental toward them. It is God's goodness that leads to repentance.[15] However, mercy does not triumph over truth. Mercy and truth co-exist, they are not mutually exclusive. "All the paths of the LORD *are* mercy and truth."[16] "His mercy *is* everlasting, and His truth *endures* to all generations."[17]

Jesus showed mercy to the woman caught in adultery, but He did not disregard truth. After those who wanted to stone her left, Jesus told her, "Neither do I condemn you; go and sin no more."[18] He did not tell her that what she had done was okay. He did not ask whether she really loved the man with whom she had committed adultery. He did not say that it was fine to live with the man to whom she was not married so that she would not be lonely and would have support. He told her to sin no more. By granting her mercy, He did not approve of her conduct or her continuing in it.

Jesus said, "Do not think I came to bring peace on earth. I did not come to bring peace but a sword."[19] He did not compromise with evil. He drove from the temple all those who bought and sold in the temple, and He overturned the tables of the moneychangers.[20] He openly rebuked the scribes and Pharisees for their hypocrisy[21] and their traditions and false doctrine.[22] He stood firm when tempted by the devil.[23] He presented people with a choice—truth or evil,[24] submission to God's authority or lawlessness,[25] salvation on God's terms or judgment without mercy.[26]

We cannot negotiate, we cannot compromise, we cannot live at peace with evil. We are to abhor evil and cling to what is good.[27] The enemy's sole purpose is to destroy us. Our only response can be to gain total victory.

However, we must not become so hardened that we fail to exercise mercy when it is appropriate according to God's will, nor must we confuse exercising mercy with endorsing sin.

---

[1] Psalm 145:8.
[2] Matthew 14:14; 15:32.
[3] Titus 3:5; 1 Peter 1:3.
[4] 2 Corinthians 1:4.
[5] Isaiah 61:1; Luke 4:18.
[6] Romans 12:15
[7] Romans 12:8.
[8] W.E. Vine, "An Expository Dictionary of New Testament Words with their Precise Meanings for English Readers," *Vine's Complete Expository Dictionary of Old and New Testament Words* (Nashville: Thomas Nelson Publishers, 1985), p. 403.
[9] Matthew 23:23.
[10] 1 Corinthians 5:1-5.
[11] Romans 9:15.
[12] Acts 22:20.
[13] 1 Timothy 1:12-16.
[14] James 2:13b.
[15] Romans 2:4.
[16] Psalm 25:10a.
[17] Psalm 100:5.
[18] John 8:11.
[19] Matthew 10:34.
[20] Matthew 21:12.
[21] Matthew 23:13-15.
[22] Mark 7:1-13.
[23] Matthew 4:1-11.
[24] John 3:19-20.
[25] Matthew 7:21-23.

[26] Hebrews 10:28-31; Matthew 25:41-42; Revelation 20:11-15; 21:1-8.
[27] Romans 12:9.

Freedom Is Your Destiny!

19

DEFENDING AND RESCUING THE HELPLESS

Defend the fatherless,
Plead for the widow.

Isaiah 1:17

Deliver the poor and needy;
Free them from the hand of the wicked.

Psalm 82:4

One morning, my helicopter and many others, including helicopters from other units, landed in a large rice paddy and shut down. It was after the harvest, and the rice paddy was dry. We were told that higher ups were trying to decide exactly what they wanted us to do and that we would be shut down for at least three hours. The rice paddy was surrounded by heavy brush and trees, and we could see some enemy bunkers in the tree line. The area had been secured, so my door gunner and I grabbed our M-16 rifles and walked off to explore it. We eventually came upon a grass hut, and looked in the doorway just to see what the inside looked like. It was pretty barren. When we turned to go, an elderly Vietnamese woman appeared. I assumed that she lived in that grass hut. Just then four American soldiers from some other unit walked up. They were each armed with an M-16 rifle. One of them said, "Let's kill the old lady." As soon as I heard those words, I resolved that they would kill her over my dead body, and I meant that literally. I decided that if he tried to shoot her, I would shoot him, and his three friends would undoubtedly then shoot me. Fortunately, it did not come to that.

I was standing between the woman and the four soldiers. I said "Leave her alone" while walking past them as if I was leaving. What I was really doing was getting in a better tactical position behind them in case one of them tried to harm her. When I was behind them, I turned around to see what they were going to do. Fortunately, they then turned and walked away in the direction from which they had come.

Why was I literally willing to die for that old woman? It was not because she was my friend, or even that she was a fellow Christian. I obviously had never met her before and knew nothing of her beliefs. It was not because of her position, power, or wealth. She had absolutely nothing of value she could give me. It was simply because it was wrong to kill her and she was powerless to defend herself.

Nothing stirs the heart of a warrior more than the helpless who are in peril from evil. God's heart was even touched by our helplessness. "For when we were still without strength [powerless], in due time Christ died for the ungodly,"[1] demonstrating His love for us.[2]

"Pure and undefiled religion before God and the Father is this: to visit orphans and widows in their trouble, *and* to keep oneself unspotted from the world."[3] Orphans and widows were the powerless and helpless in the agrarian economy existing in Biblical times. Thus, Psalm 82:3 admonishes, "Defend the poor and fatherless; do justice to the afflicted and needy. Deliver the poor and needy; free *them* from the hand of the wicked." This verse is not talking about those who are able to support themselves. "If anyone will not work, neither shall he eat."[4] However, to the extent we can, we should defend the helpless from the wicked.

Another time, we had landed at the outskirts of a village to await further orders. As was usual, some young boys crowded around the helicopters. My door gunner and I were sitting on our seats with the doors open because it was hot. He took off his sunglasses and laid them down, and a Vietnamese boy grabbed them and took off running. My door gunner swore, grabbed his M-16, got out of the helicopter, and aimed his rifle at the running boy. In about four steps I was out my door gunner's door and on the ground next to him. I pushed the muzzle of his rifle upward and said, "Don't shoot." That boy's life was certainly more valuable than a pair of sunglasses.

On November 14, 1965, lead elements of the 1st Battalion, 7th Cavalry jumped out of sixteen helicopters that had just landed in a small clearing, designated LZ X-ray, in the scrub jungle in the Ia Drang Valley in the Central Highlands of Vietnam. They were soon attacked by three battalions of North Vietnamese Army soldiers, and, outnumbered about ten to one, were engaged in a desperate fight for their lives. This battle, which was the first major battle of the Vietnam War between American and North Vietnamese soldiers, is described in the book "We Were Soldiers Once . . . and Young" and depicted in the movie "We Were Soldiers." The commander on the ground, Lt. Col. Moore, soon closed LZ X-ray because the enemy fire was so intense that he did not believe helicopters could make it in and out without being shot down. Nevertheless, after LZ X-ray was closed, he radioed a request for one helicopter to attempt to bring in ammunition, medical supplies, and water and to evacuate the wounded.

The commander of the 229th Assault Helicopter Battalion of the 1st Cavalry Division asked his pilots if one would volunteer to fly back into the hot LZ. One of his pilots was Capt. Ed Freeman, the second in command and a 17-year Army veteran. Ed had served eighteen months as an infantryman in the Korean War and had received a battlefield commission on Pork Chop Hill, where he was one of fourteen men of a 257-man company who could walk back down the hill after the battle. After Korea, he wanted to become a pilot, but at six feet four inches he was too tall according to the Army. In 1955, the Army changed its regulations, and Ed learned to fly both helicopters and fixed-wing aircraft. As a result his nickname became "Too Tall to Fly" or "Too Tall."

As soon as the request was made, Ed immediately answered, "I'll take it" and headed for his helicopter. From his experience in Korea, Ed knew that the men in LZ X-ray would soon need to be resupplied. Therefore, he had already loaded ammunition, water, and medical supplies into his helicopter. He climbed into the pilot's seat and began cranking the engine, when he noticed his door gunner, crew chief, and copilot also getting in. Ed yelled at his copilot, "Get your ass out of here!" The copilot answered, "No, I'm going with you." Ed told him again, "Get out." His copilot responded, "No." Ed said, "It may be the longest day of your life," to which his copilot answered, "I know." Ed warned, "It may be the last day of your life." His copilot's response was again, "I know." That Ed's crew would not let him fly the mission alone shows the respect that they had for him and his leadership.

During the next fourteen and one-half hours, Ed flew fourteen missions in three different helicopters through a gauntlet of enemy fire into and out of LZ X-ray, delivering critically needed ammunition, medical supplies and water, and evacuating thirty wounded soldiers. On July 16, 2001, Ed was awarded the Congressional Medal of Honor, our nation's highest award for heroism. However, probably the greatest reward was shortly after the ceremony when he received a telephone call from one of the wounded soldiers he had evacuated from LZ X-ray. The soldier stated that he was doing well, was married, and had a family, and he would not have lived had Ed not risked his life to evacuate him from LZ X-ray.

Another time, Ed was flying near Bong Son in the central highlands of Vietnam when he received a radio call from the ground commander of a unit involved in a firefight. The commander needed someone to evacuate wounded soldiers. Ed could see the artillery strikes and A-1E Skyraiders off in the distance where the firefight was ongoing. The Skyraiders were propeller-driven, attack aircraft that had been designed during World War II. They were used for close air support early in the Vietnam War.

Ed told the commander to "throw some smoke" (pop a smoke grenade to mark where he wanted Ed to land). The commander warned Ed that it is "hot" (under enemy fire), and Ed responded, "It will not be any hotter for me than it is for you."

As soon as Ed's helicopter started touching down in the LZ, an enemy machine gun opened fire from directly in front and another one opened fire from the right rear. As they were sitting there waiting for the soldiers to bring up the wounded, Ed's helicopter was being raked with machine gun fire. Ed looked over his right shoulder and saw from the blood on his door gunner's uniform that he was wounded in the arm. He looked over his left shoulder and saw that his crew chief was also wounded in the arm. He looked at his copilot, and saw his bleeding right leg. Ed was also wounded when eleven rounds tore through his windshield and one of them hit him in the side under his right arm.

He suddenly felt the helicopter rock as his copilot tried to pull up the collective lever to take off. That lever controls the pitch in the rotor blades and there is one located on the left side of both the pilot's and copilot's seats. Both levers are connected so that they move in unison. Ed pushed his collective lever down and yelled at his copilot, "We've got to get the wounded out of here." His copilot again tried to pull up on the collective, and Ed again yelled, "We've got to get the wounded out of here." This time, his copilot implored, "Don't we count?"

Ed waited until the wounded were loaded onto the helicopter, and then took off. He headed for an aid station that had been set up about five miles away. As he was en route, various warning lights flashed on as systems in the helicopter began failing due to bullet damage. The helicopter barely made it, but Ed was able to skid to a landing at the aid station and safely deliver the wounded soldiers. His helicopter had taken 52 rounds of enemy fire. For his heroism in this instance, Ed was awarded the Distinguished Service Cross, the Army's second-highest award for bravery.

In both of these instances, Ed demonstrated selflessness. He put the interests of others above his own life. A warrior is not self-centered, but will risk his or her very life to save others.

Jesus said, "And whoever desires to be first among you, let him be your slave—just as the Son of Man did not come to be served, but to serve, and to give His life a ransom for many."[5] We are "through love [to] serve one another. For all the law is fulfilled in one word, *even* in this: *'You shall love your neighbor as yourself* "[6] In response to the question of "Who is my neighbor?" Jesus explained:

> "A certain *man* went down from Jerusalem to Jericho, and fell among thieves, who stripped him of his clothing, wounded *him*, and departed, leaving *him* half dead. Now by chance a certain priest came down that road. And when he saw him, he passed by on the other side. Likewise a Levite, when he arrived at the place, came and looked, and passed by on the other side. But a certain Samaritan, as he journeyed, came where he was. And when he saw him, he had compassion. So he went to *him* and bandaged his wounds, pouring on oil and wine; and he set him on his own animal, brought him to an inn, and took care of him. On the next day, when he departed, he took out two denarii, gave *them* to the innkeeper, and said to him, 'Take care of him; and whatever more you spend, when I come again, I will repay you.' So which of these three do you think was neighbor to him who fell among the thieves?" And he [a certain lawyer] said, "He who showed mercy on him." Then Jesus said to him, "Go and do likewise."[7]

The good Samaritan gave of himself to someone in need. He bandaged the man's wounds, took him to an inn, cared for him, and paid for the man's lodging and further care. We are to do likewise. We are to give of ourselves and our provision for others. "If a brother or sister is naked and destitute of daily food, and one of you says to them, 'Depart in peace, be warmed and filled,' but you do not give them the things which are needed for the body, what *does it* profit?"[8] We must demonstrate our faith by what we are willing to risk or give up to help those in need. "Show me your faith without your works, and I will show you my faith by my works."[9] A warrior will come to the aid of those in need.

---

[1] Romans 5:6.
[2] Romans 5:8.
[3] James 1:27.
[4] 2 Thessalonians 3:10b.
[5] Matthew 20:27-28.
[6] Galatians 5:13b-14.
[7] Luke 10:30-37.
[8] James 2:15-16.
[9] James 2:18b.

20

TEAMWORK MAKES IT HAPPEN

Five of you shall chase a hundred, and a hundred of you shall put ten thousand to flight;

Leviticus 26:8

Our gunships were typically sent out in teams of two. Occasionally we operated in a team of three (a heavy team), with two gunships on the deck (flying close to the ground) and one at altitude (about 1000 feet above the ground). Two gunships would work together, with one flying lead and the other flying wing, providing cover to the lead gunship. In addition, we usually had a command helicopter flying at 1500 feet. When a gunship was shot down, the command helicopter would attempt to land as quickly as possible to pick up the crew of the downed helicopter. The other gunship would provide cover. When we were in combat, our gunships were in constant radio communication with each other and with the command helicopter. The crewmembers of a gunship were also in constant communication with each other through the intercom. Each of us had a job to do, and each of us had to do his job in order to succeed. We also worked in unison with the soldiers on the ground and, at times, with jet aircraft. To be successful, we all had to work together, each doing his assigned task. In addition, we could not have done much without the work of those who supplied us with munitions, fuel, spare parts, food, and other supplies. Combat is a team activity. A warrior must fight as part of a team, not seeking individual glory.

When Jesus sent out the Twelve to engage in spiritual warfare by preaching the gospel, healing diseases, and casting out demons, He sent them out two by two.[1] When He sent out the seventy (or seventy-two) to engage in spiritual warfare, He likewise sent them out two by two.[2] Paul did not go alone on his missionary journeys. On his first missionary journey, he went with Barnabas.[3] They were both apostles.[4] When Paul and Barnabas were sent out again, Judas (not Iscariot) and Silas, both of whom were prophets, went with them.[5] When Paul and Barnabas separated, Paul went with Silas,[6] so they were an apostle-prophet team.

Paul requested that others would fight with him in prayer. He requested prayer for himself and those with him,[7] so that "the word of the Lord may run *swiftly* and be glorified" and that they "may be delivered from unreasonable and wicked men."[8]

When you consider what we are to do for or with one another, it is obvious that we are not to fight this battle alone. We are to "[b]ear one another's burdens, and so fulfill the law of Christ"; to care for one another; to have compassion for one another; to "have fervent love for one another"; to be "hospitable to one another"; to minister to one another by the gifts we have received; to submit to one another in the fear of God; to teach and admonish one another; to restore those overtaken in any trespass in a spirit of gentleness; to comfort and edify one another; to "pray for one another"; and to "exhort one another daily."[9]

Obviously, to do this we must be in communication with each other. We are to "consider one another in order to stir up love and good works, not forsaking the assembling of ourselves together."[10]

In addition, people have different gifts and anointings, and they are more effective working together than separately. There are three classifications of spiritual giftings mentioned in Scripture: motivational gifts (Romans 12:6-8), Holy Spirit gifts (1 Corinthians 12:7-10), and ministry or five-fold gifts (Ephesians 4:11).

The motivational gifts shape our personalities, provide the motivational force of our lives, and affect how we view the world. There are seven motivational gifts, stated as follows:

> Having then gifts differing according to the grace that is given to us, *let us use them*: if prophecy, *let us prophesy* in proportion to our faith; or ministry, *let us use it* in *our* ministering; he who teaches, in teaching; he who exhorts, in exhortation; he who gives, with liberality; he who leads, with diligence; he who shows mercy, with cheerfulness.[11]

Not everyone has the same motivational gifts, or even the gifts in the same measure. We have gifts "differing according to the grace that is given to us."

There are nine Holy Spirit gifts, stated as follows:

> But the manifestation of the Spirit is given to each one for the profit of *all*: for to one is given the word of wisdom through the Spirit, to another the word of knowledge through the same Spirit, to another faith by the same Spirit, to another gifts of healings by the same Spirit, to another the working of miracles, to

another prophecy, to another discerning of spirits, to another *different* kinds of tongues, to another the interpretation of tongues.[12]

The Holy Spirit situationally distributes these spiritual gifts among us as He wills for the benefit of all.[13] As 1 Corinthians 12:29 asks rhetorically, "*Are* all workers of miracles? Do all have gifts of healings? Do all speak with tongues? Do all interpret?" The implied answer is, "No." Not all have these gifts.

The five-fold gifts are persons who have one or more of five anointings: "And He [Christ] Himself gave some *to be* apostles, some prophets, some evangelists, and some pastors and teachers."[14] Only "some" are apostles, prophets, evangelists, pastors, or teachers. Again, as 1 Corinthians 12:29 asks rhetorically, "*Are* all apostles? *Are* all prophets? *Are* all teachers?" The implied answer is, "No." Not all have one of these anointings. Persons with a five-fold anointing were given to the church "for the equipping of the saints for the work of ministry, for the edifying of the body of Christ, till we all come to the unity of the faith and of the knowledge of the Son of God, to a perfect man, to the measure of the stature of the fullness of Christ."[15]

Based upon 1 Corinthians 12:28, some mistakenly assert that the five-fold anointings are hierarchical positions of authority, like general, colonel, major, etc. That verse states, "And God has appointed these in the church: first apostles, second prophets, third teachers, after that miracles, then gifts of healings, helps, administrations, varieties of tongues." The Greek words translated "first," "second," and "third" in this verse mean "a series or succession of circumstances."[16] It is obviously not a hierarchy, because the other five-fold anointings (evangelists and pastors) are not mentioned, and "gifts of healings, helps, administrations, varieties of tongues" are not persons.

If any person had all of the giftings, he or she would be at risk of becoming proud and thinking that he or she did not need anyone else. Before listing the motivational giftings, Scripture says, "For I say, through the grace given to me, to everyone who is among you, not to think *of himself* more highly than he ought to think, but to think soberly, as God has dealt to each one a measure of faith."[17] Scripture then stresses that we each have a different function because of our differing giftings. "For as we have many members in one body, but all the members do not have the same function, so we, *being* many, are one body in Christ, and individually members of one another."[18] Scripture then states, "Having then gifts differing according to the grace that is given to us, *let us use them.*"[19] Merely having the gifts is not what is important. We are to use them.

After listing the Holy Spirit gifts, Scripture again stresses that all believers are members of one body with each believer having a different role to play. Scripture uses by analogy different parts of the human body (feet, hands, ears, eyes, and noses) to teach us that each person in the body of Christ has an important role to play, no one is unnecessary, and no one can do it all.[20] The conclusion is that "there should be no schism in the body, but *that* the members should have the same care for one another. And if one member suffers, all the members suffer with *it*; or if one member is honored, all the members rejoice with *it*."[21]

Finally, before addressing the five-fold ministry, Scripture exhorts us "to walk worthy of the calling with which you were called, with all lowliness and gentleness, with longsuffering, bearing with one another in love, endeavoring to keep the unity of the Spirit in the bond of peace."[22] The purpose of the five-fold is to equip the saints for the work of the ministry and to edify the body of Christ so that we "may grow up in all things into Him who is the head—Christ—from whom the whole body, joined and knit together by what every joint supplies, according to the effective working by which every part does its share, causes growth of the body for the edifying of itself in love."[23]

I want to emphasize two phrases: "by what every joint supplies" and "by which every part does its share." We each have something to contribute, and we each have an obligation to do our part in God's plan. You have something to provide and an obligation to do what God has called you to do. That is why you have a God-ordained destiny.

The fact that we are all part of one body does not mean that God does not see us as individuals, or that we are not each individually significant. Galatians 4:6-7 tells us that upon becoming believers in Christ Jesus, God adopts us as His children. "And because you are sons, God has sent forth the Spirit of His Son into your hearts, crying out, "Abba, Father!" Therefore you are no longer a slave but a son, and if a son, then an heir of God through Christ."

It is significant that we are His adopted children. A loving father does not look at his children as just a group of nameless family members. He views, knows, and loves each child individually. Jesus told the twelve, "[T]he very hairs of your head are all numbered."[24] That comment shows that we are each individually important to God. He loves and cares for each of us individually.

There is indication that people working together are more powerful spiritually than those working alone.[25] Leviticus 26:7-8 states, "You will chase your enemies, and they shall fall by the sword before you. Five of you shall chase a hundred, and a hundred of you shall put ten thousand to flight." A military that fights as one, with all personnel doing their part, is much more effective than one in which the different branches or units are not working together, but are in competition with each other seeking their own glory.

Jesus prayed that we who would believe in Him may be one—"that they all may be one, as You, Father, *are* in Me, and I in You; that they also may be one in Us, that the world may believe that You sent Me."[26] He did not pray for an organizational unity, or a unity that comes from outward conformity. Rather, He prayed for a spiritual unity—that we may be one because of our submission to the Father and to Jesus. That unity comes from loving and abiding in Jesus;[27] receiving, believing, and obeying God's word;[28] separating from the world and sin;[29] and demonstrating true love to the world to bring glory to God and show that Jesus is the Christ.[30] We must not permit prejudices, jealousies, selfish ambition, doctrines of men, or anything else to keep us from that unity. We must keep in mind, *"There is* one body and one Spirit, just as you were called in one hope of your calling; one Lord, one faith, one baptism; one God and Father of all, who *is* above all, and through all, and in you all."[31] We are not fighting for our own glory. We are fighting to bring glory to God.

Finally, fighting together, even in spiritual warfare, brings you closer together. Combat forges strong bonds among those who fight alongside each other.

---

[1] Mark 6:7-13.
[2] Luke 10:1-12.
[3] Acts 13:1-3.
[4] 1 Corinthians 9:1-6.
[5] Acts 15:32, 22

[6] Acts 15:39-40.

[7] 1 Thessalonians 5:25.

[8] 2 Thessalonians 3:1-2.

[9] Galatians 6:2; 1 Corinthians 12:25; 1 Peter 3:8; 4:8-10; Ephesians 5:21; Colossians 3:16; Galatians 6:1; 1 Thessalonians 5:11; James 5:16; Hebrews 3:13.

[10] Hebrews 10:24-25a.

[11] Romans 12:6-8.

[12] 1 Corinthians 12:7-10.

[13] 1 Corinthians 12:11.

[14] Ephesians 4:11.

[15] Ephesians 4:12-13.

[16] AMG Complete Word Study Dictionary, New Testament (4412 – *prōton*).

[17] Romans 12:3.

[18] Romans 12:4.

[19] Romans 12:6.

[20] 1 Corinthians 12:12-24.

[21] 1 Corinthians 12:25-27.

[22] Ephesians 4:1-3.

[23] Ephesians 4:15-16.

[24] Matthew 10:30.

[25] Genesis 11:6.

[26] John 17:21.

[27] John 17:23 with John 15:4-5.

[28] John 17:6, 8, 17, 19.

[29] John 17:14-17.

[30] John 17:21, 23 with John 15:8-10; 13:35; Matthew 5:16; John 7:25-29.

[31] Ephesians 4:4-6.

21

BE ALL YOU CAN BE

Whatever your hand finds to do, do it with all your might . . . .

Ecclesiastes 9:10

At the beginning of my second year in Vietnam, I received a new helicopter. It was not new in the sense of unused. It was new to our unit. A pilot, copilot, my door gunner, and I went to Da Nang to pick it up. We caught a ride in a C-123 to Saigon, where we spent the night in a hotel. The following morning we caught a ride in another C-123 to Da Nang. The next morning, I was to inspect the helicopter, and the unit transferring it to us was to fix anything I found wrong.

B-model Hueys develop structural cracks in the upper forward corners of their cargo doors. They come from the factory with a piece of spongy rubber covering that area. The rubber's purpose is to seal that corner when the door is closed, to keep out rain and dust. The first thing we always did whenever we received a new (to us) helicopter was to tear off those pieces of rubber to see if cracks had started to develop. The Huey in Da Nang still had the pieces of rubber attached, so the first thing I did was tear them off. Sure enough, there were large cracks in the upper forward corners of both doors. I pointed them out, and they had the sheet metal crew begin the repairs while I continued my inspection.

I found various other things that needed to be fixed, but now I only remember two of them. There is a radio antenna mounted on the top of the vertical fin at the rear of the tail boom. Because that antenna is right next to the tail rotor, there is supposed to be a wedge-shaped spacer beneath the antenna that tilts it away from the tail rotor. That spacer was missing. The other item I remember was an improper nut on a tail rotor drive shaft hanger bearing. The tail rotor drive shaft runs along the top of the tail boom, and it consists of several sections of drive shaft. Those sections are attached to hanger bearings, which simply hold the sections in place. The hanger bearings are mounted on top of the tail boom with four bolts, but the nuts attached to those bolts are visible only from inside the tail boom. There is a small storage area that is accessed by a door in the right rear part of the fuselage. By opening that door and sticking your head into the storage area, you can inspect the inside of the tail boom. When doing so, I discovered that one of the nuts screwed onto one of the bolts attaching a hanger bearing was not the required self-locking nut. There was therefore a risk that it could vibrate loose in flight.

When I pointed it out, the people from Da Nang thought I was getting too picky. They were apparently becoming exasperated with the things I was finding wrong. One of them asked my door gunner if I was a "TI" (Technical Inspector). He responded, "No, he is just a crew chief." It took all morning, but they fixed all of the items I listed.

When it came to maintaining my helicopter, I went by the book. One time during my second year I was working on my helicopter in the hangar to repair bullet damage. I usually let the maintenance crews do all of the work when my helicopter was in the hangar, but this time I was replacing the bullet riddled right fuel cell so I could get it back flying sooner. To install the new fuel cell, I had to tighten a ring of bolts that attached the top of the rubber fuel cell to the helicopter. Because the bolts were supposed to be tightened in a specific order, I was referring to the maintenance manual so I would do it right. A member of a maintenance crew, who had just been transferred to our unit and had been in my class at helicopter maintenance school, walked by and said sarcastically, "Going by the book I see, Eismann." I responded, "That's right."

During my second year, many of the mechanics working in the hangar were very sloppy in their work. Sometimes when my helicopter came out of the hangar, it was not safe to fly. A bolt that was supposed to be torqued down was merely hand tightened, or a part was installed wrong. However, there was a good side to their sloppiness. Even though crew chiefs were supposed to perform daily maintenance on their helicopters, we were not issued any tools. I began my second year with just a handful of tools that my door gunner scrounged from somewhere. Within a few months, I had a complete set of tools, including open-end wrenches, sockets, pliers, wire cutters, and twelve torque wrenches. They had all been left various places in or on my helicopter by the maintenance crews after they had finished their work and had returned my helicopter to the flight line.

The Army slogan used to be, "Be all you can be." I tried to be the best crew chief I could be. I wanted to know all I could about my helicopter. Lives depended upon how well I did my job. If the helicopter went down because of a maintenance problem, I was not the only one who would have been at risk. In addition, when you are going out daily to face an enemy who is shooting bullets at you, you have the incentive to be the best you can be.

There are two reasons that I was very thorough in my examination of that helicopter we picked up in Da Nang. First, the rest of the crew and I would be flying it from Da Nang to Soc Trang. They are about 460 miles apart, but because South Vietnam is crescent shaped, the actual flying distance was greater than that. Much of our flight would be at night, and we were armed only with pistols. If something went wrong, we were the ones who would suffer. I did not want any surprises during the journey. Second, once we arrived at Soc Trang, a TI would go over the helicopter, and I did not want to miss anything that he would catch later. My work was going to be examined. After we had flown the helicopter to Soc Trang, it was examined by a TI, and he did not find any needed repairs that I had missed.

Incidentally, on three of the first four combat missions I flew in that helicopter, it came back "red X-ed" because of bullet damage. When a helicopter was unsafe to fly for some reason (e.g., a mechanical failure, a worn or damaged part, or bullet damage), a description of the problem was written in the helicopter's log book followed by a red "X" entered next to it. The red "X" meant that the helicopter could not be flown until the problem was corrected. That may have been an omen that things were going to start heating up, which they did. My second year in Vietnam was more intense than my first.

I also tried to be the best door gunner I could be. I practiced regularly with my machine gun, and became very proficient with it. While holding it at waist level, I could easily hit targets within 50 or 60 yards of my helicopter as we flew past, and I also hit targets that were so far away I had to lob the bullets in on them. I fired my gun enough that I did not have to think about aiming; it became instinctive. At a recent reunion of my company, one of our pilots stated that I was a phenomenal shot with a machine gun.

My gunship platoon was well known to the enemy. Painted on the noses of our gunships was our platoon logo, a cartoon caricature of a Viking on a blue diamond background. The Viking was wearing a helmet with horns, and he was holding rockets under each arm and a machine gun in each hand. The logo was reportedly designed by Disney Studios. As a result of that "nose art," Hanoi Hannah, who broadcast propaganda on Radio Hanoi from North Vietnam in an attempt to demoralize American troops, called us, "The Blue Diamond Devils of the Delta." We adopted that as our platoon nickname.

Even though we were in the Mekong Delta and the southernmost Army base in Vietnam, the enemy in North Vietnam's capital city knew who we were. During my second year, the enemy placed bounties on our heads. To me, being known by the enemy was a good sign. It meant we were doing something right. My company also received a Presidential Unit Citation and a Valorous Unit Citation.

When the seven sons of Sceva attempted to exorcise an evil spirit, "the evil spirit answered and said, 'Jesus I know, and Paul I know; but who are you?' Then the man in whom the evil spirit was leaped on them, overpowered them, and prevailed against them, so that they fled out of that house naked and wounded."[1]

We should fight spiritual battles in such a way that the enemy does not ask, "Who are you?" Our desire should be that the enemy knows who we are because we have been effective in our prayer lives, as witnesses for Christ, and in what God has called us to do.

We are all going to have to give an account to God of

what we have done during our lives. "Therefore we make it our aim, whether present or absent [from the body at His coming], to be well pleasing to Him. For we must all appear before the judgment seat of Christ, that each one may receive the things *done* in the body, according to what he has done, whether good or bad."[2] Not only must we give account, but there will be differing rewards based upon what we have done. Therefore, we each should make it our aim to do all that God has set before us to do and to do it to the best of our abilities.

In Colossians we are told:

> And *whatever* you do in word or deed, *do* all in the name of the Lord Jesus, giving thanks to God the Father through Him.[3]

> And whatever you do, do it heartily, as to the Lord and not to men, knowing that from the Lord you will receive the reward of the inheritance; for you serve the Lord Christ.[4]

Whatever we do, we must do it in the name of the Lord Jesus and as if we were doing it for Him. We are ambassadors for Christ.[5] In all areas of our life, we should conduct ourselves as if we are working for the Lord, because we are. If we are His disciples, everything we do is a reflection of Him to others. Because we are working for the Lord and are His representatives, we should strive to be the best we can be.

One thing I realized when I was in Vietnam is that when you are going out on a daily basis into situations in which the enemy is actively trying to kill you, and often coming close, it tends to re-order your priorities. When each day is literally a matter of life or death, things that at one time seemed important no longer are. Similarly, this spiritual war is a matter of life or death—the spiritual lives of us and others.

Doing all things as unto Christ requires a similar re-ordering of our priorities. We must have a heavenly perspective. As stated in Colossians 3:1-3, "If then you were raised with Christ, seek those things which are above, where Christ is, sitting at the right hand of God. Set your mind on things above, not on things on the earth. For you died, and your life is hidden with Christ in God." We must view, consider, value, and judge everything from a heavenly perspective. "[W]e do not look at the things which are seen, but at the things which are not seen. For the things which are seen *are* temporary, but the things which are not seen *are* eternal."[6]

We must consider things from a spiritual, not earthly, perspective, and "avoid foolish and ignorant disputes."[7] We must not allow the cares of this world to distract us from what God has prepared for us to do. Our first priority must be things of eternal significance, not things of the world which one day will be destroyed. "[E]ach one's work will become clear; for the Day [of the Lord] will declare it, because it will be revealed by fire; and the fire will test each one's work, of what sort it is. If anyone's work which he has built on *it* endures, he will receive a reward. If anyone's work is burned, he will suffer loss; but he himself will be saved, yet so as through fire."[8]

Near the end of his life, Paul was able to write, "I have fought the good fight, I have finished the race, I have kept the faith."[9] May we each be able to say the same thing, and may we hear our Lord say, "Well done, good and faithful servant."

---

[1] Acts 19:15-16.

---

[2] 2 Corinthians 5:9-10. See also Romans 14:10-12; Hebrews 4:13.

[3] Colossians 3:17.

[4] Colossians 3:23-24.

[5] 2 Corinthians 5:20.

[6] 2 Corinthians 4:18.

[7] 2 Timothy 2:23.

[8] 1 Corinthians 3:13-15.

[9] 2 Timothy 4:7.

22

DO NOT LOSE HEART

And let us not grow weary while doing good, for in due season we shall reap if we do not lose heart.

Galatians 6:9

In Vietnam we fought a guerilla war. It was not a six-week war, like Desert Storm, or a four-year war, like World War Two. Direct combat involvement by U.S. troops lasted about twelve years. It was at that time the longest war in American history.

On a typical day, we would take off before sunrise and fly to an area where we would begin searching for the enemy. Some days, I fired over 10,000 rounds just through my machine gun. Other days, I did not fire my machine gun at all. We would return around sunset, plus or minus a few hours, and then I would prepare my helicopter to fly the next day, which would typically take from two to three hours.

Unlike conventional wars, in Vietnam we did not fight to gain control of territory, nor was there an enemy capital that we sought to conquer. There was no tangible goal we could fight towards. There was no one decisive battle that determined the outcome of the war. Rather, we simply attempted to engage the enemy on a daily basis, often taking and then abandoning enemy-held positions, only to retake them again. During my two years there, I did not know whether, overall, we were winning or losing. The war became simply a matter of body count, the number of enemy soldiers killed compared to American casualties.

I had opportunities to withdraw from combat, but I did not. During the few months I was stationed in Vinh Long at the end of my first year in Vietnam, I was a crew chief on a Cobra gunship and did not have a combat job. While I was there, two senior NCO's from Saigon came to my unit seeking a crew chief for a Colonel's helicopter. After interviewing several of us, they called me in and asked if I would be the Colonel's crew chief. In many ways it would have been an attractive assignment. I would have been living in Saigon, which had many more creature comforts (like air conditioning) than other places in Vietnam and a large PX (post exchange) where I had heard you could buy things about which those of us stationed elsewhere only dreamed (like ice cream). I also would have been flying around with this Colonel, meeting many interesting and important people, and it would have been relatively safe. I told them, "No thank you. I want to return to combat." I informed them that I had already submitted a written request to extend my tour of duty in order to return to Soc Trang so I could rejoin the gunship platoon. One of them responded, "The Colonel occasionally drops down low and allows his crew chief and door gunner to fire their machine guns." I answered, "I do not mean any disrespect, but that is not combat."

Another gunship crew chief had been transferred to Vinh Long with me. We both elected to return to Soc Trang for a second year, but when we arrived we had to wait two weeks before there were openings in the gunship platoon. During those two weeks, we were the "night crew" at the hangar, doing the final work on helicopters so that they could be returned to the flight line. Because of our experience, we were able to work much more efficiently than the work crews in the hangar. Near the end of those two weeks, the Captain in charge of maintenance asked me if I would work for him in the hangar. I declined because I wanted to get back into combat. After I had returned to the gunship platoon, the Captain again asked if I would come to work for him in the hangar after he had watched me make some repairs to my helicopter. I again declined because I wanted to stay in combat.

As we are walking out our destinies, we may be given opportunities to withdraw from the battle. They may appear as an opportunity for a more comfortable life, like when I was offered the job to be a crew chief for a Colonel in Saigon. It may be an opportunity for a less risky assignment, like when I was asked to work in the hangar. If we want to live out all that God has planned for us, we must not allow ourselves to be diverted to other things, even if they provide the comforts of the world or appear to involve less risk.

One time, my desire to be in combat actually kept me from being seriously injured. My favorite place to fly was an enemy stronghold called the U Minh Forest because every time I flew there I got bullet holes in my helicopter, which meant I was engaged in the battle. In the chapter entitled "Receiving Fire," I recount a time my helicopter was scheduled to fly airfield security, and we went out seeking enemy fire to lessen the boredom of that assignment. The next time that pilot was scheduled to fly my helicopter for airfield security, I had the option of flying with him that night or flying the next day to the U Minh Forest. To me, it was like offering me my two favorite desserts, but making me pick only one. I decided I could not pass up a trip to the U Minh Forest, and so another crew chief flew for me that night. They flew out to see if they could draw some enemy fire, like we had done. During the night, the miniguns malfunctioned, and they exchanged my helicopter for another. When they returned to engage the enemy, they were shot down, and the crew chief flying for me was seriously injured in the ensuing crash. I never saw him again. I flew out a day later and took pictures of what was left of the helicopter after it had burned up. It was not much. Jet fuel burns very hot, and the aluminum and magnesium used to build helicopters burn very thoroughly.

We spent many days providing cover for South Vietnamese (ARVN) troops. They typically did not want to engage the enemy. When we would spot enemy soldiers and radio their location to the ARVN commander, he usually led his troops in the opposite direction. One morning we provided cover for ARVN helicopters that landed about 96 ARVN soldiers in an LZ. The area where they landed was a pineapple plantation, with coconut trees and other foliage. Although there was plenty of cover, it was not dense foliage like a jungle. There were many open areas. The insertion of the soldiers went without incident, so we flew back to the staging area to refuel and have lunch. We suddenly received a frantic radio call telling us that the ARVN's were surrounded and needed our help. We immediately scrambled out, and on the way to the LZ my pilot asked the ARVN commander what the estimated enemy strength was. He responded, "Two." My pilot thought he must have misheard the transmission, and said, "Say again." The response was again, "Two." About 96 ARVN soldiers were "surrounded" by an estimated force of two enemy soldiers.

Our enemy was usually a much more tenacious

fighter than the ARVN's. One day we located some enemy soldiers in bunkers constructed in a tree line. We were able to call in two Navy jets, and they reduced that part of the tree line to stumps and mud. When they were done, we dropped down on the deck and again flew over what was left of the tree line. As we were doing so, I saw a rifle barrel protrude out of a hole in the ground and the muzzle flash as the enemy soldier began shooting at me. The enemy was still willing to fight.

Even though we were fighting for the South Vietnamese and their soldiers were often not only unwilling to fight, but shot at us, I did not lose heart. My job was to fight the enemy. That was all that mattered. I did not become discouraged by circumstances. As long as there was an enemy to fight, the war was not over.

One day we were flying over a large rice paddy that was bounded on one side by a thick band of trees. Jutting perpendicularly from that band of trees was a narrow line of small trees and brush which extended in a straight line several hundred yards into the rice paddy. My gunship was flying wing, and the lead gunship spotted two enemy soldiers in the small tree line near where it ended in the rice paddy. As our gunships circled the spot in a clockwise direction, the door gunners on each gunship opened fire, killing the two enemy soldiers. The pilot of my helicopter then said over the intercom, "I would like to have their weapons." I responded, "Land the helicopter and I will go get them."

I did not care about recovering the weapons. I had a strong feeling there was another enemy soldier still alive in the tree line, and I wanted to go after him. The pilot set the helicopter down at a point parallel to the small tree line and about 200 yards from where it ended in the rice paddy. I grabbed my M-16 rifle and jumped out of the helicopter onto the ground. It was just after the rice harvest, and so the rice paddy was flat as a table top, dry, and absolutely devoid of any cover between the tree line and me. The line of trees and brush were on a wide paddy dike that was elevated a couple feet above the rice paddy. If anyone in the tree line started shooting at me, I would be at a distinct disadvantage. I would have no place to hide. It would be like trying to hide in the middle of a football field.

Because I had not been able to see where the two enemy soldiers were and did not want an enemy soldier popping up behind me, I headed for the end of the little line of trees. I decided I would start there and work my way down the tree line until I found the third enemy soldier. As I started jogging towards it, my first thought was that if someone shot me, I hoped he shot me in the chest and not the head. The "chicken plate" (body armor) covering my chest would stop a .30-caliber round, something my plastic flight helmet could not do. I also wished that they made small radios so that if the situation turned bad, I could be in radio contact with the gunship in the air, and we could coordinate how to respond.

We did not have the compact radios that soldiers have today. The standard field radio used in Vietnam weighed twenty-five pounds and was worn on a backpack. The Army also had a smaller radio that weighed six and one-half pounds and had a two-foot-long antennae. Even the smaller of the two was not a small radio. We did not carry either of those on our gunships.

As I jogged toward the tree line, I kept a close eye on the brush at the base of the trees, looking for any movement, the glint of sunlight off a rifle barrel, or a muzzle flash. When I arrived at the end of the tree line, I started making my way down it through the brush. After several yards, I encountered a hole in the ground. I walked up to it and peered down inside. It was empty. I noticed it was cylindrical in shape with smooth, vertical walls and a flat floor, and it was large enough and deep enough to hide an enemy soldier. Some yards later, I encountered a second hole. When I approached it and peered over the edge, it too was empty. It was just like the first hole. As I continued working my way down the tree line and brush, I came upon a third hole. When I walked up to it and peered over its edge, I discovered a third enemy soldier, who was very much alive, squatting down in the bottom of the hole. I shot him before he could shoot me. After this, the men in my platoon nicknamed me "Sgt. Rock," the name of a Rambo-like comic book soldier.

The United States military soundly defeated the enemy forces in Vietnam. By 1972, General Tran Van Tra, a senior communist general, reluctantly observed that the North Vietnamese troops were no longer capable of fighting and had to be withdrawn from South Vietnam and re-organized. The North Vietnamese Defense Minister General Giap, who led Vietnam's armies from their inception in the 1940's, estimated that the NVA had to outnumber American troops by nine to one in order to win a given battle. Although there are over 58,000 names on the black granite wall of the Vietnam Veterans Memorial, North Vietnam lost about 1.1 million soldiers.

America did not win the war in part because the American people lost heart. In January 1968, the enemy launched a major offensive throughout South Vietnam during the Vietnamese holiday of Tet. The enemy had some initial successes during this "Tet Offensive," but within days American forces had turned back the offensive and recaptured most areas. Although the Tet Offensive was a devastating military defeat for the enemy, the American media portrayed it as an enemy victory, convincing much of the public that victory in Vietnam was unattainable. As a result, there was an increasing public demand to withdraw from the war and to bring our soldiers home. Fear of direct Chinese military involvement, as happened in Korea, also restricted the military action we took against North Vietnam. Years after the war ended, we learned that the enemy was very close to giving up, but was emboldened to hang on by the American anti-war movement.

Satan is a terrorist. He has lost the war. The outcome is not in doubt. His ultimate destiny is the lake of fire.[1] He simply wants to inflict as much suffering as he can before the end. He came to steal, to kill, and to destroy.[2] When he attacks us, it is nothing personal. It is simply because we are children of God—because we "keep the commandments of God and have the testimony of Jesus Christ."[3] We will meet people who will immediately dislike us, not because of anything we have done or said but because the spirit influencing them does not like the Holy Spirit living inside of us. Do not take it personally.

We cannot compromise with a terrorist. Our enemies will never be content with compromise. They will only be content with our unconditional surrender. Spiritually, we cannot negotiate truth, either moral or doctrinal, with our enemies because only God has that authority, and it is clear that He will not do so. The Laodicean church was a compromising, lukewarm church. Jesus said He would vomit it out of His mouth.[4] Our victory in this spiritual war is attained only if we stand firm. We must "be able to withstand in the evil day, and having done all, to stand."[5] We are to hate evil and love good.[6]

One of the enemies' strategies is discouragement, trying to convince us that our efforts are futile. That can occur even following great victories. Elijah had a great victory on Mount Carmel, calling fire down from heaven to consume the water-soaked sacrifice and executing the 450 prophets of Baal.[7] He then went to the top of Mount Carmel and prayed. In response to his prayers, it rained, ending a three and one-half year drought.[8] Baal was the god of fertility, including human, animal, and agricultural. His worshipers believed he brought the rain. By bringing and then ending the drought, the LORD showed that He, not Baal, was God.

Right after those victories, Jezebel sent a messenger to threaten Elijah's life, and he fled in terror and prayed that he might die.[9] When God confronted him, Elijah said, "I have been very zealous for the LORD God of hosts; for the children of Israel have forsaken Your covenant, torn down Your altars, and killed Your prophets with the sword. I alone am left; and they seek to take my life."[10] Elijah was discouraged, probably for two reasons.

First, the primary ministry of a prophet is to help keep people in covenant relationship with God. The purpose for having fire come down from heaven to burn the sacrifice was "that this people may know that You *are* the LORD God, and *that* You have turned their hearts back *to You* again."[11] Elijah may have become discouraged because the people had forsaken that covenant. He may have felt he was a failure because the people did not respond as he thought they should. As he had prayed earlier after fleeing upon hearing Jezebel's threat, "Now LORD, take my life, for I *am* no better than my fathers!"[12] If we are doing what God has called us to do, we cannot become discouraged if the results do not line up with our expectations. We are only responsible for obeying God. We must trust Him regarding the results that may flow from our obedience. We must not allow our expectations to breed discouragement when we do not see the results we wanted.

Second, Elijah said, "I alone am left; and they seek to

take my life."[13] He may have thought that the victory on Mount Carmel was the final battle. It was such a clear-cut victory that surely Jezebel would give up. She did not. Our enemy will never give up. Throughout our lives, there will always be evil in the world.

We must not become discouraged or grow weary of doing good.[14] We must not lose hope. We must endure to the end.[15] After Elijah ran in fear from Jezebel, God had him anoint Elisha to be a prophet in Elijah's place.[16] If we lose heart, God may call someone else to finish what He has called us to do. If He does, it will be our loss.

At times, the battle may seem overwhelming. There may be no relief in sight. During those times, we simply must take one day at a time. We must concentrate on getting through the day.

When you are doing what God has called you to do, you will be attacked and criticized by those who do not know God. They will even accuse you of wrongdoing for doing things that please God. For example, when the king of Assyria sent an army against Jerusalem, he had a military official seek to demoralize those in Jerusalem. He accused Hezekiah of destroying the LORD's high places and altars and proclaiming that the Israelites were to worship before the altar in Jerusalem.[17] Hezekiah had destroyed those high places and altars, but they were not the LORD's. God was pleased that Hezekiah had done so because the high places and altars were used to worship other gods.[18] The Assyrians simply did not know God. A similar attack is when those who do not know God quote Scripture out of context to attack us.

The Assyrian military official also falsely announced that God had told him to destroy Jerusalem,[19] but it would not happen if those inside Jerusalem rejected Hezekiah's advice and made peace with the king of Assyria.[20] He would then take them to a land just like their own where they could prosper. Hezekiah's response was as ours must be in such situations. He simply sought the counsel of the LORD and prayed.[21] Because he did, the LORD defended Jerusalem. The Angel of the LORD (the pre-incarnate Christ) slew 185,000 Assyrian soldiers in one night, and when the Assyrian king returned home, he was killed.[22] We must not be intimidated by threats and criticism from those who do not know God, or who claim to be speaking for Him.

Some days we will engage the enemy, and some days we will not. Some days we will have victories, and some days we will not do so well. Some days we may be wounded or shot down, but we must not lose heart. The battle will continue as long as we are in these bodies. During our lifetimes, there will be no final battle in which the enemy is defeated. This is a marathon, not a 100-yard-dash. We must never lose heart or grow weary of the struggle. As stated in 2 Corinthians 4:16-18:

> Therefore we do not lose heart. Even though our outward man is perishing, yet the inward *man* is being renewed day by day. For our light affliction, which is but for a moment, is working for us a far more exceeding *and* eternal weight of glory, while we do not look at the things which are seen, but at the things which are not seen. For the things which are seen *are* temporary, but the things which are not seen *are* eternal.

Years after I returned from Vietnam, I met a Huey gunship pilot who told me of a sign he had seen on a bunker in Vietnam. It read: "You have never really lived until you have almost died. For those who have fought for it, life has a flavor the protected will never know."

That is really true. The days the enemy did not shoot at me seemed like wasted days. If the enemy was not shooting at me, I was not in the battle. To borrow a phrase from Anita Bryant, "A day without being shot at was like a day without sunshine."[23] For those who have survived physical combat, each day should be special because each day is a gift.

It was not because I enjoyed the carnage of war. I did not. However, once you no longer fear death, there is a certain attraction to fighting and prevailing in a battle with an evil enemy where your life is on the line. It is a high stakes competition. Therefore, the only thing I wanted to do was to fly every day and engage the enemy. Nothing else mattered.

Even good food could not entice me away. During my second tour, I was appointed assistant platoon sergeant and became an acting sergeant rather than a specialist five.[24] Although the pay grade was the same, as a sergeant I was a non-commissioned officer (NCO). The First Sergeant suddenly knew my name when we met on the street, and he invited me to the next NCO barbeque. I went, but could not stay long because I was sergeant of the guard that night. There was barbequed steak and lobster and anything I wanted to drink. That was the last time I attended the NCO barbeque (which I think was held monthly, but it may have been weekly). Even barbequed steak and lobster were not sufficient to entice me away from flying all day and working evenings performing maintenance on my helicopter so that I could fly the next day. I did not want to do anything that would prevent me from flying every day.

There is an excitement and satisfaction that comes from being in the spiritual battle, whether it is publicly standing for truth, leading someone to the Lord, seeing your prayers answered, or whatever else the Lord has you doing. Using your God-given gifts to do what He has called you to do is exhilarating!

David ran to meet Goliath.[25] After the Holy Spirit had warned that Paul would face persecution in Jerusalem, his friends pleaded with him not to go there. Paul's response was, "What do you mean by weeping and breaking my heart? For I am ready not only to be bound, but also to die at Jerusalem for the name of the Lord Jesus."[26] Paul desired the battle of spreading the gospel.

You will have attractive opportunities to withdraw from the battle. They may come in many forms, but their purpose will be to divert you from your mission—from fulfilling your God-given destiny. A warrior does not shrink from the battle, but welcomes it.

You must make it your goal to be able to state at the end of your life, as did Paul, "I have fought the good fight, I have finished the race, I have kept the faith."[27] Similar to Vietnam, the battle is over body count, not bodies killed, but souls saved. The gates of Hades will not prevail against the church.[28] Each person who is pulled from the fire[29] or turned from the error of his way[30] is a victory.

At times it is difficult to have a positive attitude. We can view obstacles in the path of life as either barriers to success or challenges to overcome. As stated in the above quotation, "we do not look at the things which are seen, but at the things which are not seen." God may not respond according to our timetables. We may have to pray and endure for years before we see positive results. In some instances, we may never see the results of our obedience.

Becoming discouraged and withdrawing from the battle is simply a lack of faith in God. With God, nothing is impossible.[31] Hope is eagerly waiting for something with perseverance.[32] We must hope in God, and we must have the will to overcome! It takes patience to bear fruit,[33] to endure difficult times,[34] and to inherit God's promises.[35] During those times, we may find encouragement and hope from reading the Scriptures or remembering the times that God blessed us in the past. It also helps to keep in mind that we are each here for a purpose, that God still has plans for our lives.

During difficult times, we must maintain an attitude of thankfulness to God for all He has done. God has warned us about complaining.[36] Rather than complaining, we should be singing His praises. As we are commanded in Philippians 4:6, "Be anxious for nothing, but in everything by prayer and supplication, **with thanksgiving**, let your requests be made known to God." (Emphasis added.) We are not to waste time bemoaning what we do not have. Rather, "in everything give thanks; for this is the will of God in Christ Jesus for you."[37]

That does not mean we are to give thanks for everything that occurs. Rather, no matter what the circumstances, we have many reasons to give thanks to God. Paul and Silas are an example. After being beaten with rods and thrown in prison, they responded by "praying and singing hymns to God."[38] As stated at 1 Peter 4:13, you are to "rejoice to the extent that you partake of Christ's sufferings, that when His glory is revealed, you may also be glad with exceeding joy."

During my second year in Vietnam, it became obvious to me that the leaders of our country were no longer trying to win the war. They were simply trying to lose it gracefully. Some people I knew withdrew from combat, saying, "I do not want to be the last American to die in Vietnam." The men in my platoon did not have that attitude. As long as there was an enemy to fight, we went out every day to search for and engage the enemy.

We can be confident that our Commander will never give up. In our battle to fulfill our destinies, He will be with us always[39] to help us so that we can be victorious.

Jesus prayed for Simon Peter, that his faith would not fail.[40] "And this is the victory that has overcome the world—our faith."[41] We are to have faith in God.[42] Our faith, our trust in God, our firm conviction as to His authority and character, is essential for us to gain the victory. We remain steadfast to the end. Having done all, we must stand.[43]

Our attitude must be like that of Shadrach, Meshach, and Abed-Nego. When King Nebuchadnezzar gave them the options of either bowing down to the gold image or being thrown into the fiery furnace, they responded:

> "O Nebuchadnezzar, we have no need to answer you in this matter. If that *is the case*, our God whom we serve is able to deliver us from the burning fiery furnace, and He will deliver *us* from your hand, O King. But if not, let it be known to you, O King, that we do not serve your gods, nor will we worship the gold image which you have set up."[44]

The Soldier's Creed of the United States Army includes the following:

> I will always place the mission first.
> I will never accept defeat.
> I will never quit.
> I will never leave a fallen comrade.

That same creed applies to the spiritual war in which we are engaged. We must place the mission first. Whatever God has called us to do must be our highest priority. God sent King Saul on a mission, and he only completed part of it because he kept some of the spoil for himself. As a result, God rejected him as being king.[45] We must never accept defeat. "[H]e who endures to the end will be saved."[46] We must never quit. God will enable us to do all He has called us to do, and quitting is simply losing faith in Him. We must never leave a fallen comrade. Rather, we must reach out in love and truth.

"No temptation has overtaken you except such as is common to man; God *is* faithful, who will not allow you to be tempted beyond what you are able, but with the temptation will also make the way of escape, that you may be able to bear *it*."[47] The Greek word in this verse translated "temptation" means a "state of trial in which God brings His people through adversity and affliction in order to encourage and prove their faith and confidence in Him."[48] These words may not seem comforting when we are going through very difficult times and no end seems in sight, but accepting defeat or quitting is simply losing faith in God.

Nothing can happen to you that God did not foresee and does not allow. He has confidence in you that you can go through the tribulation without losing heart. Your opinion of yourself must match God's opinion of you. As Paul learned as a result of his sufferings, "I can do all things through Christ, who strengthens me."[49] We must learn to see ourselves as God sees us, and to love ourselves as God loves us. We must learn to trust God in all circumstances.

---

[1] Revelation 20:10.
[2] John 10:10.
[3] Revelation 12:17.
[4] Revelation 3:16.
[5] Ephesians 6:13b.
[6] Amos 5:15.
[7] 1 Kings 18:20-40.
[8] 1 Kings 18:41-45; James 5:17.

[9] 1 Kings 19:1-4.
[10] 1 Kings 19:10.
[11] 1 Kings 18:37.
[12] 1 Kings 19:4.
[13] 1 Kings 19:10b.
[14] Galatians 6:9; 2 Thessalonians 3:13.
[15] Matthew 10:22b; 24:12-13.
[16] 1 Kings 19:16.
[17] Isaiah 36:7.
[18] 2 Kings 18:1-5.
[19] Isaiah 36:10.
[20] Isaiah 36:12-17.
[21] Isaiah 37:1-4; 14-20.
[22] Isaiah 37:21-38.
[23] For those too young to remember, Anita Bryant became the spokeswoman for the Florida Citrus Commission in 1969. Its television commercials featured her saying, "A day without orange juice is like a day without sunshine."
[24] During the Vietnam era, the Army had parallel ranks for the enlisted grades, based upon command position versus technical skill. Those whose duties involved technical skills (such as helicopter maintenance) had "specialist" ranks, from specialist four through specialist nine, although it is my understanding that nobody ever actually held the ranks of specialist eight or nine. The parallel ranks, called "hard stripes," were: corporal, sergeant, staff sergeant, sergeant first class, first sergeant, and sergeant major.
[25] 1 Samuel 17:48.
[26] Acts 21:13.
[27] 2 Timothy 4:7.
[28] Matthew 16:18.
[29] Jude :23.
[30] James 5:19-20.
[31] Luke 1:37.
[32] Romans 8:25.
[33] Luke 8:15.
[34] 2 Thessalonians 1:4.
[35] Hebrews 6:12.
[36] 1 Corinthians 10:10.
[37] 1 Thessalonians 5:18.
[38] Acts 16:25.
[39] Matthew 28:20.
[40] Luke 22:32.
[41] 1 John 5:4b.
[42] Mark 11:22.
[43] Ephesians 6:13.
[44] Daniel 3:17-18.

[45] 1 Samuel 15:17-23.
[46] Matthew 10:22.
[47] 1 Corinthians 10:13.
[48] AMG Complete Word Study Dictionary New Testament, Spiros Zodhiates, gen. ed., (3986).
[49] Philippians 4:13.

23

ENJOYING THE BATTLE

My brethren, count it all joy when you fall into various trials.

James 1:2

When I was stationed in Vietnam, I had several "toys." For a while we had a Thompson submachine gun on the helicopter, but we did not have much ammunition for it. I fired it on the ground once just to see what it was like, but did not fire it from the helicopter. However, I did use it one time to break a language barrier.

One day we landed to rearm at a staging area. I threw the cardboard boxes used to hold our machine gun ammunition onto the ground so that the pilots could begin reloading them while my door gunner and I reloaded the metal boxes of minigun ammo. There was a group of Vietnamese men walking around picking up brass (empty cartridge casings) from the ground. They did not have anything to put the brass in, so when they saw the cardboard boxes they grabbed them and walked away. When I saw it, I yelled at them to bring the boxes back, but they acted like they did not understand what I was saying. I grabbed the Thompson and a magazine of ammunition, jumped out of the helicopter, and quickly walked towards the closest man. As I approached him, I slammed the magazine into the submachine gun, held the gun in my right hand with the muzzle pointing at his abdomen, extended my left hand towards him with the open palm up, and demanded the box. He suddenly understood me. He handed me the box, and the other men returned the ones they had taken. Of course I would not have shot him, but he did not know that.

I also had an M-1 carbine that I carried in the helicopter. I cut the stock off at the pistol grip to make it shorter. I would occasionally shoot it from the helicopter, just to see if I could hit anything with it. Sometimes when we landed, kids and men would gather around the helicopter, some out of curiosity and others to see what they could steal. I pulled some bullets from cartridges for the carbine and replaced the bullets with candle wax. I would occasionally fire wax bullets to keep them away, without the risk of injuring anyone.

Sometimes crew chiefs would squirt grease from a grease gun to keep people away from their helicopters. One time my gunship and another landed next to an ARVN compound and shut down. The door gunner of the other helicopter squirted grease at a group near his helicopter, hitting the pants of an ARVN soldier. The soldier became enraged and stormed back into the compound. He emerged a few minutes later with a pistol strapped to his hip. Someone from the other helicopter yelled a warning. As the ARVN soldier walked purposely towards us, he stopped and adjusted the holster as if this was going to be the showdown at the OK Corral. The crew chief and door gunner of the other gunship and my door gunner and I all grabbed our machine guns, inserted the barrels, bailed out of our helicopters, and lined up facing the ARVN soldier, with our machine guns at the ready. He stopped, turned around, and disappeared back into the compound.

I also obtained a police siren and put it on my helicopter, simply because I thought it would be fun for the pilot to be able to activate the siren in combat. The enemy may wonder what in the world that sound was. Unfortunately, the helicopter had a 28-volt system and it was a 12-volt siren. I never could find any way to reduce the voltage so that the siren would operate properly. I found one step-down transformer for sale in the PX, but it began smoking when I tried to use it to reduce the voltage. After a few short blasts of the siren, it would quit.

Occasionally, I would do a little play-acting when we were taking off and there happened to be people who I thought knew nothing about helicopters. When the pilot began to start the engine, I would grab the main rotor blade, not letting it move. As the engine increased in rpm's, I would feel the transmission tugging on the rotor blade. Eventually, I would hold it with both hands, run forward a few steps, and then push it with all my might, acting as if we had to start a helicopter like they did the engines of WWI biplanes.

One time some combat engineers gave me fifty pounds of TNT (in one-pound canisters), blasting caps, fuse, and igniters. I wanted to make a big bomb to drop from my helicopter. There was not anything in particular that I wanted to blow up. I just thought it would be fun to see the explosion.

I first determined how long it took for a six-inch section of fuse to burn, and then went into the room in which I had placed the TNT to begin making my bomb. As I was in the process of inserting blasting caps into some of the canisters and connecting them with the fuse, my platoon sergeant walked in and became rather upset. I eventually talked him into letting me make one- and two-pound bombs to carry in my helicopter. When we would swoop in low over enemy structures, I would drop the bombs on them.

One day, my helicopter was flying lead across a bare rice paddy heading towards a thick line of trees and brush bordering the rice paddy. Suddenly, a good portion of the tree line erupted in automatic weapons fire while we were a few hundred yards away. The muzzle blast of automatic weapons shooting directly at you looks white, rather than yellowish as it does when viewed from the side. Our enemy often overplays his hand. We did not know they were there. Had they waited until we were closer before opening fire, they probably would have shot us down.

My pilot immediately turned hard right so that we were flying parallel to the tree line, but a couple hundred yards from it. My machine gun malfunctioned, so all I could do was watch. As we flew parallel to the enemy position, I noted that they were pretty good shots. I was watching the bullets hit the rice paddy next to my helicopter, and they were leading us very well, just shooting about ten to twenty yards short. I contemplated grabbing my camera to take a picture, but did not because I concluded that the puffs of dirt where the enemy bullets were hitting the rice paddy next to my helicopter probably would not show up on a photograph.

Because the enemy was in well-built bunkers, we climbed to altitude (about 1000 feet). I had some of my bombs with me and asked the pilot if we could make a bombing run, and he agreed to do so. I did not think that the bomb would have any impact on the enemy bunkers, but I thought it would be a fun diversion. I wanted to see if I could accurately calculate the altitude from which to drop the bomb in order for it to explode at ground level. I had screwed a hand grenade fuse into one of the TNT bombs, so

I estimated that, given the rate of acceleration of gravity and the time delay on the fuse, we needed to be about 500 feet above the ground when I released the bomb. I knew that was a fairly risky altitude at which to fly.

When we were on the deck and flew over enemy soldiers, we were low enough that they could hit us easily with AK-47's, but since we were flying close to the ground at about 60-70 knots they had very little time to shoot at us. The foliage, bunkers, holes, or other things they were hiding in, behind, or under blocked part of their view, limiting the amount of time they could see us to shoot at us. When we were at 1000 feet, they had plenty of time to shoot at us, but we were so far away that it was hard for them to lead us properly in order to hit us. However, at 500 feet we were high enough that they had plenty of time to shoot at us, and we were low enough that we were not as hard to hit.

One time, as we were flying over an enemy area on the way to our destination, my pilot dropped down to 500 feet so we could shoot any enemy we happened to see. Within a few minutes, a bullet tore through the copilot's door, striking the map light above his head. My pilot decided that maybe cruising over enemy territory at 500 feet was not such a good idea. From that incident and conversations I had had with others in my platoon, I knew that flying over the enemy at an altitude of 500 feet was risky. Even so, that is where I calculated I needed to be for my bomb to explode at ground level.

I pulled the pin on the bomb, holding it tightly in my left hand. The pin keeps the safety lever ("spoon") on the hand grenade fuse from moving. The spoon is an L-shaped piece of metal that extends from the top of the fuse assembly down the side of the hand grenade. The spoon holds down a spring-loaded striker that is hinged on one end. When the pin is pulled and the spoon released, the spring tension on the striker forces the spoon to pivot upward far enough to come off and to release the striker, allowing it to continue pivoting so that a cone-shaped protrusion on it strikes the fuse, igniting it. The fuse will burn four to five seconds before it reaches the detonator, which is similar to a small blasting cap.

I climbed onto the rocket pod as far outside the helicopter as I could so that I was holding onto the litter pole with my right hand to keep from falling. I wanted to be as far outside the helicopter as I could so that if I was shot, the bomb would fall outside the helicopter and not inside it.

We started descending in altitude, and the enemy began shooting at us. I had not told the pilot how low I wanted to get. At about 700 feet above the ground, I began hearing the pop, pop, pop of bullets going past me. The pilot heard them also and ordered, "Drop the bomb!" From where I was standing, I could see the altimeter, and so responded, "No, we need to get lower." As we continued to descend, the pop, pop, pop of the bullets going past increased. When we finally got down to 500 feet I released the bomb. My estimation was correct, because it exploded at ground level. I doubt that it did much damage, but it was fun. Even in battle you can sometimes have fun.

In March 2008, my wife, Sheila, and I went to the house of some friends in order to see a prophet of God whom we had met before. As we were leaving later that evening, the prophet told Sheila, "You have a miracle daughter, a miracle granddaughter, and you will have another miracle before the end of the year." The prophet had no way of knowing, except by divine revelation, that we had a daughter, what had happened to her years earlier, or that she was pregnant.

We certainly had a miracle daughter. During her first year of college, our daughter Christi had been seriously injured in a traffic accident when she was riding with two other classmates to California. We lived about 45 miles from the local trauma center, and Sheila received a telephone call at home telling her that Christi had been injured and was being flown by helicopter to the trauma center. I was at a meeting, and Sheila telephoned me with the news. I immediately drove to the hospital, arriving shortly after Christi had been brought into the hospital from the helicopter. She was semi-comatose, occasionally saying nonsensical things like, "Don't drop the box!" and "Open the book!"

Our daughter had received a closed head injury and her brain was swelling due to the trauma. She lapsed into a deeper coma, and it was then a matter of waiting to see whether the brain swelling would stop before it killed her. Her neurosurgeon said it would be five "white knuckle" days to see whether the swelling would stop. After those days were past, Christi seemed to be gradually coming out of the coma. She would occasionally squeeze our hands when asked and would sometimes briefly open her eyes. On the tenth day, a Sunday, she took a turn for the worse.

Christi developed blood clots in the venous sinuses in her brain (venous sinus thrombosis) and an infection in her head (evidenced by gram negative rods in her cerebral fluid). As a result, her brain began to swell and the pressure inside her head increased dramatically. At about 2:30 p.m., the neurosurgeon on duty told us that there was nothing more they could do. He ended with, "Although her condition is compatible with life, I don't think she is going to make it." I responded by asking, "Can I go into her room and pray for her?" He answered: "You might as well. That's all you've got left." I went to her bedside and prayed for her, and then my wife and I called everyone we could think of to have her put on prayer chains.

Later that night at about 9:00, we were in her room when the hospital chaplain came in and told us: "There is nothing more that they are going to do tonight. You might as well go home, get some sleep, and come back in the morning to tell us what you want done with her body." The medical personnel were prepared to harvest her organs upon being given consent. They had already removed a brace that had been securing her torso to stabilize the compression fractures in her back. When I left her room, her lips and hands were blue, and her partially opened eyes were unblinking.

God miraculously healed her. The next morning when we arrived at the hospital, Christi was still alive! An MRI done later that day showed that the blood clots were gone. By Friday, she was awake. After she was moved from ICU, her neurosurgeon told us she would never have the mental capacity to return to college because of the brain damage that would have been caused by the high pressure inside her head. Near the end of her hospital stay, a neuropsychologist did some testing to determine the extent of her brain damage. He told us, "This is really strange. I can find evidence of damage to her lower frontal lobe that happened in the accident, but I cannot find any evidence of overall brain damage like you would expect with someone whose intracranial pressure was so high." God had not only saved her life, but He had prevented her from suffering brain damage that should have occurred as a result of her brain swelling. She not only completed college, but has a successful business career and is a wonderful wife and mother.

When Christi was in the coma, the Lord told my wife that Christi would "take up her mat and walk." After sixty-three days, she walked out of the hospital carrying under her arm a rolled up foam mat, which she slept on to prevent bed sores. The word of the Lord was fulfilled literally.

We also had a miracle granddaughter, who was born just after the prophet gave Sheila the prophecy. Christi and her husband had been trying to have a child, to no avail. For years, they had tried all of the medical procedures available at great expense, but Christi could still not conceive. Finally, she told God: "That's it, I've had it. I totally surrender to you. If you want me to adopt a child, I'll adopt a child. If you don't want me to have any children, I'll accept that. I leave it up to You." Within two months she was pregnant with our granddaughter, and she has since also given birth to a son.

Sheila and I were wondering what the third miracle would be. Little did we know what was about to happen.

On July 4th of 2008, a Friday, Sheila and I went to a distant city to watch a wonderful fireworks display. That night, I suddenly had severe chills for about ten minutes and was literally shaking violently in the hotel room. The next day I had a pain in my right side, and over the weekend it moved around to the front of my abdomen. On Monday, I went to the doctor, who diagnosed it as a kidney stone. She scheduled a CT scan later that day to see how many kidney stones there were and where they were. After the CT scan, the technologist told me that the radiologist wanted to do another one with contrast because there was something he wanted to see better. I said, "Fine," and they did the second one. At the time, I did not know the significance of that.

The following day, I received a telephone call from someone who told me that he had the radiologist's report, that the CT scan revealed masses consistent with lymphoma, that he knew it was something I did not want to hear, and that he was sorry. He then said, "Good-bye."

I did not know what lymphoma was, except that it was something one did not want to have. I went online to learn about it, and one website said that up to half of those who have it survive five years, depending upon the stage of the disease, from I to IV, with IV being the worst. The following week, I had a bone marrow biopsy, a PET scan, and a spinal MRI. On Thursday, I met with my oncologist. I learned I had stage IV lymphoma. It had spread from my lower abdomen all the way up my spinal column to the top vertebrae in my neck; through all of the bone marrow in the upper ends of my femurs, my pelvis, all of my vertebra and ribs, and my sternum; and into my spinal canal where it was pressing on my spinal cord in two places, causing the severe back pain I had been experiencing. It was also wrapped around my aorta and around the S-1 nerve root on my left side. He told me that as far as it had spread without causing any symptoms, it was probably small cell lymphoma, which is very slow growing. He was going to be leaving town on Friday and said that I would start chemotherapy in three weeks after he had returned.

The next day, I received a telephone call from another oncologist's office asking me to come see her at noon. When Sheila and I met with that oncologist, she told me they had received the pathologist's report and that I had aggressive, large-cell, non-Hodgkin's lymphoma. She said that I would be starting chemotherapy immediately, although because of another test they wanted to do, it did not start until Saturday. We later learned that it had begun as small-cell lymphoma, and, after it had spread throughout my body, it had transformed into large-cell lymphoma.

I asked God, "Does this mean that all of the days ordained for me have come to an end?" I added, as if God did not know: "This would not be a good time for me to die. Sheila needs my support right now, this is a critical time in Matt's [our son's] life, and there is more I would like to do in Your kingdom." It seemed He responded, "How was the lymphoma discovered?" I then remembered that it was simply by His intervention that it had been discovered. After I had the CT scan, the kidney stone symptoms went away, and there was **NO** kidney stone. If all my days had come to an end, there would have been no reason for the fake symptoms of a kidney stone to reveal the lymphoma because I would have been dead within less than two months. Lymphoma tries to get to the brain, and since it had invaded the bone marrow of the top vertebrae in my neck, it was close. I then prayed. My prayer was not, "God, why did this happen to me?" It was not, "God, heal me!" It was simply, "God, may You be glorified through this."

After the diagnosis, my wife, Sheila, remembered a prophecy concerning me she had received some ten months earlier at a women's conference. The prophecy was that I would go through a very difficult time, but in the end I would be closer to God.

I had total peace about going through the chemotherapy. In fact, I did not even view myself as being sick. This was just something I had to go through. If God wanted me to go through it, I would do so with a smile on my face. Anything less would be a lack of trust in God. During my weekly visits to the clinic, there were several times when the nurses said, "You're sure smiling today" and "What are you so smiley about?"

During my treatments, several of our Christian friends suggested that I fly to various places where healing revivals were being conducted. However, the prophecy stated that I would **go through** a difficult time, not that I would be delivered from a difficult time. When they made that suggestion, I would ask God if He had changed His mind. It never seemed that He had, so I did not travel to those revivals seeking a healing.

I apparently was not responding to the situation as was typical. During one of my early visits to my oncologist, he chided me, "Dan, you could die from this!" I responded, "I could die while walking across the street." Not wanting him to think I did not appreciate all he was doing, during my next appointment I told him: "I spent two years in Vietnam. Every day I flew I knew I could die, but every day I flew I believed I would live. By God's grace, I made it through relatively unscathed. I have the same attitude about this. I know I could die, but I believe I will live. I have no reason to be pessimistic. I am receiving excellent medical care."

My first course of treatment was intravenous infusions, two weeks apart, with a drug combination called R-CHOP. My first treatment was in the hospital because of the reaction one could have to the chemotherapy. While I was chatting with the oncology nurse and her assistant, the nurse said she would rather go through anything other than a bone marrow biopsy. I thought she was kidding. My first bone marrow biopsy was not painful in the least. I later learned that they typically are very painful. I had three during this process, and, by God's grace, none of them caused any discomfort.

There were some good things about the chemotherapy. After my hair fell out, I did not have to shave. To stave off weight loss, I ate five times a day, and, per doctor's orders, I consumed high-calorie foods I had not had for years, such as whole milk and croissants. I would lose eight pounds during the week following each treatment, and then gain it back the following week, just in time for my next treatment.

The first bone marrow biopsy revealed that the lymphoma had altered the DNA in my bone marrow. After I had completed the six R-CHOP treatments, my oncologist did another bone marrow biopsy. Although there was barely enough bone marrow to obtain an appropriate sample due to the damage done by the lymphoma and the chemotherapy, the biopsy revealed that the DNA in my bone marrow was back to normal. One of my oncologists said it was miraculous.

My next course of treatment was four weekly injections of a drug called methotrexate into the spinal fluid of my lumbar spine. With each of those injections, it became harder to find a pocket of spinal fluid, and so the procedure took longer. During the fourth one, the doctor tried for about thirty minutes, moving the needle around in my lower back, repeatedly hitting the nerve going down my left leg, searching for a pocket of spinal fluid. It was fairly painful. He decided to try another location, and during that short break the nurse came up to tell me that she had to leave and another nurse would take over. I was still lying on my stomach on the table, and she walked up, bent down, and said, "I have to go now. It's been nice meeting you. I hope to see you again sometime." I smiled and responded, "It was nice meeting you too, but we can't keep meeting like this." My response took her aback, but then she smiled. It took another hour of trying, in two different locations in my back, repeatedly hitting the nerve going down my left leg, before the doctor was able to complete the injection.

One side effect of the methotrexate was that the slightest cool draft on my head would trigger a severe headache. When I was home working on my computer, I would wear a winter hat with ear flaps because even the slight draft of Sheila walking by would trigger a headache. I purchased a black fleece beanie and wore it in the courtroom during oral arguments because my seat on the bench was below an air vent. The first time I wore it, there was a high school class in the courtroom. At the conclusion of the arguments, one of the justices went out to talk with the students. One of them asked, "Does he get to wear the hat because he's the Chief Justice?" The hat became known as the "Chief Justice's Hat." When Chief Justice Roberts of the United States Supreme Court came to Idaho to speak at the law school, I presented him with a Chief Justice's Hat, but he said he would not wear it in court.

My next treatment was three days in the hospital with an intravenous injection of a drug combination called R-ICE. It was uneventful, with no side effects.

After that treatment, they harvested stem cells from my blood by inserting a catheter into my jugular vein and running my blood through a centrifuge (an apheresis machine). The centrifuge stratified the blood by weight into three sections: red blood cells, white blood cells, and plasma. The stem cells were in the interface between the red and white blood cells, and the operator adjusted the machine to extract the right color of pink fluid from the interface in order to collect as many stem cells as possible.

They wanted 10 million stem cells, half to use and half to keep frozen in reserve. Due to the risk of infection, the catheter could remain in me for only five days. Each day's harvest took about five hours while all of my blood circulated four times through the machine. Before starting the process, I was told that on average it took 2.3 days to harvest ten million stem cells. Because of how badly damaged my bone marrow was, they were concerned that they would not be able to obtain enough stem cells within the five days. The woman operating the apheresis machine told my secretary that I would definitely be there for five days. By the end of the second day, they had collected 11 million. The woman operating the apheresis machine said it was a miracle.

My last treatment was six continuous days of intravenous infusions of high dose chemotherapy with a drug combination called BEAM. It would attack all of the fast-growing cells in my body, including not only the cancer cells but the mucous membranes lining my mouth, throat, and entire digestive system. The side effects could include vomiting, diarrhea, and mouth sores, along with hair loss and fatigue. I was told it would be seven days of getting really sick, seven days of being really sick, and seven days of getting better.

Another side effect would be the destruction of my remaining bone marrow, so that my body would no longer be producing red blood cells (to carry oxygen), white blood cells (to provide an immune system), and platelets (to help blood clot). Therefore, on the seventh day they would infuse back into me five million of my previously collected stem cells in order to grow new bone marrow and a new immune system.

When I checked in at the nursing station to begin the treatment, the nurse asked, "Can I help you?" I answered, "I'm here for my three week vacation." She paused for a few seconds, then smiled and responded, "I'll take you to the presidential suite." She led me to my hospital room, but it seemed small for a presidential suite.

I was connected to an IV the entire time. When I was receiving the high dose chemotherapy, they placed a semi-transparent brown plastic cover over the IV bag to warn others. The chemotherapy drugs were not only carcinogenic, but they were also toxic and would burn or damage flesh that they came in contact with. I thought the brown cover was appropriate when I would wheel the IV stand down to the first floor coffee shop for my morning latte. The first time, I told the barista that I needed a refill of my coffee IV.

God was very gracious during this treatment. I did not experience the severity of side effects that are common with this type of chemotherapy. I did not even have any nausea, much less vomiting, nor did I have any diarrhea. Although my mouth became too sore for me to chew and swallow cottage cheese, I was able to find things on the menu that I could eat, without having to resort to liquid or IV nutrition. After I had gotten through the worst of it, one of the nurses told me, "You're just sailing through this."

There was only one occurrence that caused the medical personnel concern. They tested my blood daily to monitor my blood counts, one of which was my absolute neutrophil count (ANC). Neutrophils are the most common type of white blood cell and the body's first line of defense against infection. A normal ANC is above 1,500. When mine dropped to 500, I was placed in isolation because at that point I had a severe risk of infection. When my ANC dropped to zero, I spiked a fever of 102°F. It broke during the night, but the next morning my oncologist said that I had kept him up that night.

While I was in isolation, I felt like Paul when he was in chains in Rome. I could not leave the room, but I was able to talk about spiritual things to some of the nurses who came in to attend to me.

Before I started the six days of high dose chemotherapy, I was told that it would be about four months before I would have recovered enough to be able to return to work full time. By God's grace, I was back to work full time eight days after I was discharged from the hospital. In fact, because the hospital had Wi-Fi, I actually worked most of the days I was hospitalized, doing legal research and writing opinions. When a nurse told me I had set a record for returning to work full time after that type of chemotherapy, I told her, "I would have returned to work earlier if I had known there was a record to break."

During the first month after returning home, I had to wear a HEPA filter mask in public because of the risk of infection. One day when I was entering the employee entrance at the courthouse, I was wearing the mask and my Chief Justice's Hat. The security person monitoring the security cameras in the capitol area saw me and sent security personnel to the courthouse, thinking I was a terrorist, or maybe he just wanted to know, "Who was that masked man?"

About a month after being discharged from the hospital, I had another PET scan to determine the effectiveness of the chemotherapy. It did not show any active lymphoma. After reading the report, my oncologist became emotional and stated, "This is a far better outcome than I ever expected." My wife Sheila asked, "Would you say it's a miracle?" After pausing briefly, he answered, "It's a miracle." My oncologist then commended me for my "equanimity" (mental calmness and composure) throughout it all. He added, "It must have been because of your spirituality and life experiences." Sheila answered, "No, it was because of his faith in God." I agreed, saying, "That's right."

I left the hospital on December 29, 2008. The prophecy of another miracle prior to the end of the year came true.

I do not know why God had me go through that, but I know He had a reason. It may have simply been to be a witness to others. My wife was recently going through various photos that she had taken throughout the time I was going through the treatments, and she commented that I was smiling in all of the pictures.

James 1:2 says, "My brethren, count it all joy when you fall into various trials." One reason we can consider it "all joy" is because it gives us an opportunity to demonstrate our faith in God. To me, going through the chemotherapy without a smile on my face and a thankful heart would have been indicating a lack of trust in God. This did not take Him by surprise, and He could have ended it at any time. I knew He had a reason and I trusted in His love and goodness. Demonstrating our faith is often much more powerful than talking about it.

The kingdom of God is righteousness, peace, and joy in the Holy Spirit.[1] Joy should be a hallmark of a Christian, even in the midst of battle. Joy is not dependent upon the circumstances. When we exhibit joy during persecution, it demonstrates our trust in God, and it gives the enemy fits. A smile and kind word in response to a personal attack often leaves the attacker speechless. Our attitude should be like that of the Apostles after they had been imprisoned, beaten, and threatened by the high priest and the council for preaching the name of Jesus. "So they departed from the presence of the council, rejoicing that they were counted worthy to suffer shame for His name."[2]

The more intense the battle, the sweeter the final victory. So, go forth in the strength of the Lord. "Oh, taste and see that the LORD *is* good; blessed is the man *who* trusts in Him!"[3]

As you walk down the path of life that God has set before you, you can view obstacles in your way as either barriers to success or challenges to overcome. There is no person or entity in all creation that can keep you from fulfilling your God-given destiny, but you. " 'For with God nothing will be impossible.' "[4]

In Christ we have the victory, so we might as well enjoy the battle!

---

[1] Romans 14:17.
[2] Acts 5:41.
[3] Psalm 34:8.
[4] Luke 1:37.

Freedom Is Your Destiny!

24

FREEDOM!

Now the Lord is the Spirit; and where the Spirit of the Lord is, there is liberty.

2 Corinthians 3:17

One afternoon my gunship and another were flying near the Cambodian border when we received a distress call from an Australian advisor, whose radio name was Batman. He and another Australian, whose radio name was Robin, were advisors to a South Vietnamese Army patrol that had just been ambushed on the side of a nearby mountain. They were trapped and needed our help.

The South Vietnamese Army had an outpost on top of the mountain and a training base at its foot, but the enemy controlled the remainder of the mountain. The problem was that the mountain was covered by jungle, and there was no way that we could see soldiers on the ground through that foliage. How could we help them if we could not see where they were?

After we told Batman that we were unable to see them, he suggested a plan. He would pop a smoke grenade and then move the patrol away from the smoke grenade. By the time the smoke could drift up through the trees so that we could see it, they would be out of the immediate area of the smoke grenade and the pursuing enemy soldiers would hopefully be in that area. We could then shoot at the smoke, hitting the enemy soldiers or at least slowing their pursuit. If it worked, Batman would continue to pop smoke grenades and move as they tried to make it down the mountain.

The forest was the dark domain of the enemy, but the forest ended at the foot of the mountain. If they could make it to the bottom of the mountain, they could escape from the dark jungle into the light, and be free.

My gunship was flying lead, and when we saw red smoke drift up through the tops of the trees, the pilot put the helicopter into a dive towards it. The copilot began firing the miniguns at the rate of 4,000 rounds per minute. The enemy began firing back at us, and the copilot suddenly exclaimed, "There are more tracers coming up at us than we are sending down at them!" Sometimes we could help others simply by drawing enemy fire towards us and away from them. When the enemy was shooting at us, they were not shooting at the guys on the ground.

At the conclusion of the attack, the pilot banked the helicopter into a hard left turn in order to climb back up and get into position for another gun run. When he did so, I decided to try something I had never done before, nor had anyone else to my knowledge. I flexed my right foot upward and held it rigid so it would be like a hook. I then "hooked" it against the bottom of the litter pole in front of my seat and stood up outside the helicopter with my left foot on the rocket pod. I faced to the rear of the helicopter and leaned forward as far as I could towards the rear, holding my machine gun at arms' length and using my right foot as a hook to keep me from falling. Had I relaxed my right foot, I would have fallen about 1,000 feet to the ground. Because the helicopter was in a steep bank (turned almost on its side), I was lower than the tail boom. I began firing under the tail boom at the red smoke on the far side of the helicopter, concentrating on hitting the smoke. As I was doing so, Batman radioed, "Keep it up! Keep it up! That's just where I want it!"

I do not understand the physics involved, but in this situation my machine gun had no perceived weight or recoil. With the box of ammo attached to its side, it weighed about 37 pounds. I could easily hold it at arms' length, so that it was perpendicular to my outstretched arms, and fire it. My left hand was gripping the handguard around the barrel, and my right hand was gripping the pistol grip. I had no problem controlling it, and could change the point of impact of the bullets with just slight movements of my hands. Firing it on the ground was entirely different. I had to lean into it in order to keep the recoil from causing the muzzle to start climbing upward while firing.

This was the first time I had ever attempted this maneuver, and from then on I always did it when we banked to the left after a minigun or rocket run. If my helicopter was flying lead, I did it to provide covering fire for our wingship as it was starting its attack behind us. If my helicopter was the wingship, I did it to provide covering fire for us as we turned.

Batman continued popping smoke grenades and moving, and we continued shooting at the smoke when it drifted above the trees, until he and the patrol finally made it to the bottom of the mountain. Near the end of the firefight, Batman was shot in his thumb, but he and the rest of the patrol escaped the snare of the enemy and made it to freedom. Interestingly, the enemy was using the same radio frequency as Batman. We could hear them chattering at times during the operation.

A warrior loves freedom! In Vietnam and in the

other wars in which our nation has fought during the 20th and 21st centuries, we were fighting for freedom—freedom for others and often freedom for ourselves. A nation living in bondage does not live in freedom. During those wars, the members of our military have fought and risked their lives so that others can be free.

To some it will seem strange that one can have freedom while in the military. One of the freest times of my life was when I was in combat in Vietnam. I had no concerns or worries. Material possessions were unimportant. I never thought about what kind of car I would like to drive or house I would like to live in. I never cared about whether my olive-drab clothing was in style. I had no payments or financial obligations. I would sometimes go months without even picking up my paycheck because there was nothing that I wanted to do with the money.

Those of us in the gunship platoon did not have to pull guard duty or perform tasks otherwise required of enlisted men in the company. In our platoon area and on the flight line, regulations regarding dress did not apply. We did not even have to salute. We were simply left alone to do our jobs. One of the reasons I elected to stay in combat a second year was because of the freedom that accompanies it. A warrior not only loves freedom and lives in it, but a warrior also fights for others to be free.

When Jesus came to earth, He did not simply die as a propitiation for our sins. His purpose was not simply to provide for eternal life after we died. He also died so that we could live in freedom now. As He said, "I have come that they may have life, and that they may have it more abundantly."[1] "Therefore we were buried with Him through baptism into death, that just as Christ was raised from the dead by the glory of the Father, even so we also should walk in newness of life."[2]   Jesus was anointed with the Holy Spirit "[t]o proclaim liberty to the captives" and "[t]o set at liberty those who are oppressed."[3]   "He has delivered us from the power of darkness . . . ."[4]

Because of their fleshly natures and the work of the enemy, there will always be people on earth who want to exercise control over others.   Attempting to control or manipulate others is one of the hallmarks of the work of the enemy.   He wants our worship, and if he cannot have that then he wants us in subjugation to him.   He wants to take us captive to do his will.[5]

People under his influence also seek to control others.   They believe it is their right to do so, because of their superior enlightenment, righteousness, or anointing, or simply because they are entitled by birth.   They will typically try to use the government or man-made religious rules or both to gain and exercise control, and they may also take advantage of human weaknesses.   They will often say they are doing so for the common good, or at least for the good of the individuals they seek to control.   It is certainly possible that they may even believe that.   The root of the desire to control others is pride, and pride can be very blinding.

Jesus told the apostles, "You know that the rulers of the Gentiles lord it over them and those who are great exercise authority over them.   Yet it shall not be so among you; but whoever desires to become great among you, let him be your servant."[6]   The Greek word translated "lord it over" means to have dominion over or rule over.   The apostles were not to rule over others.   Likewise, Peter wrote that elders were to shepherd the flock of God, not "as being lords over those entrusted to you, but being examples to the flock."[7]

Trying to exercise control over others comes from

the enemy. Those who seek to exercise control over others have, due to their pride, a lust for power. They want to exalt themselves by exercising power over others, and they want others to serve them, to fear them, and to seek sustenance from them. In short, they want to be gods. Their motivation corresponds to Satan's as described in Isaiah 14:13-14:

> "For you have said in your heart:
> 'I will ascend into heaven,
> I will exalt my throne above the stars of God;
> I will also sit on the mount of the congregation
> On the farthest sides of the north;
> I will ascend above the heights of the clouds,
> I will be like the Most High.'"

The framers of our Constitution knew that God has placed the desire for liberty in our hearts. As stated in the Declaration of Independence, "We hold these truths to be self-evident, that all men are created equal, that they are endowed by their Creator with certain unalienable Rights, that among these are Life, Liberty and the pursuit of Happiness." The framers also knew through history and human nature that there will always be those who will try to rule over others—to deprive them of liberty.

The religious and political leaders sought to kill Jesus because the anointing of the Holy Spirit that was upon Him threatened their power and prestige. The Pharisees wanted to keep the religious power they had gained by controlling the people through legalism and the traditions of men. The Herodians (a political party comprised primarily of Sadducees) wanted to keep the power they had gained through politics. Even though the Pharisees and Herodians were opposed to each other, they joined together to try and destroy Jesus.[8] Another means of control is using lust to entice people into conduct that results in idolatry, as Balaam did by enticing the Israelites to participate in idolatrous feasts and sexual immorality.[9]

People are in bondage to whatever they submit themselves to obey.[10] It could be lust, legalism, fear, bitterness, hatred, money, power, pride, envy, man-pleasing, drugs, worldly pleasure, false doctrine, or anything else other than God. They spend their lives seeking fulfillment through such things, but they never find it. Whatever satisfaction they experience is fleeting. They must always do just a little more. The harder they strive, the more they have to do. Each time they submit to such sinful passions, it becomes easier to do so, and the passions become stronger. The problem is that we can never find fulfillment when our focus is on self-satisfaction. True fulfillment comes only by delighting ourselves in the LORD.[11]

When I was a general-jurisdiction trial judge, I started a drug court. It uses the coercion of the criminal justice system (the threat of incarceration) to force drug addicts into treatment. They also regularly appear in court to receive rewards or sanctions for their conduct. One of the reasons I created the drug court was to free them from bondage to drugs so their lives and family relationships could be restored and, hopefully, so that they could know Jesus. Until they were set free, they could not fulfill their destinies.

We have been called to freedom so we can serve one another in love.[12] However, we cannot do so when we are in bondage. We can be in bondage to the elements of the world, or we can be bondservants of our Lord. We can serve the flesh, or we can serve Christ. Nobody can serve two masters.[13] We have to choose.

Jesus told the Jews who believed in Him: "If you abide in My word, you are My disciples indeed. And you shall know the truth, and the truth shall make you free."[14] These believing Jews responded by saying that they were Abraham's descendants and had never been in bondage to anyone.[15] Jesus answered them: "Most assuredly, I say to you, whoever commits sin is a slave of sin. And a slave does not abide in the house forever, *but* a son abides forever. Therefore if the Son makes you free, you shall be free indeed."[16]

Through Christ, we can have freedom from worry and fear and freedom from the power of sin that holds us in bondage. Through Him, we have the freedom to fulfill our destinies and to do and be all that God has planned for our lives. Through Him, we can live in freedom regardless of our circumstances or what has happened to us in the past.

One aspect of our freedom is God's forgiveness of our sins through Christ Jesus our Lord. The enemy uses condemnation regarding our past mistakes to keep us in bondage and to make us feel we are not acceptable to God. Our past conduct cannot be changed; it can only be forgiven. "*There is* therefore now no condemnation to those who are in Christ Jesus, who do not walk according to the flesh, but according to the Spirit."[17]

Salvation is by grace through faith; it is not something we can earn. "[*I*]*t is* the gift of God, not of works, lest anyone should boast."[18] In addition, God loved us before Christ died for our sins. "God demonstrates His own love toward us, in that while we were still sinners, Christ died for us."[19] Because we do not have to earn salvation or God's love, we have the freedom to make mistakes. We do not have to live our lives in fear that we will do something that displeases God. We will, but through Christ we have forgiveness. We therefore have the freedom to make mistakes.

However, we cannot use our freedom as a license to

sin, or we will become slaves to sin, which leads to death.[20] "[D]o not *use* liberty as an opportunity for the flesh."[21] However, because we have been set free from the bondage of legalism and man-made religious rules, we need not fear losing God's love when we make a mistake. Knowing that we do not have to earn His forgiveness frees us to rest in the security of His unconditional love.

---

[1] John 10:10b.
[2] Romans 6:4.
[3] Luke 4:18.
[4] Colossians 1:13.
[5] 2 Timothy 2:26.
[6] Matthew 20:25-26.
[7] 1 Peter 5:3.
[8] Mark 3:6.
[9] Revelation 2:14.
[10] 2 Peter 2:19.
[11] Psalm 37:4.
[12] Galatians 5:13.
[13] Matthew 6:24.
[14] John 8:31-32.
[15] John 8:33
[16] John 8:34-36.
[17] Romans 8:1.
[18] Ephesians 2:8-9.
[19] Romans 5:8.
[20] Romans 6:15-18.
[21] Galatians 5:13.

Freedom Is Your Destiny!

25

GOING HOME

"In my Father's house are many mansions; if it were not so, I would have told you. I go to prepare a place for you."

John 14:2

Soldiers in Vietnam knew their DEROS (date eligible for return from overseas). It was the date they would be going home. They would climb aboard that freedom bird for the flight back to the United States. For them, the war would be over. They would be reunited with their families and friends and would be able to enjoy the many blessings of living in "the world" (America). Compared to Vietnam, America seemed like heaven.

Soldiers who were nearing their DEROS were called "short timers" or simply "short." Many of them created visual reminders of how many days they had left "in country." It may have been a calendar with the number of days remaining until their DEROS written in it, or a short-timer's stick. I had a section of small chain with one link for each day I had remaining "in country." Each day I removed one more link until the day I departed Vietnam.

As my second year in Vietnam was coming to an end, I knew it was time to leave. My tour of duty had come to an end. I had done all I could do and had no desire to remain any longer. Vietnam was not my home. It was not where my heart was. It was not where I wanted to spend the rest of my life. I had been sent there temporarily, to do a job, and now it was time to go home.

Unfortunately, many soldiers did not make it home alive. The names of over 58,000 who died are etched in the black granite wall that is the Vietnam Veterans Memorial. The names listed include soldiers of every rank from major general down to private. Death is no respecter of persons. Some died in combat, others died in accidents or from illnesses or other causes. Some were taken early in their tours of duty, and some were taken just before they would have left Vietnam for home. None of them wanted to die in Vietnam. They all hoped to make it home alive. Most probably thought they would.

Are you going to make it home alive? As I mentioned at the beginning of my book, we were all born into a war, a spiritual war that began with Satan's rebellion against God. Most will not make it home alive from that war.[1] I do not mean they will die physically. None of us will live forever in these bodies. Rather, they will not make it home alive because they will be dead spiritually. This present world in which we live is not our eternal home. "[I]t is appointed for men to die once, but after this the judgment."[2] We do not cease to exist when we die physically; we each have a spirit that will live on for eternity. If we ceased to exist at death, there would be no judgment because there would be nothing left to judge.

The judgment will not be an inquiry into whether you are guilty of sinning against God. You are. To sin simply means to miss the mark set by God. It is an act of disobedience to God, whether intentional or unintentional. It can be doing what you should not do, or not doing what you should. None of us have lived a sinless life. None of us can live a sinless life. "[F]or all have sinned and fall short of the glory of God,"[3] and the punishment for sin is death.[4] The judgment will be whether you have been pardoned by accepting Jesus Christ as your Savior and Lord. "He who believes in Him is not condemned; but he who does not believe is condemned already, because he has not believed in the name of the only begotten Son of God."[5]

Those who believe in Jesus will make it home alive. They will inherit eternal life and have an eternal home with God.[6] They will live in Paradise. We cannot even imagine or comprehend the glorious place God has prepared for those who will make it home to Paradise.

Those who do not believe in Jesus, however, will be excluded. They will not make it home. They will be spiritually dead, "punished with everlasting destruction from the presence of the Lord and from the glory of His power."[7] They will receive eternal punishment in the lake of fire, what we call hell.[8] We sometimes joke about hell, but for those who end up there it will be no laughing matter. Jesus described it as "the fire that shall never be quenched,"[9] where there will be "wailing and gnashing of teeth."[10]

So, how do you make it home alive? Romans 10:9-10 says that "if you confess with your mouth the Lord Jesus and believe in your heart that God has raised Him from the dead, you will be saved. For with the heart one believes unto righteousness, and with the mouth confession is made unto salvation."

Confess with your mouth the Lord Jesus. We must confess Jesus as Lord, but what does that mean? To confess the Lord Jesus, we must first know who Jesus is. That is probably the primary issue that we must decide. Was He simply a righteous man, merely a teacher of morality, only a prophet, nothing but a man? Was He created by God?

The Gospel According to Matthew recounts "the birth of Jesus Christ."[11] When I was young, I thought "Christ" was simply Jesus's last name. However, when Jesus asked the disciples who they said He was, Peter answered, "You are the Christ, the Son of the living God."[12] They said He was "the Christ." Christ was not His last name. It is the role He played in salvation. As Jesus explained to His disciples after His resurrection, "Thus it is written, and thus it was necessary for the Christ to suffer and to rise from the dead the third day, and that repentance and remission of sins should be preached in His name to all nations, beginning at Jerusalem."[13]

The Gospel According to John was written so that you "may believe that Jesus is the Christ, the Son of God, and that believing you may have life in His name."[14] One who denies that Jesus is the Christ "denies the Father and the Son."[15] When the Bible says that Jesus is the Christ, it means "this *Jesus* is the Christ."[16] "**This** Jesus" means that this particular Jesus—the Jesus of the Bible— is the Christ. Jesus warned that there would be false christs.[17] It is not the name "Jesus," or some other real or imagined person with that name, who is **the** Christ. It is only "**this** Jesus" who was described in the Bible. So who is "this Jesus?"

As stated above, Peter stated that Jesus was "the Christ, the Son of the living God."[18] What did he mean by "the Son of the living God"? The phrase "Son of God" did not mean descendant of God. It meant having the nature of or being the same as God. When Jesus said that God was His Father, the Jews sought to kill Him because He had said "that God was His Father, making Himself equal with God."[19] The only one who could be equal with God is God. Thus, another time when Jesus said that God was His Father, the Jews again took up stones to kill Him because

"You, being a Man, make Yourself God."[20]

Thus, this Jesus is God. As stated in Philippians 2:5-7, "Let this mind be in you which was also in Christ Jesus, who, being in the form of God, did not consider it robbery to be equal with God, but made Himself of no reputation, taking the form of a bondservant, *and* coming in the likeness of men." No one could be in the form of God but God. That is why He could say, "He who has seen Me has seen the Father."[21]

The plan of salvation had Jesus being born as a man. "For God so loved the world that He gave His only begotten Son, that whoever believes in Him should not perish but have everlasting life."[22] Jesus was God's "**only** begotten Son." In foretelling the Christ's birth, the Bible stated that He would be "Mighty God."

> For unto us a Child is born,
> Unto us a Son is given;
> And the government will be upon His shoulder.
> And His name will be called
> Wonderful, Counselor, Mighty God,
> Everlasting Father, Prince of Peace.[23]

Jesus is unique. He is the only one Who was both man and God. He "was born of the seed of David according to the flesh, *and* declared *to be* the Son of God with power according to the Spirit of holiness, by the resurrection from the dead."[24]

Genesis 1:1 states, "In the beginning God created the heavens and the earth." Yet, Scripture also tells us that Jesus was the Creator. "For by Him all things were created that are in heaven and that are on earth, visible and invisible, whether thrones or dominions or principalities or powers. All things were created through Him and for Him."[25]

"All things were made through Him, and without Him nothing was made that was made."[26] Obviously, Jesus was not a created being because "by Him all things were created that are in heaven and that are on earth, visible and invisible." That would include all of the angels, both the faithful angels, who are "ministering spirits sent forth to minister for those who will inherit salvation,"[27] and the fallen angels (Satan and his angels), who deceive the whole world.[28]

Satan was a created being, an "anointed cherub,"[29] cast down because he said in his pride, "I will be like the Most High."[30] Jesus actually is like the Most High because He is God. He is "the brightness of *His* [God's] glory and the express image of His person."[31]

How could Jesus be God and the Father be God, when the Bible says that there is only one God? For example Deuteronomy 6:4 says, "Hear, O Israel: The LORD our God, the LORD *is* one!" Likewise, 1 Kings 8:60 states that "the LORD *is* God; *there is* no other." Indeed, God Himself said, "I *am* the First and I *am* the Last; Besides Me *there is* no God,"[32] and "*there is* none besides Me. I *am* the LORD, and *there is* no other."[33] God even asked "Is there a God besides Me?" and then answered that question by stating, "Indeed *there is* no other Rock; I know not *one*."[34]

So, how could the Father and Jesus both be God? God is three divine persons who exist in such unity that they are one God. They are God the Father, God the Son, and God the Holy Spirit—sometimes collectively called the Godhead. They are each fully divine, equal with the other two, but they are not three separate gods. Likewise, they are not simply three parts or expressions of God. The triune nature of God is something we cannot understand. What is important in this discussion is that they took differing roles with respect to our salvation.

We must confess that Jesus is Lord. What does that mean? The Greek word translated "Lord" is *kurios*, and it means master, owner. You have to confess that Jesus is your master. That confession is not merely reciting empty words. Jesus made that clear when He said, "Not everyone who says to Me, 'Lord, Lord,' shall enter the kingdom of heaven, but he who does the will of My Father in heaven."[35] The issue is one of the heart—do you have a sincere, heartfelt desire to obey God? To those who call Jesus Lord but do not seek to obey God, He will declare, "I never knew you; depart from Me, you who practice lawlessness!"[36] Practicing lawlessness is living a life in rebellion against God. It is being self-seeking and not obeying the truth.[37] It is refusing to submit to God's law and instead living a life guided by our own desires and our own views of right and wrong.

Confessing that Jesus truly is our Lord, our Master, entails: (a) agreeing that we have been disobedient to God by failing to live in accordance with His will; (b) turning to God in repentance; and (c) sincerely seeking to obey Him out of gratitude and love. Repentance is being truly sorry for our sinful conduct, not simply because of the consequences, but because it is an offense against God.[38] We can profess to know God, but deny Him by our conduct.[39] True repentance will produce a change in heart, which will result in a change in conduct.[40] That does not mean we will suddenly be able to live perfect lives, free from sin. None of us can do that, even after being saved. It simply means that our conduct will begin conforming to God's will. Thus, we must "repent, turn to God, and do works befitting repentance."[41] As we do so, and allow Christ to work through us, we will be changed.

Believe in your heart that God raised Jesus from the dead. Repentance and good works will not, by themselves, get you home. Nobody can be good enough to deserve to go to heaven. You cannot earn your way there. It is not a matter of the good you do outweighing the bad. To earn your way to heaven, you would have to never sin throughout your entire life. Only the arrogant believe they can do that. If you think you never sin, even after coming to Christ, you deceive yourself.[42] From God's perspective, violating one aspect of His moral law is the same as violating the entire law. "For whoever shall keep the whole law, and yet stumble in one *point*, he is guilty of all."[43] Your only hope is to receive forgiveness for your sins, to be pardoned. Your only hope is a Savior.

The gospel (literally "good news") is that Jesus has provided that forgiveness by His sacrifice on the cross. Because God is righteous, the penalty of death had to be paid for our sins. "[W]ithout shedding of blood there is no remission [forgiveness of sins]."[44] Jesus paid that penalty for you and for me by dying for our sins on the cross.[45]

The role taken by Jesus was to become incarnated in human form so that He could be born the Son of God. He was born of a virgin (to show he did not have an earthly father), but was both fully man and fully God.[46] He suffered and died for our sins and was buried.[47] What happened next is the key. God raised Him bodily from the dead.[48]

By raising Jesus from the dead, God showed that Jesus was the "Son of God."[49] As I explained above, the phrase "Son of God" does not mean descendant of God. It means having the nature of or being the same as God. That is why the Jews believed that it was blasphemy for Jesus to say He was the Son of God because by doing so He was saying He was God.[50]

By raising Jesus from the dead, God also showed that Jesus had accomplished what He came to earth to do—

to pay the penalty for our sins. In order to pay for our sins, Jesus had to live a sinless life as a man on the earth. If He had sinned, His death would have been only the just penalty for His own sin, not ours. That God raised Jesus from the dead showed that Jesus lived a sinless life[51] and could therefore die for us. "If Christ is not risen, your faith *is* futile; you are still in your sins!"[52]

Jesus was "delivered up [killed] because of our offenses, and was raised because of our justification."[53] Justification is God's act of declaring us free from guilt and condemnation because Jesus took the punishment we deserve by dying on the cross. As a result, there is no condemnation for those who are in Christ Jesus.[54] "He who believes in Him is not condemned; but he who does not is condemned already, because he has not believed in the name of the only begotten Son of God."[55]

By raising Jesus from the dead, God showed that He would also raise from the dead those who turn to God through Jesus.[56] We have that hope as an anchor for our souls. Death has no power over us. God will raise us up to live with Him for eternity. However, there is only one way to God. As Jesus said: "I am the way, the truth, and the life. No one comes to the Father except through Me."[57]

God loves you and wants you to come home. God loves you so much that He gave His only begotten Son, that whoever believes in Him shall not perish but have everlasting life.[58] What more could He give for you than His only Son? How better could He prove His love for you? He wants you to be His child. He wants you to come home. The choice is yours. I hope you have chosen life. I hope to see you in heaven.

Thank you for taking this journey with me.

---

[1] Matthew 7:13-14.
[2] Hebrews 9:27.
[3] Romans 3:23.
[4] Romans 5:12; 6:23.
[5] John 3:18.
[6] John 14:2.
[7] 2 Thessalonians 1:9.
[8] Matthew 25:41; Revelation 20:12-15.
[9] Mark 9:43.
[10] Matthew 13:50.
[11] Matthew 1:18-25.
[12] Matthew 16:16.
[13] Luke 24:46-47.
[14] John 20:31.
[15] 1 John 2:22.
[16] Acts 9:22.
[17] Matthew 24:5, 24.
[18] Matthew 16:16.
[19] John 5:18.
[20] John 10:33.
[21] John 14:9.
[22] John 3:16.
[23] Isaiah 9:6.
[24] Romans 1:3-4.
[25] Colossians 1:16.
[26] John 1:3.
[27] Hebrews 1:14.
[28] Revelation 12:9.
[29] Ezekiel 28:11-16.
[30] Isaiah 14:14.
[31] Hebrews 1:3.
[32] Isaiah 44:6.
[33] Isaiah 45:6.
[34] Isaiah 44:8.
[35] Matthew 7:21.
[36] Matthew 7:23.
[37] Romans 2:5.
[38] Psalm 51:4.
[39] Titus 1:16; James 2:26.
[40] Matthew 3:8.
[41] Acts 26:20.
[42] 1 John 1:8.
[43] James 2:10.
[44] Hebrews 9:22.
[45] 1 Corinthians 15:3.

[46] Romans 1:3-4; 8:3; Galatians 3:16, 4:4; Philippians 2:5-7; 1 Timothy 3:16.

[47] Romans 5:8-10; 1 Corinthians 15:3; 1 Peter 3:18.

[48] Acts 2:31; 13:32-39; Romans 4:24; 1 Thessalonians 1:10; 1 Corinthians 15:3-5; 2 Timothy 2:8.

[49] Romans 1:4.

[50] Matthew 26:62-66; John 5:17-18; 10:30-33; 19:7.

[51] Hebrews 4:15.

[52] 1 Corinthians 15:17.

[53] Romans 4:25.

[54] Romans 8:1.

[55] John 3:18.

[56] 1 Corinthians 6:14.

[57] John 14:6.

[58] John 3:16.

Daniel T. Eismann

ABOUT THE AUTHOR

Dan Eismann is a decorated combat veteran who served two tours of duty in Vietnam, graduated from the University of Idaho College of Law, practiced law for ten years, and has served in the Idaho Judiciary for over 26 years as a trial judge and Supreme Court Justice. He has taught Adult Sunday School and led Bible Study groups for many years.

Daniel T. Eismann

(Me, standing at left), one of my door gunners (squatting), and one of my pilots. This shows the police siren I had on my gunship for a while.

Approaching the airfield at Soc Trang from the south. The southern end of the airfield is just past the grove of trees in the left center of the picture. There is just one runway, which is basically aligned with the center trees. The area to the right that may look like a runway is water.

Trolling for bullets.

A Chinook taking off with my gunship.

Exit hole made by a .50 caliber machine gun bullet in the copilot's door of my gunship. The window was rolled down at the time, so that is why there is also a hole in the Plexiglas window. (We were on the deck in a slight right turn when we were hit. The pilot and copilot sat on a tubular frame covered with nylon netting. That frame was mounted inside an assembly of armor plating that protected them from the back, bottom, and sides. The bullet entered through the triangular window in the pilot's door; passed in front of the pilot and over the armor plating on the right side of the copilot's seat; cut the webbing he was sitting on, scorching his pants; ricocheted off the inside of the armor plating on the back of his seat; went through a slot in the armor plating through which the seat belt passed on the left side of his seat, enlarging the slot; and exited out the copilot's door.)

The remains of one of our gunships after it was shot down, crashed, and burned.

Our gunship flight line at Soc Trang at night.

Damage to one of our slicks after an ARVN soldier shot it with an M-79 grenade launcher. With allies like that, you do not need enemies.

Minigun and rockets on my gunship. The rockets protruding out the fronts of the rocket tubes have 17-pound warheads. The other tubes have rockets with 10-pound warheads.

Nose art on my Viking UH-1B Gunship.

The second time I was shot down. The cowling is open because I had assessed the damage while waiting to be picked up. After the area was secured, the pilot and I returned. I replaced the damaged part, and we flew it out.

Laying a smoke screen.

The result after a gunship lost its tail rotor assembly while flying on the deck. This probably resulted from enemy fire. Miraculously, nobody was killed.

Gunship taking off at night. The person sitting by the open door is the crew chief and was about the same size I was at the time. The vertical pole in front of him is the "litter pole."

Small village.

A little girl to whom I had given my C-rations (the box she is holding in this picture). She is standing on the runway made of interlocking pierced steel plates (PSP).

Me, after being hit in the head with shrapnel.

The North Vietnamese army shot at us with the three types of cartridges on the left as seen in the picture above. Beginning with the smallest, they were fired from an AK-47, a .30 caliber machine gun, and a .50 caliber machine gun. The South Vietnamese army shot at us with the two types of cartridges on the right. The smaller one was fired from an M-16, and the larger from an M-79 grenade launcher. The cartridge in the middle was the type we fired from our M-60 guns and miniguns.

OTHER BOOKS AVAILABLE FROM DESERT SAGE PRESS @ www.desertsagepress.com

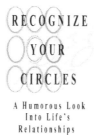

In this collection of true stories titled **Stirrings of The Spirit**, author Sheila F. Eismann invites you to walk through several valleys en route to some mountain tops with her family as they learned to rely on God in the most harrowing of circumstances.

RECOGNIZE YOUR CIRCLES

A Humorous Look Into Life's Relationships

Have you ever wondered why you were the last one to hear of THE big social event of the year? Well, wonder no longer after reading this e-book titled **Recognize Your Circles**! When volunteering for an organization years ago, author Sheila F. Eismann was introduced to the concept of "the circles of your life." Since the idea was so beneficial to her, she decided to share it with all of you.

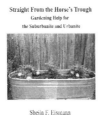

Straight From the Horse's Trough
Gardening Help for
the Suburbanite and Urbanite

Sheila F. Eismann

Straight from the Horse's Trough is a humorous read to render assistance to the suburbanite or urbanite who desires to live a healthier lifestyle by growing his or her own food but is faced with the challenge of a small space in which to do so. This e-book is chock full of how-to steps and includes pictures to remove guesswork from the project.

The Christmas Tin

By Sheila Faye Eismann • Ali Faith Putz
Illustrated by Connie Richardson

The Christmas Tin is a most delightful read for the young at heart anytime during the year! This endearing book is based upon a true story featuring the older of the two authors when she was a young girl and conveys the timeless message that "love truly is the best gift of all." Children will especially enjoy all of the colorful illustrations contained within this treasure!

Freedom Is Your Destiny!

Daniel T. Eismann